Understanding Changes in Poverty

DIRECTIONS IN DEVELOPMENT
Poverty

Understanding Changes in Poverty

Gabriela Inchauste, João Pedro Azevedo, B. Essama-Nssah, Sergio Olivieri, Trang Van Nguyen, Jaime Saavedra-Chanduvi, and Hernan Winkler

1818 H Street NW, Washington DC 20433
Telephone: 202-473-1000; Internet: www.worldbank.org

1 2 3 4 17 16 15 14

ISBN (paper): 978-1-4648-0299-7
ISBN (electronic): 978-1-4648-0300-0
DOI: 10.1596/978-1-4648-0299-7

Cover art: © Thomas Sennett / World Bank. Used with permission. Further permission required for reuse.
Cover design: Debra Naylor, Naylor Design, Inc.

Library of Congress Cataloging-in-Publication Data has been requested.

Contents

Figures

Tables

Acknowledgments

This book was cofunded by the Poverty Reduction and Economic Management Network and the Multi-Donor Trust Fund for the Diagnostic Facility on Shared Growth.

The team was led by Gabriela Inchauste (task team leader and senior economist, Poverty Reduction and Equity Department [PRMPR]) under the guidance of Jaime Saavedra-Chanduvi (Director, PRMPR) and Christina Malmberg Calvo (Acting Director, PRMPR). Members of the team and tasks were as follows:

Chapter 1	Gabriela Inchauste Jaime Saavedra-Chanduvi
Chapter 2	João Pedro Azevedo B. Essama-Nssah Gabriela Inchauste Sergio Olivieri
Chapter 3	João Pedro Azevedo Gabriela Inchauste Trang Van Nguyen Sergio Olivieri Hernan Winkler
Chapter 4	B. Essama-Nssah
Chapter 5	Gabriela Inchauste Sergio Olivieri Hernan Winkler
Chapter 6	Gabriela Inchauste Sergio Olivieri Hernan Winkler

The team is grateful to Mary A. Anderson (consultant, PRMPR) for providing feedback on organization and content as well as for formatting and editing the manuscript. The authors acknowledge analytical inputs provided by Reena Badiani-Magnusson (economist, EASHS); Reno Dewina (consultant, EASPW); Jenny Lighthart (consultant, EAP); Minh Cong Nguyen (economist, ECSP3); and Viviane Sanfelice (consultant, LCSPP).

The authors thank colleagues for their insightful suggestions, in particular, Kathleen Beegle (lead economist, AFRCE); Francisco Ferreira (chief economist, AFRCE); Samuel Freije (lead economist and sector leader, LCSPR); and Emmanuel Skoufias (lead economist, LCSPP). The authors are grateful to colleagues from the World Bank for their comments at various stages in developing the concept note and the drafts and presentations of the book. The authors thank all of them, in particular Dean Joliffe (senior economist, DECPI); Ambar Narayan (lead economist, PRMPR); Luis Servén (senior advisor, DECMG); Erwing Tiongson (senior economist, LCSPP); and Renos Vakis (lead economist, DECPI).

The research also benefited from presentations of draft papers at the Latin American and Caribbean Economic Association meetings in Lima, 2012; at the Network of Inequality and Poverty meetings at Columbia University, 2012; at Tulane University, 2013; and at World Bank workshops between 2011 and 2013. The authors gratefully acknowledge the insightful comments and suggestions of participants at these workshops.

About the Authors

João Pedro Azevedo is a senior economist at the World Bank, where he currently works for the Europe and Central Asia region, focusing on Turkey and Central Asia and leading the region's Statistical Team. Azevedo has focused much of his work on helping developing countries to improve their systems for evidence-based decision making. Before joining the World Bank, he served as the superintendent of monitoring and evaluation at the Secretary of Finance for the State of Rio de Janeiro, Brazil. He was also a research fellow at the Brazilian Institute of Applied Economic Research. He is a former chairman of the Latin American Network on Inequality and Poverty. He holds a PhD in economics from the University of Newcastle upon Tyne.

B. Essama-Nssah worked for 17 years for the World Bank in Washington, DC, before he retired as a senior economist in 2011. During his tenure at the World Bank, he performed economic analyses, prepared policy research and technical papers, and conducted an annual training course on impact evaluation methodologies for staff from the World Bank and client countries. Before joining the World Bank, he worked for 2 years as a senior research associate on the Food and Nutrition Program at Cornell University, and for 6 years as head of the Economics Department and vice dean of the Faculty of Law and Economics of the University of Yaoundé, Cameroon. He currently works as a consultant focusing on poverty and growth incidence analysis, program evaluation, and analysis of the social impact of public policy. He holds a PhD in economics from the University of Michigan in Ann Arbor.

Gabriela Inchauste is a senior economist in the Poverty Reduction and Equity Department at the World Bank. Her research interests include poverty, macro-micro linkages, and the distributional impact of fiscal policy. She has published in academic volumes and peer-reviewed journals in the areas of fiscal policy, the informal sector, the impact of crises on the poor, and the role of remittances in developing countries. Before joining the World Bank, she was a senior economist at the Inter-American Development Bank and the International Monetary Fund, where she contributed to operational and analytical activities in numerous countries on topics including macroeconomic forecasting, public expenditure policy, poverty and social impact analysis, fiscal and debt sustainability analysis, postdisaster needs assessments, and subsidy reform. Inchauste holds a PhD in economics from the University of Texas at Austin.

Trang Van Nguyen is a senior economist in the Poverty Reduction and Equity Department at the World Bank. Previously, she worked in the East Asia and Pacific, Africa, and Europe and Central Asia Regions of the World Bank, in the areas of labor, poverty and inequality, education, health, social protection, and gender and development. Nguyen is one of the lead authors of the World Bank's regional flagship report, *East Asia Pacific at Work: Employment, Enterprise, and Well-Being*. She is also coauthor of two other World Bank flagship publications: *Toward Gender Equality in East Asia and the Pacific: A Companion to the World Development Report* (2012) on gender equality and development and *International Migration and Development in the East Asia and Pacific Region*. She holds a PhD in economics from the Massachusetts Institute of Technology.

Sergio Olivieri is an economist in the Poverty Reduction and Equity Department at the World Bank. His main research areas are ex ante analysis of the distributional impact of macroeconomic shocks, understanding how economic growth affects poverty, poverty measurement, and multidimensional poverty. He has published articles in peer-reviewed journals on labor informality, polarization, and multidimensional poverty and has contributed to edited volumes on inequality, poverty, and social cohesion. Previously, he was an assistant professor of labor economics in the Department of Economics of University of La Plata, Argentina, and as a researcher in the university's Center of Distributional, Labor and Social Studies.

Jaime Saavedra-Chanduvi is Minister of Education in Peru. He was previously the director of the Poverty Reduction and Equity Department at the World Bank. His major areas of interest include education policy, poverty reduction, inequality, labor markets, and social policies. He was executive director and principal researcher at Grupo de Análisis para el Desarollo, a nonpartisan think tank based in Lima, and a principal advisor to the Ministry of Labor and Social Promotion in Peru. He has been a consultant and researcher for the World Bank, the Economic Commission for Latin America and the Caribbean, the Inter-American Development Bank, and the International Labour Organization. He has been president of the executive committee of the Network on Inequity and Poverty of the Inter-American Development Bank–World Bank–Latin American and Caribbean Economic Association as well as a board member of Latin American and Caribbean Economic Association, the Nutrition Research Institute, and the National Council of Labor in Peru. He has held teaching positions at Pontificia Universidad Católica del Peru and Universidad del Pacífico in Peru, and has been a visiting researcher at the University of Toronto. Saavedra-Chanduvi holds a PhD in economics from Columbia University.

Hernan Winkler is an economist in the Office of the Chief Economist for Europe and Central Asia at the World Bank. He specializes in applied microeconomics, with a particular focus on labor market issues and the sources and consequences of inequality and poverty. He was part of the core team of the World Bank's regional flagship report, *Diversified Development: Making the Most of Natural Resources in Eurasia* (2014), and also on the core team of the next regional flagship report on the aging populations of Europe and Central Asia. Before joining the World Bank, Winkler was a researcher at the Center of Distributional, Labor and Social Studies at the University of La Plata, Argentina. He holds a PhD in economics from the University of California at Los Angeles.

Abbreviations

ATET	average treatment effect on the treated
ENAHO	Encuesta Nacional de Hogares (Peru National Institute of Statistics and Information)
FAO	Food and Agriculture Organization of the United Nations
GDP	gross domestic product
GIC	growth incidence curve
HIES	Household Income and Expenditure Survey (Bangladesh Bureau of Statistics)
PPP	purchasing power parity
RIGA	Rural Income-Generating Activities (datasets compiled jointly by the Food and Agriculture Organization of the United Nations and the World Bank)
SEDLAC	Socio-Economic Database for Latin America and the Caribbean
SES	Household Socio-Economic Survey (Thailand National Statistical Office)

Currency is in U.S. dollars unless specified otherwise.

CHAPTER 1

Opportunity Knocks: Deepening Our Understanding of Poverty Reduction

Introduction

A 2013 cover of *The Economist* virtually declared victory: "Towards the End of Poverty" (*Economist* 2013). Given international benchmarks, a battle has indeed been won—to cut in half the share of the world's population living in extreme poverty. In fact, the achievement of this 2015 Millennium Development Goal was met with time to spare.[1] By 2013, the percentage of developing-country populations living under the direst conditions—measured by the extreme poverty line, typically set at $1.25 a day[2]—decreased from 43 percent in 1990 (1.9 billion people) to 21 percent by 2010 (1.2 billion people). Clearly there is still a long way to go, with 1.2 billion people still struggling to get enough to eat. But what can we learn from the recent success?

For example, how much do we truly understand about the specific drivers of such momentous changes in poverty—be they reductions or increases, in low-income or middle-income countries, at extreme or moderate poverty levels? To be sure, 21st-century poverty reduction is largely a growth story, and one that is indisputable by either national or international poverty lines.[3] Even knowing that growth correlates strongly with poverty reduction (Ravallion and Chen 2007), economists and policy makers want to "drill down" into the data to answer many more questions:

- What role have demographic changes and lower dependency ratios had on the reduction in poverty?
- What was the role of higher employment and higher real earnings? Did higher labor productivity lead to higher real earnings? Or did earnings growth result either from improved human capital (in education, training, or experience) or from changes in the *returns* to those characteristics?

- To what extent did changes in the sectoral composition of employment lead to higher productivity and higher earnings? For instance, how did movements from agriculture to the services or industry sectors contribute to poverty reduction?
- What was the role of transfers from the government, including the new generation of social safety net programs that have begun to proliferate?
- What was the role of private transfers in the form of international remittances?

International bodies and financial institutions are setting ambitious new poverty reduction targets for 2030. Similarly, many developing countries have clear development goals and national plans to reduce poverty and promote inclusive growth. The methods and results presented in this book are envisioned to contribute to the evidence base that governments can use in setting the policy agenda.

Decomposing Poverty Reduction

The links between economic growth, income redistribution, and poverty reduction have long interested economists. Growth, at the end of the day, is a means to an end. Bolstered by decades of previous work, recent methods can be used to decompose the contributions to poverty reduction.

Decomposition methods originated in the seminal papers of Oaxaca (1973) and Blinder (1973), which aimed to decompose changes in wages over time. Since then, the increase in wage inequality observed in the United States and several other countries since the late 1970s has led to the development of new methods, including those introduced by Juhn, Murphy, and Pierce (1993) and Bourguignon, Ferreira, and Lustig (2005). Although these methods were focused on better understanding distributional changes, they can also be used to better understand changes in poverty.

In particular, we focus on two questions: What was the main contributor to poverty reduction? What was behind the poverty reduction due to labor income growth in particular? The first question can be addressed with a simple accounting approach that quantifies the contributions to poverty reduction on account of changes in demographics, changes in employment and labor income, and changes in nonlabor income (including remittances, public transfers, and other private transfers). The second question requires a more complex approach to further distinguish between distributional changes because of changes in endowments or returns to those endowments; changes in occupational choice; and changes in the geographical, age, and gender structure of the population, along with the nonlabor dimensions mentioned above. Such an approach can, for instance, help distinguish whether improvements in human capital (via a more educated work force) have been accompanied by increases in the returns to education (and potential improvements in productivity).

What Was the Main Contributor to Poverty Reduction?

By covering and expanding upon existing decomposition methods, chapters 2 and 3 describe and apply the first of these methods to identify the forces that account for substantial declines[4] in moderate poverty over the past decade[5] in a selected set of 21 developing nations. The main results are as follows:

- *Labor income growth* (comprising growth of employment and earnings) clearly contributed the most to poverty reduction in the studied countries (figure 1.1). Being the main asset of the poor, increased labor income accounts for more than half of the poverty reduction in 12 of the 21 countries with substantial poverty reduction. In another 6 countries, it accounted for more than 40 percent of the reduction in poverty. Moreover, in most cases, it was the growth in income per worker that contributed the most to poverty reduction, rather than an increase in employment (measured by the share of working adults).

- *Demographic changes* (primarily increases in the share of adults per household) led to declining age-dependency rates, which in turn can lead to increases in per capita income and consumption. This effect occurred in most of the

Figure 1.1 Decomposition of Changes in Moderate Poverty, by Income Level, in Selected Developing Countries, 2000s

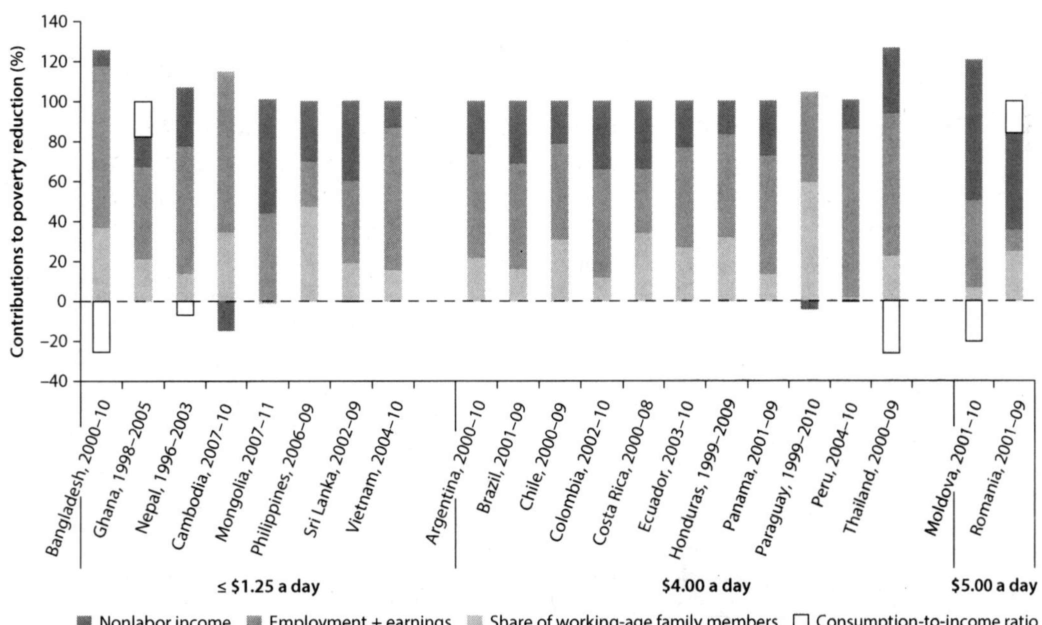

Sources: Data from SEDLAC, various years; FAO n.d.; and national household surveys.
Note: "Nonlabor income" refers to public and private transfers (including remittances), pensions, capital, and other nonlabor income. "Employment + earnings" refers to the combined change in employment and earnings per working-age adult (aged 15–64 years). The "consumption-to-income ratio" represents the ratio of measured consumption to measured income. Changes in this ratio capture changes in savings patterns of households as well as measurement errors in household consumption and income. Consumption-based measures of poverty are used in Bangladesh, Ghana, Moldova, Nepal, Peru, Romania, and Thailand. The remaining countries use income-based measures of poverty.

countries considered here over the past decade and was especially important in Costa Rica, Paraguay, and the Philippines. However, in most of the countries studied, the magnitude of this effect was small relative to the effect of labor income growth.

- *Nonlabor income* (such as government spending for subsidies or public transfers)[6] grew, as a share of gross domestic product (GDP), more than sixfold in Ghana and by more than 60 percent in Bangladesh, Moldova, Mongolia, and Romania. Remittances also grew strongly, especially in Honduras (to an average of 17.8 percent of GDP in 2009) and Nepal (to an average of 12 percent of GDP in 2003). Although transfers contributed to poverty reduction, they played a relatively smaller role in explaining declines in moderate poverty for most countries in the sample. Three notable exceptions were Moldova, Mongolia, and Romania. Moldova's poor benefited mostly from an increase in international remittances, whereas in Romania, the increase was related to both transfers and capital income. However, public transfers clearly play an increasingly important role in reducing extreme poverty. In other words, increases in transfers to the extremely poor were critical in reducing the severity of poverty.

Why Did Labor Income Grow?

Although the results clearly point to growth in income per worker as the main contributor to poverty reduction in most of the countries studied, the method is unable to discern why labor income grew. In many developing countries, poverty reduction has coincided with the labor force's increasing education and health—as well as, in some cases, more equitable distribution of land or other productive assets. Did earnings increase because of changes in the endowments of the population (such as higher educational levels or increases in other productive assets)? Or did marketplace premiums (that is, the returns to endowments) rise for workers with those endowments?

The rest of the book explores alternative methods to better understand the roots of these changes. After a review of the literature, the book's final two chapters describe and implement a second method based on Bourguignon, Ferreira, and Lustig (2005) and impose an underlying labor model and greater structure to understand why earnings increased. This decomposition approach is applied to Bangladesh, Peru, and Thailand. The results show that changes in individual characteristics (such as education, work experience, and region of residence) were influential, but that, overall, labor income grew mainly because of higher returns to endowments—signaling an increase in the marginal value of work as a result of increases in productivity or in the relative price of labor.

In Bangladesh and Peru, this increase in the marginal value of work was not driven by higher returns to education, but rather by higher returns to labor with low levels of education. In the case of Bangladesh, the increase in the marginal value of work seems to have been associated with higher food prices in the farm sector, while in Peru it was associated with higher premiums in the service sector, potentially resulting from improving productivity. Thailand, in contrast, demonstrated that greater specialization and higher returns to education can boost the marginal value of work, potentially through productivity increases.

The past decade affords us a fantastic opportunity to study the most significant factors that worked in favor of the poor. The decomposition methods reviewed in this volume provide a window to quantify the contributions to changes in poverty at a finer level of detail than ever before. The results point to the centrality of jobs in reducing poverty—particularly through increases in labor productivity—that will lead to sustained income growth for the poor. It is the authors' hope that the decompositions developed in this volume can expand the evidence base to establish the necessary conditions for future poverty reduction and therefore guide policy to enable these conditions to take hold.

Contributions of This Volume

The decomposition methods developed in this volume make some distinct contributions, further described in the chapter synopses below and summarized as follows:

- *Focus on consumption as a measure of welfare.* Up until now, decomposition methods often focused on income-based measures of welfare. These methods are adapted in this volume to focus on consumption, given that most developing countries use a consumption aggregate to measure poverty.

- *Address path dependence by calculating the Shapley-Shorrocks estimate of each component.* Like most micro-decomposition approaches in the literature, the methods proposed in this volume suffer from path dependence. In other words, the order in which the cumulative effects are calculated matters. The best-known remedy for path dependence is to calculate the decomposition across all possible paths and then take the average between them. Following the algorithm proposed by Azevedo, Nguyen, and Sanfelice (2012a, 2012b), we calculate the Shapley-Shorrocks (Shapley 1953; Shorrocks 1999) estimate of each component.

- *Apply to a wide set of countries experiencing poverty reduction around the world.* This volume presents the most comprehensive application of these techniques across countries that have experienced substantial declines in poverty over the past decade. Previous efforts typically included only a limited number of countries. The ease of use of this technique now allows for replication in a variety of contexts and can serve to decompose changes in poverty, inequality, or any other distributional change.

- *Propose a structural model that allows for household and individual decision making.* Previous approaches typically modeled only individual decision making. The proposed approach models farm income at the household level, including earnings of farm household members who have secondary occupations, thus recognizing not only that farm households typically make labor decisions as a unit but also that these households can be highly diversified.

The chapter summaries below offer only snapshots of the issues and techniques involved in understanding changes in poverty, allowing the full chapters to speak for themselves.

Chapter 2: A Simple Approach to Understanding Changes in Poverty and Inequality

Chapter 2 provides a unifying framework and a theoretical foundation for the decomposition methods commonly used in the literature. The chapter begins with the simplest decompositions—in which poverty changes can be decomposed into the growth effect and the redistribution effect (also known as the size and redistribution effects)—often referred to as the Datt and Ravallion (1992) decomposition. The chapter discusses the underpinnings of this decomposition and notes that in its original form, the Datt-Ravallion method includes a residual term. Moreover, the value of any effect (size or redistribution) depends on the chosen period of reference. To solve this problem, the standard practice is to compute the decomposition in both ways and then take the average.

As it turns out, this average Datt-Ravallion decomposition is precisely the procedure proposed by Shorrocks (1999) based on the Shapley (1953) value. Indeed, the Shapely allocation rule, based in game theory, provides a framework that can be extended to more complex decompositions, including those that decompose changes in poverty on account of changes within and between groups.

Although these decompositions are interesting, analysts often want to go beyond these summary statistics. We describe an approach that quantifies the contributions to poverty reduction on account of changes in demographics, employment, earnings, and public and private transfers based on a simple accounting identity. The method is adapted from Barros et al. (2006) and has the distinct advantage of being easy to apply and easy to understand. In contrast with the methods that use aggregate measures, such as "growth" and "redistribution" effects, this approach generates entire counterfactual distributions, allowing us to quantify the contributions to poverty reduction stemming from changes in demographics, employment, earnings, and public and private transfers by changing each one of these elements at a time.[7] To avoid path dependence, the proposed method calculates the Shapley-Shorrocks estimates of each component to find the contribution of each component.

Chapter 3: What Accounts for Changes in Poverty over the Past Decade?

Chapter 3 implements both the Datt-Ravallion decomposition and the method proposed in chapter 2 for a sample of 21 countries where moderate poverty had declined substantially between 2000 and 2010. The chapter quantifies, by generating entire counterfactual distributions, contributions to poverty reduction from changes in labor income, nonlabor income, and demographic characteristics.

Because most countries measure welfare through household expenditures or consumption (as opposed to income), this chapter modifies the Barros et al. (2006) methodology in three important respects: It decomposes consumption-based measures of poverty, computes a cumulative counterfactual distribution by adding one variable at a time, and it calculates the Shapley-Shorrocks estimates of each component.

The decompositions across the 21 countries resulted in the following general findings:

- *Labor income growth*, by far, was the main driver of poverty reduction. Moreover, an increase in workers' earnings was relatively more important in reducing poverty than the increases in the share of employed adults per household.
- *Demographic changes*—increased percentages of working-age adults per household (and thus declining dependency ratios)—also mattered in poverty reduction, particularly in seven of the countries. In general, however, the magnitude of this effect is small relative to labor income growth.
- *Nonlabor income increases*, such as public and private transfers, were important, but, for most countries in the sample, played the smallest role in explaining declines in moderate poverty. However, they were far more important in reducing extreme poverty. From decomposition of the extreme-poverty headcount, poverty gap, and poverty severity, transfers and pensions contributed a relatively higher share to poverty reduction than labor income growth.[8] These results point to the crucial role that social protection systems play in reaching the ultrapoor.

Although these methods are useful to distinguish the main contributors to poverty reduction, they cannot explain *why* workers' earnings increased. To resolve that issue, the subsequent chapters consider alternative decomposition techniques that impose an underlying labor model and greater structure.

Chapter 4: Counterfactual Decomposition of Changes in Poverty Outcomes

Chapter 4 presents a literature review of commonly used micro-decomposition methods to identify key drivers of changes in poverty. The chapter begins with the standard Oaxaca-Blinder decomposition, which aimed to understand changes in between-group differences in average wages, and reviews how this technique has since been extended to the analysis of variation in other distributional statistics, such as quantiles, poverty, and inequality measures.

The chapter first reviews methods to identify and estimate the composition (or endowment) effect and structural (or price) effect associated with variation in a general distributional statistic. The methods underlying this decomposition are considered statistical to the extent that they do not involve causal models of the observed outcomes. In this context, nonparametric estimation has the advantage of not imposing a functional form on the relationship between the outcome and its determinants. Because these statistical methods cannot shed light on the causal mechanism driving the outcome, their ability to inform policymaking is somewhat limited.

Therefore, the review also considers methods that account for behavioral responses to changes in the socioeconomic environment. These methods rely on the specification and estimation of a microeconometric model based on some theory of individual (or household) behavior and social interaction. These methods go a step further toward identifying factors associated with structural elements underpinning the observed changes in poverty outcomes. These structural methods—combining economics and statistics—can be *predictive*. In this context, chapter 5 proposes one such structural approach.

Finally, the chapter discusses the analogy between these decomposition methods and treatment effect analysis. The chapter also notes that these decomposition methods can be used in the study of the distributional and poverty impacts of an assigned intervention.

Chapter 5: Why Has Labor Income Increased? An In-Depth Approach to Understanding Poverty Reduction

The literature review presented in chapter 4 concludes that structural decomposition methods enable an analyst to study the distributional and poverty impacts of an assigned intervention by taking into account how agents respond to changes in their socioeconomic environments. This chapter presents a structure for modeling distributional changes over time that allows us to account for the contributions to poverty reduction stemming from both changes in endowments and changes in the returns to those endowments.

The proposed approach[9] estimates an educational choice model, a sectoral choice model, an activity choice model, and individual and household earnings equations. Once all of these models are estimated for individuals and households in each time period, the estimated coefficients from one year can be replaced with the estimates from another year to simulate the impact of changes in each element at a time. A series of counterfactual income distributions can then be constructed from which a counterfactual poverty measure can be estimated. This new poverty measure is then compared with the observed outcome while holding everything else constant. By changing one element at a time, these decompositions allow us to account for the observed changes in poverty.

In addition, we present a method to estimate these counterfactuals cumulatively, thereby accounting for the impact of concurrent changes. Although the method presented here draws heavily from Bourguignon and Ferreira (2005) and Bourguignon, Ferreira, and Leite (2008), it also offers some innovations:

- It assumes that welfare is measured using a consumption aggregate and accounts for the contribution of changes in the consumption-to-income ratio.
- It models farm household income at the household level and models the earnings of individuals in those farm households who have a secondary occupation, thus recognizing not only that farm households typically make labor decisions as a unit but also that these households can be highly diversified.

- It ensures that changes in the composition of activities, sectors, and education of the work force are consistent with the counterfactual choices.

Chapter 6: Understanding Poverty Reduction in Bangladesh, Peru, and Thailand

The method proposed in chapter 5 is applied in the volume's concluding chapter to understand the drastic reduction in poverty in three countries between 2000 and 2010: Bangladesh, Peru, and Thailand. While diverse in their levels of income and urbanization, these three economies each reduced moderate national poverty headcount rates by more than 14 percentage points.

In each case, GDP growth remained high, well exceeding 4 percent between 2002 and 2008. Peru and Thailand had sharp deceleration in 2009 because of the global financial crisis but rebounded quickly in 2010. Bangladesh got through the crisis virtually unscathed given the country's weaker integration into global financial markets. In addition to healthy economic growth, the countries had further similarities in potential poverty-reduction factors:

- Increases in employment, public social transfers, and remittances
- Changes in the populations' occupational structure, with workers moving away from farm and daily work and toward more salaried employment and to jobs of relatively high productivity
- Workers' sharp shifts away from agriculture and toward the higher-productivity manufacturing and service sectors
- Improvements in the work force's educational composition for several dimensions over the past 10 years, a result of each country's higher investment in education in previous decades.

Once the decompositions were performed, the main result, consistent with the findings mentioned above, was that the largest contributions to poverty reduction in all three countries were labor market–related factors, including changes in the sectoral, occupational, and educational structure of the labor force, as well as changes in the returns to individual and household characteristics. These changes cumulatively reduced moderate poverty levels in Bangladesh by 80 percent, in Peru by 69 percent, and in Thailand by 62 percent (figure 1.2).

Furthermore, within these results, we can finally explain *why* labor income increased. Through the micro-decomposition methods employed here, it was ascertained that labor income grew mainly because of higher *returns* to human capital endowments. In other words, the marginal value of work increased, and that's what made such a difference. This could signal increases in productivity, a higher relative price of labor, or both.

In Bangladesh and Peru, this increase in the marginal value of work was not driven by higher returns to education, but rather by higher returns to workers with low levels of education. To the extent that these higher returns to low-educated workers were accompanied by changes in the sectoral and occupational structure of the work force, these premiums may be reflecting improvements in

Figure 1.2 Cumulative Contributions to Moderate Poverty Reduction in Bangladesh, Peru, and Thailand, 2000s

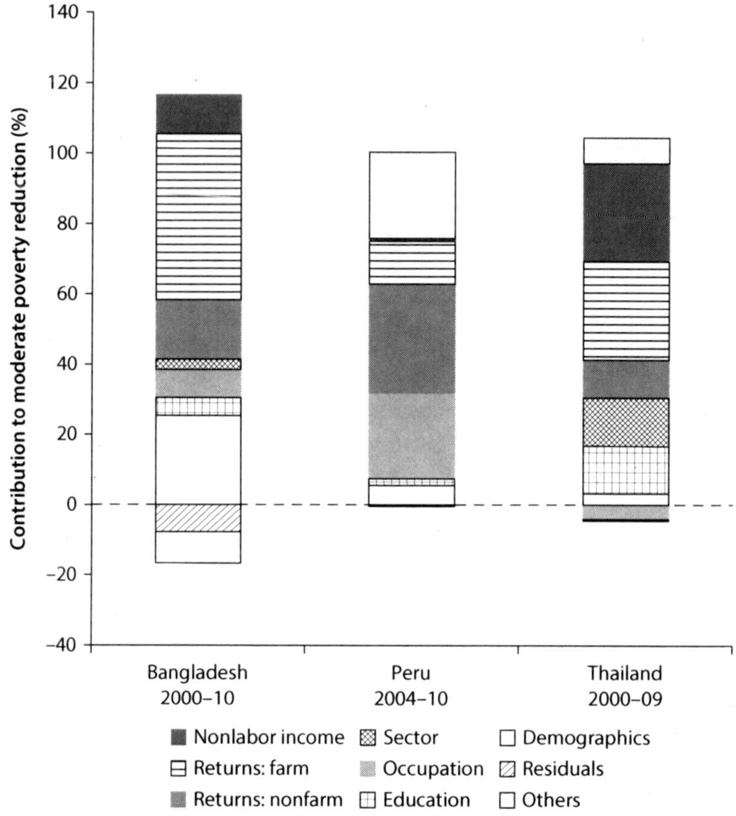

Sources: Calculations derived from household survey data from Bangladesh (HIES 2000–10), Peru (ENAHO 2004–10), and Thailand (SES 2000–09).
Note: "Moderate poverty" refers to each country's moderate poverty line. "Sector" refers to the sectoral composition of the workforce, including agriculture, industry, services. "Occupation" refers to the activity type of the workforce including daily workers, wage workers, self-employed, and unemployed. "Demographics" refers to changes in the age, gender, and regional composition of the population. "Others" includes changes in the consumption-to-income ratio and unexplained portion. HIES = Household Income and Expenditure Survey (Bangladesh Bureau of Statistics); ENAHO = Encuesta Nacional de Hogares (Peru National Institute of Statistics and Information); SES = Household Socio-Economic Survey (Thailand National Statistical Office).

the productivity of these unskilled workers. However, these higher returns might also simply reflect higher food prices, which have led to relative increases in the earnings of agricultural workers.

In contrast, in Thailand, poverty decreased because of both improvements in the education of the work force and higher returns to education. In this case, the marginal value of work increased through higher labor productivity increases.

Beyond increases in the returns to labor, all three countries showed reductions in poverty as a result of

- *A falling earnings penalty* for living outside of the capital city
- *A shift in sectoral choices* away from agriculture and toward services—reducing poverty only slightly in Bangladesh and Peru and a bit more in Thailand

- *A shift in occupational choices* among nonfarm workers away from daily-wage and self-employed work and toward salaried jobs, all of which contributed to poverty reduction, particularly in Peru.

Beyond the effects of labor income growth, the decomposition method showed that a greater share of working-age adults helped to reduce poverty, particularly in Bangladesh.

Finally, although most poverty reduction was the result of labor income growth, it is important to recognize that nonlabor income in the form of transfers did play a role: International remittances accounted for 11 and 17 percent of poverty reduction in Bangladesh and Thailand, respectively. Public transfers accounted for about 9 percent of Peru's poverty reduction, while Thailand's generous new pension scheme, combined with various private and other transfers, accounted for more than 40 percent of its poverty reduction.

Decompositions Can Inform Policy Priorities

International bodies and financial institutions are setting ambitious new poverty reduction targets for 2030. Similarly, many developing countries have clear development goals and national plans to reduce poverty and promote inclusive growth. Some are facing clear challenges to improve well-being through employment; some are facing the question of how to best design the tax-transfer system; others are undergoing tremendous demographic changes.

A first step in putting together a policy agenda is to frame the issues with respect to achieving these poverty reduction goals. As such, understanding poverty trends and the factors underlying these trends is critical. In particular, a better understanding of the roles of growth vis-à-vis distributional changes and the role of labor versus nonlabor income in explaining poverty reduction in the past 5–10 years can usefully shed light on what has worked to date and where there is room for improvement. The methods presented in this book can be applied to analyze changes in poverty, inequality, or any other distributional change over time. Both the methods and the emerging results presented here are envisioned to contribute to the evidence base that governments can use in setting the policy agenda.

Notes

1. For more information about the United Nations' Millennium Development Goals (MDGs), see the website http://www.un.org/millenniumgoals/.
2. The lower-bound poverty line, being initially set at a 1990 baseline rate of $1 a day (at 1993 purchasing power), was increased after economists gathered a new set of global poverty measures that spanned 116 countries (Ravallion, Chen, and Sangraula 2008). The new international poverty line (of $1.25 a day in 2005 prices) was calculated from "the average of the 15 poorest countries' own poverty lines in 2005 prices, adjusted for differences in purchasing power" (*Economist* 2013).

3. For more details about global changes in poverty and how poverty is measured, see Chen and Ravallion 2008 and World Bank 2012.
4. A "substantial" decline in poverty is defined as an average reduction of 1 percentage point per year over the data period.
5. "Moderate" poverty is a country-specific poverty line referring to the international poverty line that is closest to the country's moderate poverty rate (in some cases $1.25 a day, in others $2.50, and in still others $4–$5 per day.
6. Note that this exercise does not take into account the payoff of increased access to many public services that are not part of household income, nor does it account for the poverty impact of improvements in the quality of public services.
7. Counterfactual distributions are obtained by changing one determining factor at a time while holding all the other factors fixed (a straight application of *ceteris paribus* variation).
8. The poverty headcount, poverty gap, and severity of poverty refer to the Foster, Greer, and Thorbecke (1984) measures. The poverty headcount index is the proportion of the population that is counted as poor because their consumption or income is below a certain poverty line. The poverty gap adds up the extent to which individuals on average fall below the poverty line and expresses it as a percentage of the poverty line. The severity of poverty is calculated as the poverty gap index squared, which implicitly puts more weight on observations that fall well below the poverty line.
9. Our model takes into account the Roy (1951) model of choice and consequences (which stems from the optimization principle and applies to discrete choice problems), using it to model individuals' educational levels, sectors, and activity choices. We then adapt the Bourguignon, Ferreira, and Leite (2008) methodology to distinguish between distributional changes on account of (a) changes in endowments and the returns to those endowments; (b) changes in occupational and sectoral choice; and (c) changes in geographical, age, and gender structure of the population, along with the nonlabor dimensions.

Bibliography

Azevedo, Joao Pedro, Minh Cong Nguyen, and Viviane Sanfelice. 2012a. "Adecomp: Stata Module to Estimate Shapley Decomposition by Components of a Welfare Measure." Statistical Software Components S457562, Boston College, Department of Economics.

———. 2012b. "Shapley Decomposition by Components of a Welfare Aggregate." Policy Research Working Paper 6414, World Bank, Washington, DC.

Barros, Ricardo Paes de, Mirela de Carvalho, Samuel Franco, and Rosane Mendonça. 2006. "Uma Análise das Principais Causas da Queda Recente na Desigualdade de Renda Brasileira." *Revista Econômica* 8 (1): 117–47.

Blinder, Alan S. 1973. "Wage Discrimination: Reduced Form and Structural Estimates." *Journal of Human Resources* 8 (4): 436–55.

Bourguignon, François, and Francisco H. G. Ferreira. 2005. "Decomposing Changes in the Distribution of Household Incomes: Methodological Aspects." In *The Microeconomics of Income Distribution Dynamics in East Asia and Latin America*, edited by François Bourguignon, Francisco Ferreira, and Nora Lustig, 17–46. Washington, DC: World Bank.

Bourguignon, François, Francisco H. G. Ferreira, and Phillippe G. Leite. 2008. "Beyond Oaxaca-Blinder: Accounting for Differences in Household Income Distributions." *Journal of Economic Inequality* 6 (2): 117–48.

Bourguignon, François, Francisco H. G. Ferreira, and Nora Lustig, eds. 2005. *The Microeconomics of Income Distribution Dynamics in East Asia and Latin America.* Washington, DC: World Bank.

Chen, Shaohua, and Martin Ravallion. 2008. "The Developing World Is Poorer Than We Thought, But No Less Successful in the Fight against Poverty." Policy Research Working Paper 4703, World Bank, Washington, DC.

Datt, Gaurav, and Martin Ravallion. 1992. "Growth and Redistribution Components of Changes in Poverty Measures: A Decomposition with Applications to Brazil and India in the 1980s." *Journal of Development Economics* 38 (2): 275–96.

Economist. 2013. "Not Always with Us." June 1–7.

FAO (Food and Agriculture Organization of the United Nations). n.d. Rural Income Generating Activities (RIGA). Database, FAO, Rome; World Bank and American University, Washington, DC. http://www.fao.org/economic/riga/riga-database/en/.

Ferreira, Francisco. 2010. "Distributions in Motion: Economic Growth, Inequality and Poverty Dynamics." Policy Research Working Paper 5424, World Bank, Washington, DC.

Foster, James, Joel Greer, and Erik Thorbecke. 1984. "A Class of Decomposable Poverty Measures." *Econometrica* 52 (3): 761–65.

Juhn, Chinhui, Kevin M. Murphy, and Brooks Pierce. 1993. "Wage Inequality and the Rise of Returns to Skill." *Journal of Political Economy* 101 (3): 410–42.

Oaxaca, Ronald L. 1973. "Male-Female Wage Differentials in Urban Labor Markets." *International Economic Review* 14 (3): 693–709.

Ravallion, Martin, and Shaohua Chen. 2007. "China's (Uneven) Progress against Poverty." *Journal of Development Economics* 82 (1): 1–42.

Ravallion, Martin, Shaohua Chen, and Prem Sangraula. 2008. "A Dollar a Day Revisited." Policy Research Working Paper 4620, World Bank, Washington, DC.

Roy, Arthur D. 1951. "Some Thoughts on the Distribution of Earnings." *Oxford Economic Papers* 3 (2): 135–46.

SEDLAC (Socio-Economic Database for Latin America and the Caribbean). Various years. Statistical database produced by CEDLAS (Center for Distributional, Labor and Social Studies) of the Universidad Nacional de la Plata, Buenos Aires; and World Bank, Washington, DC. http://sedlac.econo.unlp.edu.ar/eng/.

Shapley, Lloyd S. 1953. "A Value for *n*-Person Games." In *Contributions to the Theory of Games*, Vol. 2, edited by H. W. Kuhn and A. W. Tucker, 307–17. Princeton, NJ: Princeton University Press.

Shorrocks, Anthony F. 1999. "Decomposition Procedures for Distributional Analysis: A Unified Framework Based on Shapley Value." Paper for the University of Essex and Institute for Fiscal Studies.

World Bank. 2012. "An Update to the World Bank's Estimates of Consumption Poverty in the Developing World." Briefing note prepared by Shaohua Chen and Martin Ravallion, Development Research Group, World Bank, Washington, DC.

CHAPTER 2

A Simple Approach to Understanding Changes in Poverty and Inequality

Introduction

The link between economic growth and poverty reduction has long been of interest to economists. The literature has proposed counterfactual decomposition methods to identify the relative contributions of different factors to variations in overall poverty.[1] These decompositions include the Datt and Ravallion (1992) method, which decomposes observed changes in poverty into a distribution-neutral growth effect and a redistribution effect. Kolenikov and Shorrocks (2005) decompose changes in poverty into growth, distribution, and price components, while Ravallion and Huppi (1991) offer a way of decomposing changes in poverty over time into intrasectoral effects and population shifts.

However, the usefulness of these decomposition methods is severely limited in policy making because they explain changes in poverty on the basis of changes only in summary statistics that are hard to target with policy instruments. For instance, it is hard to see what role demographics played in reducing poverty—or what the roles of employment and labor income were—relative to the roles of remittances and public transfers. Unfortunately, methods such as Datt-Ravallion (1992) are unable to make these explicit links because growth, inequality, and poverty measures are actually just three different aggregations of information about individual income dynamics. Moreover, they are jointly determined, such that cross-country estimates are unlikely to shed much light on the fundamental factors underlying distributional change (Ferreira 2012).

In addition to methods that focus on aggregate summary statistics, this chapter reviews a simple method to generate entire counterfactual distributions, allowing us to quantify the contributions to poverty reduction stemming from changes in demographics, changes in the share of employed adults, changes in labor income, and changes in nonlabor income, such as public transfers and remittances.

Although it follows the approach first discussed by Barros et al. (2006), the proposed method is new in three important respects:

- It extends the approach to cases where poverty is measured by consumption, as opposed to income.
- It calculates the cumulative effect of all of these changes and ensures that the sum of the components is equal to the total change in poverty.
- To avoid path dependence, every possible path is considered, and the average contribution of each factor is computed over all possible paths, leading to what is known as Shapley-Shorrocks estimates of the contribution of each component (Shapley 1953; Shorrocks [1999] 2013).

It is important to explain at the outset that these decompositions are essentially accounting exercises and do not allow for the identification of causal effects. For example, increases in cash transfers or noncontributory pensions may in some circumstances deter participation in the labor market, thus affecting labor incomes. Similarly, increases in labor income can make some households ineligible for transfer programs. For those reasons, we caution against interpreting changes in labor income (or, for that matter, changes in pensions or transfers) as "causing" changes in the poverty rate. Still, the decompositions are useful in identifying empirical regularities and, as accounting tools, can help focus attention on factors that are quantitatively more important in describing distributional changes.

The rest of the chapter is organized as follows: The next section provides background on decomposition methods used to account for variation in poverty outcomes in terms of changes in the mean and in relative inequality of the underlying outcome distribution. In particular, we review the Datt and Ravallion (1992) and Shapley (1953) decomposition methods. This is followed by a decomposition methodology that aims to quantify the contributions of labor income, transfers, and demographic effects to the observed changes in poverty, based on the Shapley approach. The last section reviews the contributions and limitations of the decomposition methods discussed in this chapter.

The Size and Redistribution Effects

This section first frames the decomposition problem by providing a unifying framework and a theoretical foundation for the decomposition methods commonly used in the literature. In particular, we note that changes in the distribution can be characterized in terms of the level of growth and the degree of relative inequality. The most common method stemming from this approach is the Datt and Ravallion (1992) decomposition, to which we turn first. However, as described in detail below, this method faces at least two important methodological issues: whether to use the initial or end period as the reference period, and how to interpret the residual change in poverty that is not accounted for.

Indeed, all decomposition methods seek to identify the contributions of factors influencing the distribution, as measured by a particular statistic, such as poverty or inequality. Ideally, these contributions should exhaust the observed distributional change, and it should not matter whether one chooses the initial or end period as a reference. However, this is not always the case, because a residual may be left unaccounted for, and the decomposition results could suffer from path dependence. Therefore, in the second part of this section, we present the Shapley (1953) method, which provides a unified framework to assess the relative importance of determining factors (Shorrocks [1999] 2013). The final part of this section considers application of the Shapley method to the decomposition of change in poverty over time.

Framing the Decomposition

Given that poverty measures are computed on the basis of a distribution of living standards that is fully characterized by its location parameter μ (the mean of the distribution) and the associated Lorenz curve L, it is reasonable to express a poverty measure P as a function of these elements along with the poverty line, z, as follows: $P_t = P(\mu_t, L_t, Z_t)$. The overall variation in poverty, as measured by P_t, from a base period ($t = 0$) to an end period ($t = 1$) can be written as follows:[2]

$$\Delta_O^P = P(\mu_1, L_1, z_1) - P(\mu_0, L_0, z_0) = \int_0^1 \frac{dP}{dt} dt. \tag{2.1}$$

Equivalently, we have

$$\Delta_O^P = \int_0^1 \frac{\partial P}{\partial \mu} \frac{\partial \mu}{\partial t} dt + \int_0^1 \frac{\partial P}{\partial L} \frac{\partial L}{\partial t} dt + \int_0^1 \frac{\partial P}{\partial z} \frac{\partial z}{\partial t} dt. \tag{2.2}$$

Equation (2.2) clearly indicates that we can think of the variation in poverty over time as consisting of three basic components: the *size effect* associated with the change in the mean of the underlying distribution, the *redistribution effect* resulting from changes in the Lorenz curve (an indicator of relative inequality), and a third component linked to the variation in the poverty line.

When working with real income (or expenditure) as an indicator of economic welfare, the poverty line is considered fixed so that we write the overall level of poverty as a function only of mean real income (or expenditure) and the Lorenz function. With this assumption, the overall change in poverty defined by equation (2.2) can be written as

$$\Delta_O^P = \int_0^1 \frac{\partial P}{\partial \mu} \frac{\partial \mu}{\partial t} dt + \int_0^1 \frac{\partial P}{\partial L} \frac{\partial L}{\partial t} dt, \tag{2.3}$$

so that any variation in poverty consists only of the *size* and the *redistribution effects*. Note that these effects are defined in terms of partial derivatives of the poverty measure. For a differentiable function of several variables, it is well known that the partial derivative of that function at a particular point is the rate of change of the function near the point with respect to one of the variables *with the other variables held constant*. This notion of *ceteris paribus* variation that underlies the definition of the decomposition terms presented in equation (2.3) also suggests a clear strategy for the identification (and hence the estimation) of those effects. The size effect, for instance, is defined as a variation in the poverty outcome with respect to a variation in the average income, holding inequality constant. Similarly, the redistribution effect is defined under the assumption of size neutrality. The identification strategy underlying all decomposition methods designed to implement equation (2.3) empirically relies on these definitions.

Decomposing changes in a variable over time can be viewed as a problem of integral approximation (Müller 2008).[3] Therefore, equation (2.1) provides a unifying framework and a clear theoretical foundation for the decomposition methods commonly discussed in the literature. In particular, its expression by equation (2.3) provides an analytical framework for the study of the poverty implications of a growth pattern, given that such a pattern can be characterized in terms of the level of growth and the degree of relative inequality.

For example, Kraay (2006) proposes a decomposition of changes in poverty that is consistent with the fundamental equation for dynamic decomposition that is equation (2.1). Consider the class of additive poverty measures defined by $P = \int_0^z \psi(y \mid z) f(y) dy$, where y is the outcome variable (for example, a living-standard indicator, such as income or consumption expenditure), z is the poverty line, and $f(y)$ is the density function associated with the distribution of y. The term $\psi(y|z)$ is a convex and decreasing function measuring deprivation for an individual with a level of economic welfare equal to y. This function is equal to zero when the welfare indicator is greater than or equal to the poverty line.

Applying Leibnitz's rule of differentiation under the integral sign and rearranging terms, one gets the following expression for the proportionate change in poverty,

$$\frac{dP}{P} = \frac{1}{P} \int_0^z y\psi'(y \mid z) g(y) f(y) dy, \tag{2.4}$$

where ψ' is the first-order derivative of the indicator of individual deprivation and $g(y)$ is the *growth incidence curve*[4] (GIC) as defined by Ravallion and Chen (2003). Equation (2.4) reveals that for the class of additively separable poverty measures, a change in poverty over time can be written as a weighted sum of points along the GIC.[5] This fact implies that variation in poverty outcomes, as measured by the class of additively separable poverty measures, inherits the decomposability of the GIC. In particular, using the neutral element for addition, one can split the GIC into one component showing the growth rate of average income $\left(\gamma = \frac{d\mu}{\mu}\right)$ and another showing the deviation of each point on the curve from the overall growth rate. We therefore have $g(y) = \gamma + [g(y) - \gamma]$. In fact, the first component is the rate of growth that would be experienced at every quantile if the growth process were distribution neutral. This is essentially the *size effect*. It can be shown that the second component is equal to the change in the slope of the Lorenz curve between the base and end periods (Ravallion and Chen 2003). Thus, this component measures the *redistribution effect*. Equivalently, we can express equation (2.4) as follows:

$$\frac{dP}{P}=\frac{\gamma}{P}\int_{0}^{z}y\psi'(y\mid z)f(y)dy+\frac{1}{P}\int_{0}^{z}y\psi'(y\mid z)\left[g(y)-\gamma\right]f(y)dy. \quad (2.5)$$

Equation (2.5) therefore shows that the proportionate change in poverty over time can be split into two components representing the size and redistribution effects.[6] It is clear from this equation that when growth is distribution neutral—that is, $g(y) = \gamma$—the redistribution effect disappears.

The size effect is a product of two terms: the growth rate of per capita income and the responsiveness of the chosen poverty measure to variations in incomes. Ultimately, this responsiveness depends on the value judgments underpinning poverty measurement. Such judgments are reflected in the specification of the individual deprivation function,[7] $\psi(y|z)$. The size effect measures the extent to which poverty would have changed had the growth process been distribution neutral. Similarly, the redistribution effect measures the extent to which poverty would have changed had growth left per capita income unchanged (that is, had the growth process been size neutral). This effect, too, depends on the elasticity of poverty with respect to income.

Economic growth is pro-poor if it leads to poverty reduction for some choice of poverty measure. On the basis of equation (2.5), Kraay (2006) identifies three potential sources of pro-poor growth: (a) growth in income per capita (γ); (b) the responsiveness of poverty to growth in average income (the coefficient of η_P in the size effect; see endnote 4); and (c) the pattern of relative inequality.

The Datt-Ravallion Method

When the poverty line is held constant over time, the overall change in poverty from the base period to the end period is equal to

$$\Delta_O^P = P(\mu_1, L_1) - P(\mu_0, L_0). \quad (2.6)$$

Datt and Ravallion (1992) propose a threefold decomposition procedure that allows an analyst to express that variation in poverty in terms of three components: the size effect, the redistribution effect, and a residual interpreted as an interaction effect. According to the *ceteris paribus* strategy, the identification of each of these effects entails a comparison of observed outcomes with counterfactual ones. For instance, the size effect is the change in poverty resulting from a variation in the mean while the Lorenz curve is held at some reference level. The identification of this effect requires that we compare the observed poverty outcome with a counterfactual based on the same level of inequality. In other words, the only difference between the two states is the mean income. Similarly, the redistribution effect is the change in poverty resulting from a change in the Lorenz curve while holding the mean constant at some reference level. Both the observed and counterfactual outcomes are based on the same mean but different Lorenz curves.

A key methodological issue here is this: Which period should be used as reference for the factor that must be common to both the counterfactual and the observed state of affairs? In principle, one could choose either the base period or the end period as reference. However, Datt and Ravallion (1992) argue that the base period is a natural choice for the decomposition and conduct their analysis on that basis. Within that framework, the size effect is equal to the following expression:

$$\Delta_{\mu}^{P} = P(\mu_1, L_0) - P(\mu_0, L_0). \tag{2.7}$$

Similarly, the redistribution effect is

$$\Delta_{L}^{P} = P(\mu_0, L_1) - P(\mu_0, L_0). \tag{2.8}$$

Note that these two expressions describe counterfactual outcomes. The size effect entails *distribution neutral* growth (the Lorenz curve does not change). The redistribution effect implies that growth is *size neutral* (the mean does not change).

To obtain the Datt-Ravallion decomposition, we can add and subtract these counterfactual outcomes to and from the right-hand side of equation (2.6). Upon rearranging terms, we get the following:

$$\Delta_{O}^{P} = \Delta_{\mu}^{P} + \Delta_{L}^{P} + \left[\left[P(\mu_1, L_1) - P(\mu_1, L_0)\right] - \left[P(\mu_0, L_1) - P(\mu_0, L_0)\right]\right]. \tag{2.9}$$

The third term in brackets on the right-hand side of equation (2.9) is the residual interpreted as the interaction effect. It is the difference between two ways of computing the redistributive effect depending on whether one fixes the end-period mean or the base-period mean. In other words, the residual is the difference between the redistribution effect computed on the basis of the end-period mean and the same effect evaluated at the initial mean (Datt and Ravallion 1992; Ravallion 2000). This is an indicator of the extent to which changes in per capita income matter to the responsiveness of poverty to inequality.

Interestingly, we can rearrange terms within the residual and get the following equivalent expression:

$$\Delta_{R}^{P} = \left[P(\mu_1, L_1) - P(\mu_0, L_1)\right] - \left[P(\mu_1, L_0) - P(\mu_0, L_0)\right]. \tag{2.10}$$

This expression reveals that the residual is also equal to the difference between the size effect computed on the basis of the end-period Lorenz curve and the same effect evaluated at the initial-period Lorenz curve. Thus the residual also shows the importance of inequality in determining the effect of changes in per capita income on poverty. The structure of the residual revealed by equations (2.9) and (2.10) led Datt and Ravallion (1992) to interpret this residual as the *interaction effect* between the size and redistribution effects.

Indeed, if the size effect depends on the reference Lorenz curve, or the redistribution effect on the reference mean, the residual would not equal zero. Thus, the interaction term would vanish if the poverty measure is additively separable between μ and L.[8] The residual would also vanish if one were to use the initial year as the reference point in the computation of the size effect and switch to the final year for the redistribution effect.

Finally, no residual would be involved if one performed the Datt-Ravallion decomposition twice and took the average result. The first decomposition uses the initial year as reference, while the second uses the end year (Ravallion 2000). As it turns out, this average Datt-Ravallion decomposition is precisely the procedure proposed by Shorrocks ([1999] 2013) based on the Shapley (1953) value. Kakwani (2000) proposes the same procedure but does not refer to the Shapley value. Instead, he invokes a series of axioms that the decomposition must satisfy.[9]

The Shapley Decomposition

In general, all decomposition methods used in distributional analysis seek to identify and assign contributions to factors influencing some distributional statistic. Ideally, the assignment is done in a manner that exhausts the quantity under consideration. The Shapley method provides a unified framework to deal not only with the identification and estimation of the size and redistribution effects but also with many other situations in applied economics where there is a need to assess the relative importance of determining factors (Shorrocks [1999] 2013). In this section, we first review the definition of the Shapley value that motivates the method. Then we consider its application to the decomposition of change in poverty over time.

The Shapley Value

The Shapley value provides a formula for dividing a joint cost or a jointly produced output on the basis of a fair assessment of individual contributions to the formation of total cost or the production of a surplus. Thus, it can be viewed as an interpretation of the *reward* principle of distributive justice (Moulin 2003).[10]

Formally, the Shapley value is a solution to a cooperative game with transferable utility (Shapley 1953). The problem of the *commons* is used often to explain the nature of such games. A commons is a technology that is jointly owned and operated by a group of agents. Consider a fixed set of agents engaged in such a venture. Their problem is to share fairly the fruit of this collaboration. Starting from scratch, let the agents join the venture one at a time in some predetermined order. As each agent joins, the value (to be shared) increases. Thus the contribution of a given agent is the value added when he or she joins the venture.

The Shapley value of a partner is her or his average contribution to value over all possible orderings of the partners.

The Shapley allocation rule respects the following restrictions: (a) there must be *symmetry* or *anonymity*; (b) the result must be an exact and *additive decomposition*; and (c) the contribution of each factor is taken to be equal to its (first-round) *marginal impact*. Symmetry means that the value assigned to players does not depend on their traits or identities. This property stems from the fact that the value of a coalitional game to a player depends only on the characteristic function that maps the set of all possible coalitions of players to a set of payoffs. This function determines the payoff a group of players can expect by forming a coalition.

To illustrate the basic idea underlying the Shapley value, consider a coalition game with a set A of three players, A = {a, b, c}, and a characteristic (or value) function v. The value of the grand coalition to be distributed among the three players is equal to $v(A)$. The number of all possible coalitions is equal to $2^3 = 8$, the number of all possible subsets of A (including the empty set). Thus there are seven possible nonempty coalitions. By definition, the payoff to an empty coalition is zero ($v(\emptyset) = 0$). Table 2.1 shows how to derive the Shapley value of each player.

Given an ordering, the computation of the marginal contribution depends on the rank of the player in that ordering. Take, for instance, the first ordering in table 2.1: (a, b, c). Since a is first, the marginal contribution of a is $m_a = v(\{a\}) - v(\emptyset) = v(\{a\})$. This is what he or she can achieve alone. We interpret this situation as joining an empty coalition. Since b is in second position, the corresponding marginal contribution is what he or she can achieve in a coalition with a, minus what a can achieve alone. The same reasoning applies to the case of c. The Shapley payoff to each player equals the arithmetic mean of her or his marginal contributions over the six possible orderings. Thus, to obtain the Shapley value for each player, we add up the marginal contributions in that player's column and divide the result by six. In the case of player a, the Shapley value is equal to the following expression:

$$S_a = \frac{1}{3}v(\{a, b, c\}) + \frac{1}{6}\left[v(\{a, b\}) + v(\{a, c\}) - 2v(b, c)\right] + \frac{1}{6}\left[2v(\{a\}) - v(\{b\}) - v(\{c\})\right]. \tag{2.11}$$

Table 2.1 Shapley Allocations for a Three-Player Game

Ordering	*a*	*b*	*c*
(a, b, c)	v({a})	v({a, b}) – v({a})	v({a, b, c}) – v({a, b})
(a, c, b)	v({a})	v({a, b, c}) – v({a, c})	v({a, c}) – v({a})
(c, a, b)	v({a, c}) – v({c})	v({a, b, c}) – v({a, c})	v({c})
(c, b, a)	v({a, b, c}) – v({b, c})	v({b, c}) – v({c})	v({c})
(b, c, a)	v({a, b, c}) – v({b, c})	v({b})	v({b, c}) – v({b})
(b, a, c)	v({a, b}) – v({b})	v({b})	v({a, b, c}) – v({a, b})
Shapley value	S_a	S_b	S_c

We have written equation (2.11) in a way that makes transparent the fact that it involves all nonempty coalitions that can be formed out of three players. It is consistent with the general Shapley formula involving combinatorial analysis. Let A be a fixed set of n players. Moulin (2003) explains that the Shapley value can be viewed as a translation of the reward principle of fairness into an explicit allocation of $v(A)$ on the basis of $(2^n - 1)$ values $v(C)$, for all nonempty coalitions of the n players involved. Let B_j be the set of coalitions that exclude player j, and $B_j(k)$ the subset of B_j containing all coalitions of size k = 0, 1, 2, ..., $n-1$. The Shapley value of player j is given by the following formula:[11]

$$S_j = \sum_{k=0}^{n-1} \sum_{C \in B_j(k)} \frac{k!(n-k-1)!}{n!} \left(v(C \cup \{j\}) - v(C)\right). \tag{2.12}$$

The term $m_j = v(C \cup \{j\}) - v(C)$ is the marginal contribution of player j if she joins coalition C. The coefficient of the marginal value in equation (2.12) represents the probability that the coalition C of size k contains exactly all the players preceding j in a random ordering of the grand coalition A. All marginal contributions involved in that expression are counterfactual outcomes. We now apply this logic to the decomposition of change in poverty over time.

Application to Change in Poverty Over Time

To see how the above principle translates into a decomposition procedure, consider a distributional statistic, such as the overall level of poverty or inequality. For instance, let the poverty be a function of m contributory factors, which together account for the value of the indicator. The m factors are thus analogous to the players in a cooperative game. The decomposition approach proposed by Shorrocks ([1999] 2013) is based on the marginal effect on the value of the indicator resulting from eliminating sequentially each of the contributory factors and computing the corresponding marginal change in the statistic. The method then assigns to each factor the (arithmetic) average of its marginal contributions in all possible elimination sequences.

Consider again the problem of decomposing a change in poverty over time into a size and a redistribution effect using the Shapley method to implement equation (2.3). We rewrite the overall variation in poverty as a function, H, of two factors as follows:

$$\Delta_O^P = H(\Delta\mu, \Delta L). \tag{2.13}$$

In other words, the overall change in poverty is fully determined by two contributory factors[12]—namely, the change in the mean of the distribution $\Delta\mu = \mu_1 - \mu_0$ and the change in the Lorenz curve $\Delta L = L_1 - L_0$. As seen in the Datt-Ravallion method, the value of any effect (size or redistribution) depends on the chosen period of reference. This *path dependence* violates the anonymity constraint that the Shapley method must respect. We therefore need to consider all possible sequences of elimination and the associated marginal contributions that must be averaged in the end. In this simple case, we have only two possible sequences: either we eliminate the size factor first by setting $\Delta\mu = 0$ and then the redistribution factor by setting $\Delta L = 0$, or we start with the redistribution factor to end with the size factor.

The Shapley contribution of the size factor to change in poverty is equal to the average (over the two possible elimination sequences) of the relevant marginal contributions. That is,

$$S_\mu = \frac{1}{2}\left[\left[P(\mu_1, L_1) - P(\mu_0, L_1)\right] + \left[P(\mu_1, L_0) - P(\mu_0, L_0)\right]\right]. \tag{2.14}$$

Similarly, the Shapley contribution of the redistribution factor to change in poverty is equal to

$$S_L = \frac{1}{2}\left[\left[P(\mu_1, L_1) - P(\mu_1, L_0)\right] + \left[P(\mu_0, L_1) - P(\mu_0, L_0)\right]\right]. \tag{2.15}$$

The overall change in poverty can therefore be expressed as $\Delta_O^P = S_\mu + S_L$, which depends on the contribution of growth and redistribution with no remaining residual.

Beyond the standard Datt-Ravallion partitioning, the decomposition of a change in poverty over time in terms of the size and redistribution effects can be embedded in a broader context to account for the effect of population shifts or for the relative importance of components of an aggregate living- standard indicator. The flexibility of the Shapley method makes it a strong candidate for handling these integrated decompositions. Let the total population of a given country be partitioned exhaustively into m socioeconomic groups. For instance, these groups could represent different groups according to geographic location, ethnicity, or other socioeconomic dimensions. Let w_{kt} be the share of population in group k at time t for $t = \{0, 1\}$ and P_{kt} the level of poverty in that group at the same time. For additively decomposable poverty measures, overall poverty at time t can be written as follows:

$$P_t = \sum_{k=1}^{m} w_{kt} P_{kt}. \tag{2.16}$$

The change in aggregate poverty over time can now be written as follows:

$$\Delta_O^P = \sum_{k=1}^{m} \left[w_{k1} P_{k1} - w_{k0} P_{k0}\right]. \tag{2.17}$$

Suppose we are interested in accounting for the overall change in poverty Δ_O^P in terms of changes in within-group poverty, $\Delta P_k = P_{k1} - P_{k0}$, and the population shifts between groups, $\Delta w_k = w_{k1} - w_{k0}$. We note that the contribution of group k in the change of aggregate poverty is equal to the following expression:

$$C_k = w_{k1}P_{k1} - w_{k0}P_{k0}. \tag{2.18}$$

If the population share of this group were fixed at the baseline level, the contribution of this group to overall poverty change would be $w_{k0}\Delta P_k$. We can add and subtract this counterfactual to equation (2.18), rearrange terms, and sum over k. We get the following decomposition presented in Bourguignon and Ferreira (2005):[13]

$$\Delta_O^P = \sum_{k=1}^{m} w_{k0}\Delta P_k + \sum_{k=1}^{m} P_{k1}\Delta w_k. \tag{2.19}$$

According to equation (2.19), the overall change in poverty can be split into two components: one representing the contribution of changes in within-group poverty and the other the contribution of population shifts.

The decomposition presented in equation (2.19) is path dependent since changes in poverty are weighted by the base-year population shares while changes in population shares are weighted by the end-year poverty level. The Shapley principle leads to the following twofold decomposition (Shorrocks [1999] 2013):[14]

$$\Delta_O^P = \sum_{k=1}^{m}\left(\frac{w_{k0}+w_{k1}}{2}\right)\Delta P_k + \sum_{k=1}^{m}\left(\frac{P_{k0}+P_{k1}}{2}\right)\Delta w_k. \tag{2.20}$$

Equation (2.20) therefore allows for a decomposition of changes in poverty on account of changes in within-group poverty and changes in population between groups.

Accounting for the Contribution of Demographics and Income Components

So far we have seen decompositions of changes in poverty on account of changes in growth and redistribution and decompositions of within-group changes in poverty as opposed to changes in population between groups. However, there is also interest in decomposing changes in poverty into the contributions that changes in demographics, employment, public transfers, and remittances could have made. In this section, we describe an approach to undertake these sorts of decompositions involving the Shapley method described above.

As proposed by Azevedo et al. (2013), we begin with a household consumption identity whereby household consumption, C_h, per capita is defined by

$$C_h = \theta_h \frac{Y_h}{n}, \tag{2.21}$$

where Y_h is total household income, n is the number of household members, and θ_h is the consumption-to-income ratio. Because poverty depends on the distribution of consumption, changes in any of the factors on the right-hand side of equation (2.21) will lead to changes in poverty: demographic changes (n), growth in labor and nonlabor income (which make up Y_h), and changes in consumption patterns (θ_h).

Following Barros et al. (2006), household per capita income can be modeled as

$$Y_{pc} = \frac{Y_h}{n} = \frac{1}{n}\sum_{i=1}^{n} y_i. \tag{2.22}$$

Income per capita is based on the sum of each individual's income as well as the number of household members, n. If we recognize that only individuals 15 years and older contribute to family income, income per capita depends on the number of adults in the family, n_A, so income per capita can be written as

$$Y_{pc} = \frac{n_A}{n}\left(\frac{1}{n_A}\sum_{i=1}^{n} y_i\right). \tag{2.23}$$

Income per adult includes labor income, y_i^L, and nonlabor income, y_i^{NL}, where nonlabor income includes public social transfers, pensions, remittances, and other private transfers. Specifying each type of income, we have

$$Y_{pc} = \frac{n_A}{n}\left(\frac{1}{n_A}\sum_{i \in A}^{n} y_i^L + \frac{1}{n_A}\sum_{i \in A}^{n} y_i^{NL}\right). \tag{2.24}$$

Finally, not all adults in the household are occupied (working), and household labor income per capita depends on the income of employed adults. Therefore, we can decompose the labor income per occupied adult as

$$Y_{pc} = \frac{n_A}{n}\left[\frac{n_o}{n_A}\left(\frac{1}{n_o}\sum_{i \in A}^{n} y_i^L\right) + \frac{1}{n_A}\sum_{i \in A}^{n} y_i^{NL}\right], \tag{2.25}$$

where n_o is the number of occupied adults.

Note that official poverty rates in some countries are calculated on the basis of household income. In these cases, equation (2.25) is sufficient to decompose the contribution of demographic factors, labor income, and nonlabor income to observed poverty reduction. However, most countries measure the distribution of welfare, and poverty in particular, using household consumption. Therefore, we modify the Barros et al. (2006) approach by mapping consumption to income. In particular, we refer to the household consumption identity in (2.21).

Combining (2.21) and (2.25) above, we can express household consumption per capita, C_{pc}, as

$$C_{pc} = \theta_h \left[\frac{n_A}{n} \left[\frac{n_o}{n_A} \left(\frac{1}{n_o} \sum_{i \in A}^{n} y_i^L \right) + \frac{1}{n_A} \sum_{i \in A}^{n} y_i^{NL} \right] \right]. \tag{2.26}$$

With this framework, whether countries measure welfare by per capita household income or consumption, we can separate the demographic, labor, and nonlabor components discussed earlier. In addition, we can separate the contribution of changes in consumption patterns over time in poverty reduction. The determinants of per capita consumption are summarized in figure 2.1.

Contributions of Determinants of Consumption to Poverty Reduction

Let $F(.)$ be the cumulative distribution function (CDF) of the distribution of welfare. Since the factors in equation (2.6) determine the changes in the CDF of consumption underlying changes in poverty outcomes, we can trace the effect of those factors on poverty. As a result, any poverty measure can be written as a function of each of these components. Therefore, the contribution of

Figure 2.1 Determinants of Consumption per Capita

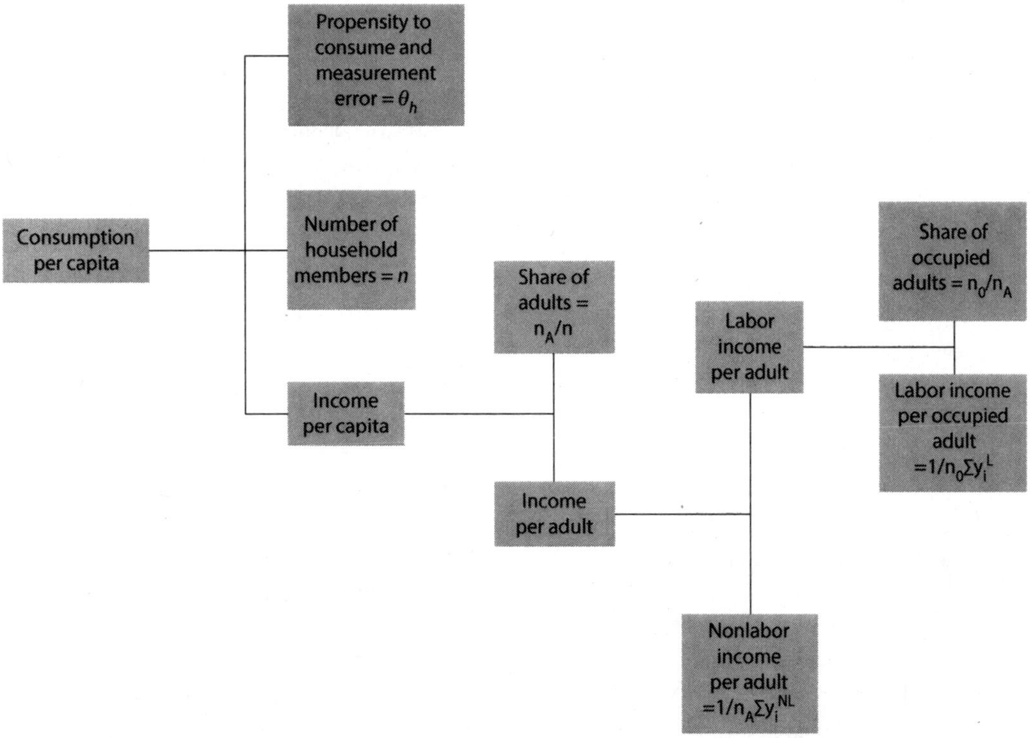

Source: Adaptation of Barros et al. 2006.

each component toward changes in poverty or distribution can be expressed as a function of these indicators in the initial and end periods.

Following Barros et al. (2006), we can then simulate the distribution of welfare by changing each of these components, one at a time, to calculate its contribution to the observed changes in poverty. In particular, let v be a measure of poverty, inequality, or any other distributional statistic. Then, this measure will be a function of the cumulative density function, $F(.)$, which in turn depends on each of the factors above, as follows:

$$\vartheta = \Phi\left(F\left(C_{pc}\left(\theta_h, \frac{n_A}{n}, \frac{n_o}{n_A}, y_{PO}^{L}, y_{PA}^{NL}\right)\right)\right), \tag{2.27}$$

where

$$y_{PO}^{L} = \frac{1}{n_o}\sum_{i \in A}^{n} y_i^{L}$$

and

$$y_{PA}^{NL} = \frac{1}{n_A}\sum_{i \in A}^{n} y_i^{NL}.$$

Given that the distribution of per capita consumption for period 0 and period 1 are known, we can construct counterfactual distributions for period 1 by substituting the observed level of the indicators in period 0, one at a time. For each counterfactual distribution, we can compute the poverty measure and interpret those counterfactuals as the poverty that would have prevailed in the absence of a change in that indicator. For example, to see the impact of the change in the share of occupied adults, we compute $\hat{\vartheta}$, where we substitute the value of $\frac{n_o}{n_A}$ observed in period 0 to the observed distribution in period 1 as follows,

$$\hat{\vartheta} = \Phi\left(F\left(C_{pc}\left(\theta_h, \frac{n_A}{n}, \frac{\hat{n}_0}{n_A}, y_{PO}^{L}, y_{PA}^{NL}\right)\right)\right), \tag{2.28}$$

such that the contribution of the share of occupied adults is the difference between the observed ϑ in period 1 and the estimated counterfactual, $\hat{\vartheta}$. Similarly, each of the other components in the consumption per capita distribution in period 1 can be substituted by its value in period 0 so that its contribution to changes in poverty can be computed.

Since we don't have panel data, we do not observe period 1 households in period 0. Therefore, we use a rank-preserving transformation to assign first-period characteristics to the second-period observations. This method uses an idea first proposed by Juhn, Murphy, and Pierce (1993), who decomposed changes in wages by running Mincer-type ordinary least squares (OLS) regressions that make it possible to decompose labor income inequality, using any measure of inequality, into three parts:

- *Quantity effects*, referring to the distribution of observable workers' characteristics, such as education and labor market experience, and are included as regressors in the equation;
- *Price effects*, which capture changes in returns to observed characteristics through the regression's coefficients;
- *The regression residual* (unobservables), which reflects changes in inequality within education and experience groups.

Counterfactuals for the quantity effects can be created by assigning the mean observable characteristic from one period to the other, and the counterfactual for the price effects can be created by substituting regression coefficients from one period to another. However, to complete that analysis, the authors needed to assign a value to the residuals in each period. So they created a counterfactual by ordering households by their earnings in each period and then taking the average residual value in each quantile from the first period and assigning it to all households in the same quantile in the second period.

In this case, instead of running a Mincer regression, we create counterfactuals by ordering households by their level of welfare (measured by either household per capita consumption or income) and then taking the average value of each characteristic in equation (2.25) for each quantile in period 0 and assigning it to each household in that same quantile in period 1. For example, if we are decomposing the effect of labor income, we order households into quantiles by their observed total household income in periods 0 and 1. Then, for every quantile in period 1, we replace the period 1 labor income with the average labor income in period 0 from households that were in the same quantile.

Barros et al. (2006) compute each counterfactual simulation in a nested fashion (table 2.2). They identify the contribution that interactions between variables have in poverty reduction by first computing the joint impact of a subset of variables, and then subtracting the marginal impact of each variable, one at a time. For instance, in step 2 in table 2.2, they first compute the joint impact of inserting both the share of adults and the income per adult from the first period into the distribution of the second period. They then compute the impact of changing only the share of adults and take the difference of these two simulations to approximate the marginal impact that changing the share of adults had on the distribution. However, in step 4, instead of computing the impact of income per adult on its own, they compute the impact of changing both the labor and nonlabor income per adult. This is done because the sum of labor and nonlabor income should be equivalent to changing total income per adult. The results of these two simulations are different, however, and the simulation of labor income is not done explicitly, but rather ends up being a "residual" in step 8 to ensure that the cumulative effect adds up to the total distributional change.

Table 2.2 Application of Barros Methodology to Measure Contributions of Variables to Change in Poverty

Step	*Estimate*	*Variable or interaction being measured*
1.	$\vartheta_0 = \Phi\left(F\left(Y_{pc}\left(\frac{n_A}{n}, \frac{n_o}{n_A}, y_{PO}^{L}, y_{PA}^{NL}\right)\right)\right)$	Initial poverty rate is ϑ_0.
2.	$\widehat{\vartheta_{a1}} = \Phi\left(F\left(Y_{pc}\left(\widehat{\frac{n_A}{n}}, \widehat{y_{PA}}\right)\right)\right)$	Contribution of the interaction between share of adults and income per adult is $\widehat{\vartheta_{a1}} - \vartheta_0$.
3.	$\widehat{\vartheta_{nA}} = \Phi\left(F\left(Y_{pc}\left(\widehat{\frac{n_A}{n}}, y_{PA}\right)\right)\right)$	Contribution of share of household adults is $\widehat{\vartheta_{nA}} - \widehat{\vartheta_{a1}}$.
4.	$\widehat{\vartheta_{a2}} = \Phi\left(F\left(Y_{pc}\left(\frac{n_A}{n}, \frac{n_o}{n_A}, \widehat{y_{PO}^{L}}, \widehat{y_{PA}^{NL}}\right)\right)\right)$	Contribution of the interaction between labor and nonlabor income is $\widehat{\vartheta_{a2}} - \widehat{\vartheta_{nA}}$.
5.	$\widehat{\vartheta_{NL}} = \Phi\left(F\left(Y_{pc}\left(\frac{n_A}{n}, \frac{n_o}{n_A}, y_{PO}^{L}, \widehat{y_{PA}^{NL}}\right)\right)\right)$	Contribution of nonlabor income is $\widehat{\vartheta_{NL}} - \widehat{\vartheta_{a1}}$.
6.	$\widehat{\vartheta_{a3}} = \Phi\left(F\left(Y_{pc}\left(\frac{n_A}{n}, \widehat{\frac{n_o}{n_A}}, \widehat{y_{PO}^{L}}, y_{PA}^{NL}\right)\right)\right)$	Contribution of the interaction between labor income and the share of occupied adults is $\widehat{\vartheta_{a3}} - \widehat{\vartheta_{NL}}$.
7.	$\widehat{\vartheta_{no}} = \Phi\left(F\left(Y_{pc}\left(\frac{n_A}{n}, \widehat{\frac{n_o}{n_A}}, y_{PO}^{L}, y_{PA}^{NL}\right)\right)\right)$	Contribution of the share of occupied adults is $\widehat{\vartheta_{no}} - \widehat{\vartheta_{a3}}$.
8.	$\vartheta_F = \Phi\left(F\left(Y_{pc}\left(\frac{n_A}{n}, \frac{n_o}{n_A}, y_{PO}^{L}, y_{PA}^{NL}\right)\right)\right)$	Final poverty rate is ϑ_F. The contribution of labor income, y_{PO}^{L}, is calculated as a residual: $\vartheta_F - \widehat{\vartheta_{a3}}$.

Azevedo et al. (2013) modify this procedure in three important ways:

- They focus on consumption as a measure of welfare.
- They compute a cumulative counterfactual distribution by adding one variable at a time.
- They compute Shapley-Shorrocks estimates of each component.

The first change –the focus on consumption—is made because most developing countries use a consumption aggregate to measure poverty. Second, in contrast to the Barros et al. (2006) approach, the proposed method does not separately identify the contribution of the interaction between variables in the observed distributional changes; doing so is partial at best, given that changing any variable can potentially affect all other variables. Instead, the impact of changes in each variable and its interactions with all other variables is calculated as the difference between the cumulative counterfactuals. Table 2.3 shows an example for one possible path, taking into account the fact that nonlabor income is made up of pensions, transfers, capital income, and other income.

The third methodological change—computing Shapley-Shorrocks estimates of each component—addresses the fact that this methodology suffers from path dependence, described in the previous section. In other words, the order in which the cumulative effects are calculated matters.[15] The best-known remedy for this is to calculate the cumulative decomposition in every possible order and then

Table 2.3 Proposed Methodology to Decompose Change in Poverty along One Possible Path

Step	Estimate	Variable measured
1.	$\vartheta_0 = \Phi\left(F\left(C_{pc}\left(\theta_h, \frac{n_A}{n}, \frac{n_o}{n_A}, y^L_{PO}, y^{NL}_{PA}\right)\right)\right)$	Initial poverty rate is ϑ_0.
2.	$\widehat{\vartheta_1} = \Phi\left(F\left(C_{pc}\left(\theta_h, \widehat{\frac{n_A}{n}}, \frac{n_o}{n_A}, y^L_{PO}, y^{NL}_{PA}\right)\right)\right)$	Contribution of share of household adults is $\widehat{\vartheta_1} - \vartheta_0$.
3.	$\widehat{\vartheta_2} = \Phi\left(F\left(C_{pc}\left(\theta_h, \widehat{\frac{n_A}{n}}, \widehat{\frac{n_o}{n_A}}, y^L_{PO}, y^{NL}_{PA}\right)\right)\right)$	Contribution of the share of occupied adults is $\widehat{\vartheta_2} - \widehat{\vartheta_1}$.
4.	$\widehat{\vartheta_3} = \Phi\left(F\left(C_{pc}\left(\theta_h, \widehat{\frac{n_A}{n}}, \widehat{\frac{n_o}{n_A}}, y^L_{PO}, \widehat{y^{Pens}_{PA}}, y^{Trans}_{PA}, y^{Cap}_{PA}, y^{Oth\ NL}_{PA}\right)\right)\right)$	Contribution of pensions is $\widehat{\vartheta_3} - \widehat{\vartheta_2}$.
5.	$\widehat{\vartheta_4} = \Phi\left(F\left(C_{pc}\left(\theta_h, \widehat{\frac{n_A}{n}}, \widehat{\frac{n_o}{n_A}}, y^L_{PO}, \widehat{y^{Pens}_{PA}}, \widehat{y^{Trans}_{PA}}, y^{Cap}_{PA}, y^{Oth\ NL}_{PA}\right)\right)\right)$	Contribution of transfers is $\widehat{\vartheta_4} - \widehat{\vartheta_3}$.
6.	$\widehat{\vartheta_5} = \Phi\left(F\left(C_{pc}\left(\theta_h, \widehat{\frac{n_A}{n}}, \widehat{\frac{n_o}{n_A}}, y^L_{PO}, \widehat{y^{Pens}_{PA}}, \widehat{y^{Trans}_{PA}}, \widehat{y^{Cap}_{PA}}, y^{Oth\ NL}_{PA}\right)\right)\right)$	Contribution of capital income is $\widehat{\vartheta_5} - \widehat{\vartheta_4}$.
7.	$\widehat{\vartheta_6} = \Phi\left(F\left(C_{pc}\left(\theta_h, \widehat{\frac{n_A}{n}}, \widehat{\frac{n_o}{n_A}}, y^L_{PO}, \widehat{y^{Pens}_{PA}}, \widehat{y^{Trans}_{PA}}, \widehat{y^{Cap}_{PA}}, \widehat{y^{Oth\ NL}_{PA}}\right)\right)\right)$	Contribution of other nonlabor income is $\widehat{\vartheta_6} - \widehat{\vartheta_5}$.
8.	$\vartheta_F = \Phi\left(F\left(C_{pc}\left(\theta_h, \frac{n_A}{n}, \frac{n_o}{n_A}, y^L_{PO}, y^{NL}_{PA}\right)\right)\right)$	Final poverty rate is ϑ_F. Contribution of labor income is $\widehat{\vartheta_F} - \widehat{\vartheta_6}$.

average the results for each component to get the Shapley-Shorrocks estimate of the contribution of each component, as described earlier (Shapley 1953; Shorrocks [1999] 2013).

Summary and Conclusions

This chapter provides a unifying framework and a theoretical foundation for the decomposition methods commonly used in the literature. We began with the simplest decompositions, noting that changes in poverty can be characterized in terms of the level of growth and the degree of relative inequality.

The most common method stemming from this view is the Datt and Ravallion (1992) decomposition. Ideally, the contribution of growth and inequality should exhaust the observed change in poverty, and the results should be the same regardless of the reference period. However, this is not the case, because a residual is typically left unaccounted for in the standard Datt-Ravallion method, and the choice of reference period can affect the results. As described in this chapter, the Shapley method provides a unified framework to assess the relative importance of determining factors (Shorrocks [1999] 2013) and addresses both of these concerns. Use of the Shapley method can be extended to more complex decompositions, such as one that accounts for changes to poverty resulting from changes within socioeconomic groups as opposed to population shifts between groups.

Although these decompositions are interesting, analysts often want to go beyond these summary statistics to decompose the contributions that changes in demographics, employment, public transfers, and remittances could have made toward poverty reduction. We described an approach to undertake these sorts of decompositions, as proposed by Azevedo et al. (2013), that involves the Shapley method described above. In contrast to the simpler methods, this approach recognizes that poverty is a function of total household per capita consumption, which can be written as an accounting identity that depends on the number of household members, the consumption-to-income ratio, and household income. Based on these identities, we can simulate changes in the distribution of welfare by changing each component, one at a time, to calculate its contribution to the observed changes in poverty.

Assuming that only cross-sectional data are available, counterfactuals can be created nonparametrically, by ordering households according to their total income, creating quantiles for the initial and end periods, and then taking the average value of each component for each quantile in one period and assigning it to each household in that same quantile in the other period. When the cumulative impact of each of the components is analyzed, the methodology suffers from path dependence. Therefore, the proposed method calculates the Shapley-Shorrocks estimates of each component to find the contribution of each component.

With chapter 2 having described a set of relatively simple decompositions, chapter 3 will apply the proposed methods to a large set of countries that have seen significant declines in poverty over the past decade. However, before proceeding, it is important to point out two remaining caveats in this approach, the first of which is addressed later in the book.

First, although the decomposition method proposed here is useful to distinguish the main contributors to poverty reduction, its main limitation is the fact that it cannot shed light on whether the decline in poverty was the result of changes in the endowments of the population (such as higher educational levels or increases in other productive assets) or the result of changes in returns to those endowments. For this, one must turn to alternative decomposition techniques that impose an underlying labor model and greater structure (such as the methods proposed in chapters 4 and 6), compared with the nonparametric approach adopted here.

The second caveat to this approach is that the counterfactual income distributions on which these decompositions rely suffer from equilibrium inconsistency. Because the decomposition modifies only one element at a time, the counterfactuals do not result from an economic equilibrium, but rather from a *ceteris paribus* exercise in which we assume that we can, in fact, modify one factor at a time and keep everything else constant. To address this concern, one would need to employ general equilibrium modeling, which is outside the scope of this book.

Notes

1. For a recent review of micro-decomposition methods, see Fortin, Lemieux, and Firpo 2011; Essama-Nssah 2012; and chapter 6 of this volume.
2. By the fundamental theorem of calculus, we know that if a primitive function F of another function f is known for $a \le x \le b$, then $\int_a^b f(x)dx = \int_a^b F'(x)dx = F(b) - F(a)$ (Kaplan 1991).
3. Let $Q(t) = Q(x_1(t), x_2(t), \ldots, x_m(t))$ be a quantity of interest that is a function of m time-dependent variables $x_k(t)$, $k = 1, 2, \ldots, m$. The fundamental equation for decomposition analogous to equation (2.1) or (2.2) can be written as $\Delta Q = \sum_{k=1}^{m} \int_0^1 \frac{\partial Q}{\partial x_k} \frac{\partial x_k}{\partial t} dt$. Any component of this expression that contains the derivative with respect to x_k is taken to represent the contribution of changes in this factor to the overall change in Q. A successful implementation of this decomposition requires the ability to solve the integrals involved or to approximate them. Müller (2008) explains that terms in this expression can be approximated by their values at the upper boundary, computing each derivative as the slope of the straight line joining the endpoints. He further points out that even though static decomposition of cross-sectional variations is formally equivalent to dynamic decomposition, for static decomposition to be meaningful there would need to be a continuous range of the variables involved between spatial or socioeconomic groups. Thus, the framework of integral approximation may not be appropriate for static decomposition. The notion of a path connecting socioeconomic groups does not necessarily make sense.

4. Suppose that y is continuously distributed over the population of interest. Denote by $F_t(y)$ the cumulative distribution function (CDF) of income showing the proportion, $\tau = \int_0^y f(y)dy$, of the population with income less than y at time t. The income level at the τth quantile is given by the inverse of the CDF: $y_t(\tau) = F_t^{-1}(\tau)$. The growth rate of income at the τth quantile between $t = 0$ and $t = 1$ is equal to $g(\tau) = \left(\frac{y_1(\tau)}{y_0(\tau)} - 1\right)$.

   The growth incidence curve is obtained by letting τ vary from zero to one and plotting against the corresponding values of $g(\tau)$. The quantiles involved are based on the ranking of individuals in an increasing order of their baseline income.
5. See Essama-Nssah and Lambert (2009) for an alternative derivation of this result.
6. Kakwani (1993) proposes a similar decomposition of a proportionate change in poverty based on the responsiveness of the chosen poverty measure to changes in mean income and to variation in the Gini coefficient.
7. Members of the additively separable poverty measures include, among others, the Watts (1968) index (W) and the Foster, Greer, and Thorbecke (1984) family (FGT). The associated deprivation functions are $\psi_W(y \mid z) = ln(z/y)$ for the Watts index, and $\psi_{FGT}(y \mid z) = \left(1 - \frac{y}{z}\right)^\alpha$, $\alpha \geq 0$, for the FGT family. When $\alpha = 0$, the deprivation leads to the headcount index: the proportion of individuals with living standards below the poverty line. When $\alpha = 1$, we get the normalized poverty deficit. Finally, when the same parameter is equal to 2, we get the "squared poverty gap."
8. Ravallion (2000) clarifies this point by noting that, in general, if a variable v is a function of two variables x and y and if this function is additively separable in x and y, then we can write: $v = g(x) + h(y)$. In these circumstances, the change in v when x changes holding y constant depends only on the initial and final values of x. Without this additive separability, we should expect the variation in v to depend on the particular value of y chosen.
9. In particular, Kakwani (2000) stipulates the following three axioms: First, the size and redistribution effects must exhaust the total change in poverty. Second, if both the size and the redistribution effects have the same sign (either [a] less than or equal to zero, or [b] greater than or equal to zero), then the overall change in poverty must have the same sign; otherwise, the total change in poverty must depend on the magnitude of the size and the redistribution effects. Third, both the size and the redistribution effects must be symmetric with respect to the base and end years. The latter axiom means that if changes in per capita income, for instance, induce poverty reduction as we go from the base to the end year, we must accept that moving from the end state to the initial state would increase poverty. A similar logic applies to the redistribution effect.
10. Moulin (2003) argues that the concept of *fairness* can be interpreted in terms of four basic principles: *exogenous rights*, *compensation*, *reward*, and *fitness*. An *exogenous right* is a normative postulate that dictates how a resource must be distributed among claimants. Equal treatment of equals is an example of such a postulate. In general, exogenous rights set claims to resources independently of the use of such resources and of the contribution to their production, while compensation and reward relate

fairness to individual characteristics relevant to the use or production of the resources under consideration. The *compensation principle* advocates giving extra resources to people who find themselves in unfortunate circumstances for which they cannot be held (morally) responsible. The *reward principle* bases allocation on individual behavior to the extent that it affects the overall burden or advantage under distribution. Finally, according to the *fitness principle*, resources must go to the person who can make the best use of them.

11. The Shapley value of player j can be equivalently expressed as $S_j = \sum_{C \subseteq A \setminus \{j\}} \frac{k!(n-k-1)!}{n!}\left(v\left(C \cup \{j\}\right) - v(C)\right)$, where the sum is taken over all possible coalitions (including the empty one) that can be built on the basis of the members of A.
12. Thus $H(0,0) = 0$.
13. It is possible to further transform this twofold decomposition as follows. Consider a counterfactual situation in which within-group poverty does not change. On the basis of equation (2.19), the contribution of group k to change in poverty can be written as $C_k = w_{k0}\left(P_{k1} - P_{k0}\right) + P_{k1}\left(w_{k1} - w_{k0}\right)$. Fixing group-level poverty at the base level reduces this contribution to $P_{k0}\left(w_{k1} - w_{k0}\right)$. We can add and subtract this counterfactual outcome to and from C_k, rearrange terms, and sum up over k to get the threefold decomposition proposed by Ravallion and Huppi (1991): $\Delta_O^P = \sum_{k=1}^{m} w_{k0}\Delta P_k + \sum_{k=1}^{m} P_{k0}\Delta w_k + \sum_{k=1}^{m} \Delta w_k \Delta P_k$. This expression shows that change in aggregate poverty over time can be decomposed into three components representing, respectively, within-group effects, the effect associated with population shifts, and interaction effects. This is analogous to the Datt-Ravallion decomposition for the size and redistribution effects.
14. Son (2003) proposes a similar expression in percentage change: $\frac{\Delta_O^P}{P_0} = \sum_{k=1}^{m} \frac{P_{k0}}{P_0}\left(\frac{w_{k0} + w_{k1}}{2}\right)\frac{\Delta P_k}{P_{k0}} + \sum_{k=1}^{m} \frac{w_{k0}}{P_0}\left(\frac{P_{k0} + P_{k1}}{2}\right)\frac{\Delta w_k}{w_{k0}}$.
15. Path dependence is common in the micro-decomposition literature. For recent reviews of the literature, see Chapter 6 of this volume; Essama-Nssah 2012; Fortin, Lemieux, and Firpo 2011; and Ferreira 2012.

Bibliography

Azevedo, João Pedro, Gabriela Inchauste, Sergio Olivieri, Jaime Saavedra, and Hernan Winkler. 2013. "Is Labor Income Responsible for Poverty Reduction? A Decomposition Approach." Policy Research Working Paper 6414, World Bank, Washington, DC.

Barros, Ricardo Paes, Mirela de Carvalho, Samuel Franco, and Rosane Mendonça. 2006. "Uma Análise das Principais Causas da Queda Recente na Desigualdade de Renda Brasileira." *Revista Econômica* 8 (1): 117–47.

Bourguignon François, and Francisco H. G. Ferreira. 2005. "Decomposing Changes in the Distribution of Household Incomes: Methodological Aspects." In *The Microeconomics of Income Distribution Dynamics in East Asia and Latin America*, edited by François

Bourguignon, Francisco H. G. Ferreira, and Nora Lustig, 17–46. Washington, DC: World Bank.

Datt, Gaurav, and Martin Ravallion. 1992. "Growth and Redistribution Components of Changes in Poverty Measures: A Decomposition with Applications to Brazil and India in the 1980s." *Journal of Development Economics* 38 (2): 275–96.

Essama-Nssah, B. 2012. "Identification of Sources of Variation in Poverty Outcomes." Policy Research Working Paper 5954, World Bank, Washington, DC.

Essama-Nssah, B., and Peter J. Lambert. 2009. "Measuring Pro-Poorness: A Unifying Approach with New Results." *Review of Income and Wealth* 55 (3): 752–78.

Ferreira, Francisco H. G. 2012. "Distributions in Motion: Economic Growth, Inequality, and Poverty Dynamics." In *The Oxford Handbook of the Economics of Poverty*, edited by Philip N. Jefferson, 427–62. New York: Oxford University Press.

Fortin, Nicole, Thomas Lemieux, and Sergio Firpo. 2011. "Decomposition Methods in Economics." In *Handbook of Labor Economics*, Vol. 4A, edited by Orley Ashenfelter and David Card, 1–102. Amsterdam, the Netherlands: North-Holland.

Foster, James, Joel Greer, and Erik Thorbecke. 1984. "A Class of Decomposable Poverty Measures." *Econometrica* 52 (3): 761–65.

Juhn, Chinhui, Kevin M. Murphy, and Brooks Pierce. 1993. "Wage Inequality and the Rise of Returns to Skill." *Journal of Political Economy* 101 (3): 410–42.

Kakwani, Nanak. 1993. "Poverty and Economic Growth with Application to Côte d'Ivoire." *Review of Income and Wealth* 39 (2): 121–39.

———. 2000. "On Measuring Growth and Inequality Components of Poverty with Application to Thailand." *Journal of Quantitative Economics* 16 (1): 67–79.

Kaplan, Wilfred. 1991. *Advanced Calculus*. Redwood City, CA: Addison-Wesley.

Kolenikov, Stanislav, and Anthony Shorrocks. 2005. "A Decomposition Analysis of Regional Poverty in Russia." *Review of Development Economics* 9 (1): 25–46.

Kraay, Aart. 2006. "When Is Growth Pro-Poor? Evidence from a Panel of Countries." *Journal of Development Economics* 80 (1): 198–227.

Moulin, Hervé. 2003. *Fair Division and Collective Welfare*. Cambridge, MA: MIT Press.

Müller, Adrian. 2008. "Clarifying Poverty Decomposition." Conference Paper 30, Proceedings of the German Development Economics Conference, Zurich.

Ravallion, Martin. 2000. "On Decomposing Changes in Poverty into 'Growth' and 'Redistribution' Components." *Journal of Quantitative Economics* 16 (1): 105–18.

Ravallion, Martin, and Monika Huppi. 1991. "Measuring Changes in Poverty: A Methodological Case Study of Indonesia during an Adjustment Period." *World Bank Economic Review* 5 (5): 57–82.

Ravallion, Martin, and Shaohua Chen. 2003. "Measuring Pro Poor Growth." *Economic Letters* 78 (1): 93–99.

Shapley, Lloyd. S. 1953. "A Value for *n*-Person Games." In *Contributions to the Theory of Games*, Vol. 2, edited by H. W. Kuhn and A. W. Tucker, 307–17. Princeton, NJ: Princeton University Press.

Shorrocks, Anthony. F. (1999) 2013. "Decomposition Procedures for Distributional Analysis: A Unified Framework Based on Shapley Value." *Journal of Economic Inequality* 11 (1): 1–28. doi: 10.1007/s10888-011-9214-z.

Son, Hyun Hwa. 2003. "A New Poverty Decomposition." *Journal of Economic Inequality* 1 (2): 181–87.

Watts, Harold. 1968. "An Economic Definition of Poverty." In *On Understanding Poverty: Perspectives from the Social Sciences*, edited by Daniel P. Moynihan, 316–29. New York: Basic Books.

CHAPTER 3

What Accounts for Changes in Poverty over the Past Decade?

Introduction

The reduction in poverty observed during the 2000s throughout the developing world provides an opportunity to study the most significant factors at work in favor of the poor. Did poverty decrease because of

- Demographic changes that led to lower dependency ratios;
- Labor market improvements that boosted employment or labor income;
- Improved and more effective social policies; or
- Increased remittances to poorer countries?

To answer these questions, and to contribute to the evidence base for future policy, this chapter focuses on a subsample of 21 countries where poverty declined substantially in the decade from 2000 to 2010. Particularly in some Latin American countries, debate focuses on whether better job opportunities or improved transfer policies can best explain the observed reductions in poverty and inequality. In some South Asian and Eastern European countries, observers question whether it was better job opportunities or higher remittances that reduced poverty. As for several East Asian countries—where poverty reduction has coincided with strong growth and job creation—questions arise about whether social policy should focus more on redistribution.

This chapter quantifies, based on a series of counterfactual simulations, the contribution of labor income to changes in poverty across countries. Based on the "simple" methodology described in chapter 2—which improved on methods that focus on aggregate summary statistics—this chapter generates entire counterfactual distributions, allowing us to quantify the relative contributions to poverty reduction as a result of changes in labor income, nonlabor income, and demographic characteristics. Because most countries measure welfare through household expenditures or consumption (as opposed to income), this chapter modifies existing methods and proposes a decomposition methodology for consumption-based measures of poverty.

The next section, "Growth and Poverty Reduction," describes the evolution of poverty across our 21-country sample, highlighting the links between poverty, growth and redistribution outcomes. "The Forces behind Poverty Reduction" discusses four potentially influential factors: demographic change, increased labor income, increased nonlabor income, and changed consumption patterns. We then present the data and the results for each country, highlighting similarities and differences. The concluding section summarizes the findings and assesses the decomposition methodology and its limitations. Annex 3A lists the specific data sources for each country in the sample.

Growth and Poverty Reduction

We focus here on 21 countries that exhibited substantial declines in moderate poverty (defined below) using comparable consumption or income data in the decade from 2000 to 2010. The countries included in this analysis are Argentina, Bangladesh, Brazil, Cambodia, Chile, Colombia, Costa Rica, Ecuador, Ghana, Honduras, Moldova, Mongolia, Nepal, Panama, Paraguay, Peru, the Philippines, Romania, Sri Lanka, Thailand, and Vietnam.

Data Sources and Distinctions

The analysis focuses on reductions in poverty during the 2000s. Most Latin American countries in the sample use income-based measures of poverty. For these countries, data come from national household surveys that have been harmonized and compiled in the Socio-Economic Database for Latin America and the Caribbean (SEDLAC).[1]

Other countries in the sample use consumption-based measures of poverty, with data provided by national household surveys. For Bangladesh, Moldova, Peru, the Philippines, Romania, Sri Lanka, and Thailand, household surveys were standardized by the World Bank. For Ghana's and Nepal's consumption-based measures, we use the Rural Income Generating Activities (RIGA) datasets, a harmonized database of household surveys compiled jointly by the Food and Agriculture Organization of the United Nations (FAO) and the World Bank (FAO n.d.).[2] Table 3A.1 (in annex 3A) provides more detail about the countries, exact years, and surveys included in this study. Regarding Cambodia, Mongolia, Vietnam, and the Philippines, household surveys were harmonized by the World Bank to generate comparable income data and income-based poverty measures. The official national poverty measurements in Cambodia, Mongolia, and Vietnam are based on the consumption welfare aggregate.

Poverty Reduction in Sample Countries

All countries in our sample had substantial poverty-reduction episodes, defined as an average decline in moderate poverty of 1 percentage point or more per year over a period of four years or more. Because the national moderate poverty line varies from country to country, we base the analysis on the international poverty line that is closest in magnitude to the national moderate poverty line in that country. For example, the moderate poverty line in Bangladesh is closer to the $1.25-a-day poverty line, while the moderate poverty line in Peru is closer to the $4-a-day poverty line, as shown in table 3.1.[3]

GDP Growth and Poverty Reduction

Poverty reduction in each of the sample countries was accompanied by strong economic growth (figure 3.1), albeit at different rates, ranging from an average of 3 percent in real gross domestic product (GDP) in Paraguay to an average of 8.4 percent in Mongolia. The 2008–09 global financial crisis increased volatility and vulnerability in middle-income countries, such as Romania, Thailand, and several countries in Latin America, while other countries, such as Bangladesh, enjoyed continued, almost uninterrupted real GDP growth of about 6 percent a year throughout the decade.

For the countries whose moderate poverty lines came closest to the $1.25-a-day level, the poverty reduction rate varied from an average of 1.3 percentage points a year in the Philippines to 2.9 percentage points a year in Nepal (figure 3.2). Among countries whose national moderate poverty lines approach the $4-a-day level, the decline varied from an average of 1 percentage point per year in Paraguay to an average of 2.8 percentage points per year in Colombia.

The link between economic growth and poverty reduction has long interested economists. As detailed in Ferreira (2012), the cross-country literature has found considerable evidence that economic growth is strongly and negatively correlated with changes in poverty (Ravallion and Chen 2007). In addition, the higher a country's initial level of inequality, the higher the growth rate needed to reduce poverty by a given amount (World Bank 2005; Ravallion and Chen 2007).

One common way to assess these relations is by using the Datt and Ravallion (1992) decomposition, which splits the change in poverty into distribution-neutral growth and redistribution effects. Using this method, we found that growth explains most of the observed reduction in moderate poverty for 17 of the 21 countries in this study (as shown in figure 3.2). Redistribution, which can be thought of as a reduction in inequality, was found to be more important in the cases of Argentina, Mongolia, Paraguay, and the Philippines.

Poverty Effects beyond Aggregate Economic Growth

In the places where most of the poverty reduction was the result of growth, some obvious questions arise: *How* did growth lead to poverty reduction? Were redistributional changes associated with the introduction of public transfers, or were they a result of market forces? Unfortunately, the Datt-Ravallion (1992) method cannot make these explicit links because growth, inequality, and poverty measures are just three different aggregations of information about individual income

Table 3.1 Poverty Headcount Rates, by Benchmark, in Selected Developing Countries, 2000s

	a. Income-based poverty headcount rate[a]											
	$4.00-a-day PPP[c]				*$2.50-a-day PPP*				*$1.25-a-day PPP*			
	Initial period (%)	*Final period (%)*	*Total reduction (ppts)*	*Annual change (%)*	*Initial period (%)*	*Final period (%)*	*Total reduction (ppts)*	*Annual change (%)*	*Initial period (%)*	*Final period (%)*	*Total reduction (ppts)*	*Annual change (%)*
Argentina, 2000–10	27.5	14.6	−13.0	−6.2	14.2	6.4	−7.8	−7.7	5.1	1.8	−3.3	−9.8
Brazil, 2001–09	43.1	27.6	−15.5	−5.4	27.4	15.1	−12.3	−7.2	11.8	6.1	−5.7	−7.9
Cambodia, 2007–10[b]	75.1	75.7	0.5	0.2	57.3	60.1	2.8	1.6	34.0	29.6	−4.4	−4.5
Chile, 2000–09	23.2	11.8	−11.4	−7.2	9.0	4.3	−4.7	−7.9	2.3	1.3	−0.9	−5.6
Colombia, 2002–10	61.6	39.5	−22.1	−5.4	42.3	22.0	−20.3	−7.8	20.7	8.2	−12.6	−11.0
Costa Rica, 2000–08	29.2	18.9	−10.2	−5.3	14.7	7.6	−7.1	−7.9	5.5	2.4	−3.1	−9.8
Ecuador, 2003–10	51.5	33.4	−18.1	−6.0	31.5	15.9	−15.6	−9.3	12.2	4.6	−7.6	−13.0
Honduras, 1999–2009	66.1	52.1	−14.1	−2.4	47.9	36.2	−11.6	−2.7	24.9	17.8	−7.1	−3.3
Mongolia, 2007–11[b]	56.6	44.3	−12.3	−6.0	35.7	22.5	−13.2	−10.9	13.1	6.0	−7.1	−17.8
Panama, 2001–09	43.4	29.9	−13.5	−4.6	28.7	16.1	−12.6	−6.9	15.4	4.6	−10.8	−14.0
Paraguay, 1999–2010	43.3	32.8	−10.6	−2.5	26.7	18.4	−8.3	−3.3	14.0	7.2	−6.8	−5.9
Philippines, 2006–09[b]	78.3	77.9	−0.4	−0.2	62.2	60.3	−1.9	−1.0	31.7	27.6	−4.1	−4.5
Vietnam, 2004–10[b]	79.9	58.9	−21.0	−5.0	56.4	33.2	−23.2	−8.5	18.1	8.7	−9.4	−11.5

table continues next page

Table 3.1 Poverty Headcount Rates, by Benchmark, in Selected Developing Countries, 2000s *(continued)*

	b. Consumption-based poverty headcount rate[c]											
	$4.00 or $5.00-a-day PPP[d]				*$2.50-a-day PPP*				*$1.25-a-day PPP*			
	Initial period (%)	*Final period (%)*	*Total reduction (ppts)*	*Annual change (%)*	*Initial period (%)*	*Final period (%)*	*Total reduction (ppts)*	*Annual change (%)*	*Initial period (%)*	*Final period (%)*	*Total reduction (ppts)*	*Annual change (%)*
Bangladesh, 2000–10	—	—	—	—	89.2	84.0	−5.2	−0.6	57.7	40.3	−17.4	−3.5
Ghana, 1998–2005	—	—	—	—	71.8	58.3	−13.5	−2.9	38.2	23.5	−14.7	−6.7
Moldova, 2001–10	93.8	58.7	−35.1	−5.1	71.4	12.9	−58.5	−17.3	27.5	0.5	−27.0	−35.4
Nepal, 1996–2003	—	—	—	—	94.3	84.9	−9.5	−1.5	54.0	25.9	−28.2	−10.0
Peru, 2004–10	45.8	30.0	−15.8	−6.8	22.9	11.7	−11.2	−10.6	3.5	0.8	−2.6	−21.1
Romania, 2001–09	75.3	33.2	−42.1	−9.7	23.7	4.2	−19.5	−19.6	2.6	0.0	−2.6	−100.0
Sri Lanka, 2002–09	84.7	78.09	−6.6	−1.2	61.9	45.1	−16.8	−4.4	14.8	4.7	−10.1	−15.1
Thailand, 2000–09	31.3	16.6	−14.7	−6.8	7.9	2.5	−5.3	−11.8	3.7	1.4	−2.3	−10.3

Sources: Data for Ghana and Nepal from FAO n.d. Data for Bangladesh, Moldova, Peru, Romania, and Thailand from national household surveys. Data for Cambodia, Mongolia, the Philippines, and Vietnam from the World Bank's East Asia and Pacific region harmonized household surveys.

Note: PPP = purchasing power parity; — = not available. Latin American countries typically measure poverty using a household income aggregate, while most other countries around the world use a consumption aggregate. Because these measures are not comparable, we present them separately.

a. The decomposition analysis for countries listed in panel a use income-based poverty estimates.

b. The income-based figures for Cambodia, Mongolia, the Philippines, and Vietnam are not the official poverty figures because these countries (except the Philippines) use consumption-based poverty estimates. However, the analysis was undertaken using income measures of poverty because of the large discrepancy between consumption and income in these countries.

c. The decomposition analysis for countries listed in panel b use consumption-based poverty estimates.

d. Moldova and Romania measure moderate poverty at rates close to $5-a-day, while Peru, Sri Lanka, and Thailand measure moderate poverty at rates close to $4-a day.

Figure 3.1 Average Real GDP Growth in Selected Developing Countries, 2000s

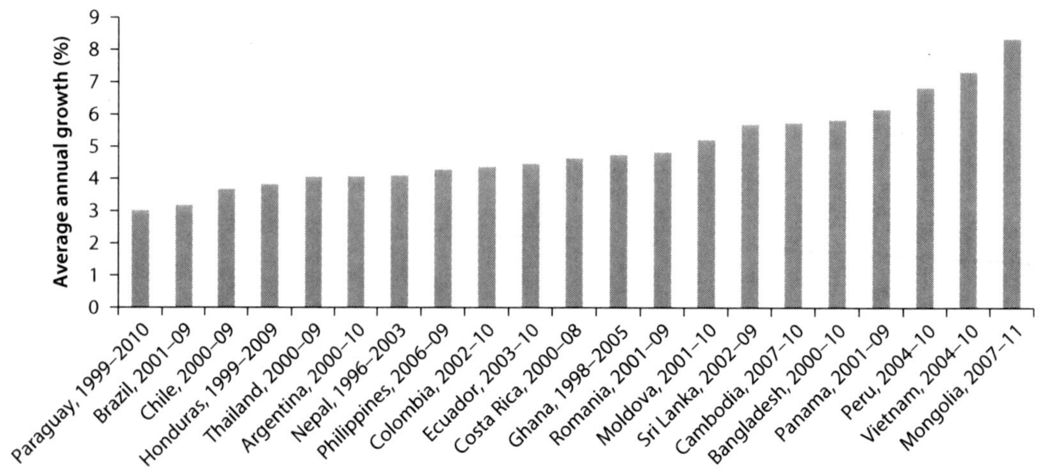

Source: World Bank 2013.
Note: GDP = gross domestic product.

dynamics. Moreover, they are jointly determined, such that cross-country estimates are unlikely to shed much light on the fundamental factors underlying distributional change (Ferreira 2012).

Therefore, instead of relying on summary measures of poverty, one could better understand distributional changes by using full distributions of income or consumption expenditures from representative household surveys. Instead of focusing on economic growth—which can also be thought of as the proportional change in the mean of the income distribution—it is best to analyze how the entire distribution changes over time. Moreover, given the richness of data available in household income and expenditure surveys, one can further disaggregate the observed distributional changes by decomposing the factors that underlie these distributions. The rest of the chapter focuses on applying the method discussed in detail in chapter 2 to further disaggregate these distributional changes.

Forces behind Poverty Reduction

We begin by noting that at least four factors could have influenced poverty reduction:

- *Demographic change*, particularly the share of adults per household
- *Growth in labor income*, either because more people are employed or because their earnings have increased
- *Growth in nonlabor income*, in the form of public or private transfers
- *Changes in consumption or savings patterns*

Figure 3.2 Contribution of Growth and Redistribution to Poverty Reduction in Selected Developing Countries, by Poverty Line, 2000s

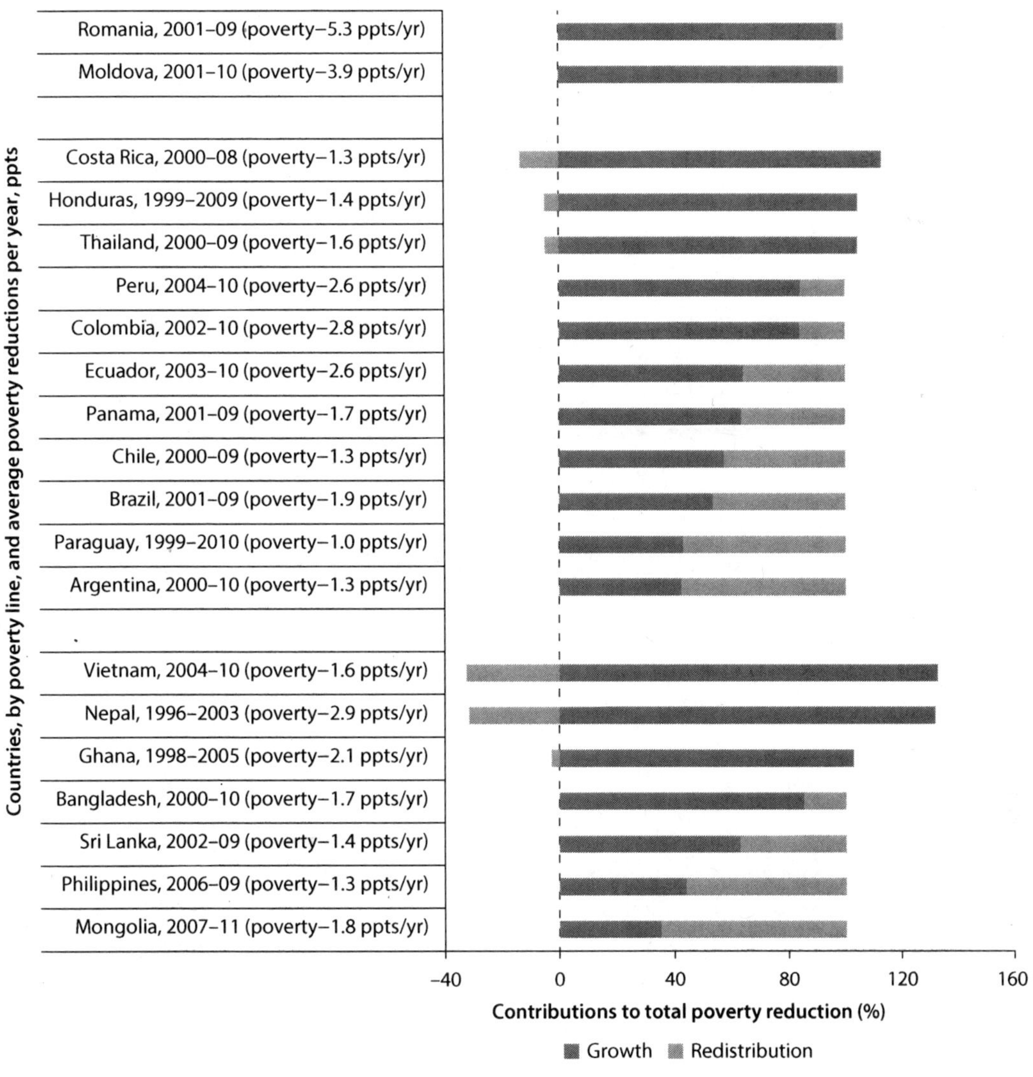

Sources: Data from SEDLAC, various years; FAO n.d.; and national household surveys.
Note: ppts = percentage points; PPP = purchasing power parity. Countries are listed in order of growth's contribution to the decline of poverty. "Growth" refers to the distribution neutral mean growth of household consumption (also known as the size effect, in which the Lorenz curve does not change), and the "redistribution" effect measures the change in poverty resulting from a change in the Lorenz curve while holding the mean constant. Shapely-Shorrocks estimates are used, see chapter 2 for a full explanation.

Demographic Change

Demographic change could play a role by affecting the dependency ratio: the number of earners relative to the number of consumers in a household. Among the countries considered here, the population of Bangladesh grew by 25 percent between 2000 and 2010, adding 19 million people to its total, while Brazil has added 18 million (a 16 percent increase) during the same time period.

Figure 3.3 Change in Age-Dependency Ratio of Selected Developing Countries, 2000s

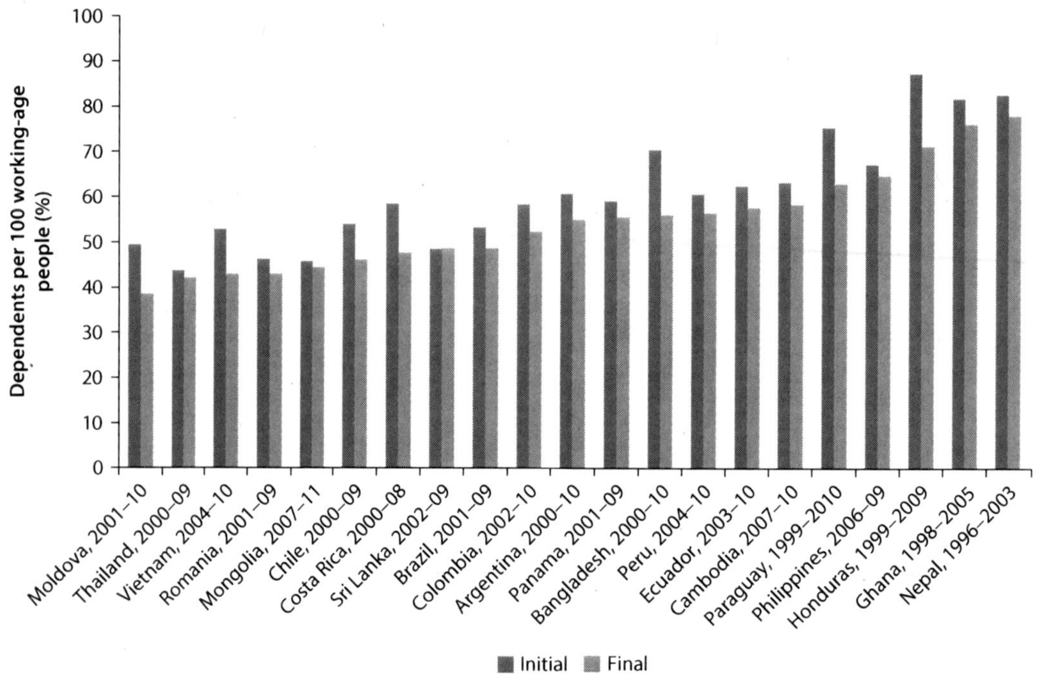

Source: World Bank 2012.
Note: The age-dependency ratio is the ratio of dependents (people younger than 15 or older than 64) to the working-age population (those aged 15–64 years). Data are shown as the proportion of dependents per 100 working-age population.

Despite these increases in population, the *rate* of population growth has decelerated enough to begin shrinking the proportion of dependents relative to the working-age population across almost all countries in our sample, as shown in figure 3.3. The exception is Sri Lanka, which has seen higher births after the end of many years of conflict in 2009.

Similarly, taking into account the fact that the elderly often continue to work beyond age 64, the share of adults (ages 15 and above) per household has increased in all countries in the sample (table 3.2). However, this overall similarity still masks the heterogeneity across households within each country. Most important, the share of adults per poor household *decreased* in Mongolia, Peru, Romania, Colombia, Panama, and Moldova—potentially pointing to an unequalizing force in these countries.

Growth in Labor Income

Growth in labor income could be the main driver in the observed poverty reductions—either because of higher employment rates or because of increased earnings. The share of occupied (working) adults per household increased in 12 of the 21 countries in our sample, as table 3.3 illustrates. In some countries, increased female employment was an important factor. For example, in Costa Rica,

Table 3.2 Share of Adults per Household, by Poverty Level, Selected Developing Countries, 2000s

	All households			*Poor households (≤ $1.25-a-day PPP)*			*Poor households (≤ $2.50-a-day PPP)*		
Country and years of data	*Initial year (%)*	*Final year (%)*	*Annual average change (%)*	*Initial year (%)*	*Final year (%)*	*Annual average change (%)*	*Initial year (%)*	*Final year (%)*	*Annual average change (%)*
Countries measuring poverty based on income									
Argentina, 2000–10	72.3	76.2	0.5	51.5	62.5	2.0	53.5	57.7	0.8
Brazil, 2001–09	71.3	75.7	0.8	50.9	56.8	1.4	55.0	55.7	0.2
Chile, 2000–09	72.6	78.0	0.8	57.5	68.4	1.9	58.8	65.6	1.2
Colombia, 2002–10	68.0	71.1	0.6	62.1	59.6	−0.5	61.4	59.1	−0.5
Costa Rica, 2000–08	67.1	73.3	1.1	58.1	64.3	1.3	56.3	60.0	0.8
Ecuador, 2003–10	66.2	72.1	1.2	56.4	61.5	1.2	56.8	60.4	0.9
Honduras, 1999–2009	57.2	63.5	1.1	48.7	53.5	0.9	50.3	55.3	1.0
Panama, 2001–09	68.1	70.0	0.3	53.7	52.2	−0.3	56.0	54.0	−0.5
Paraguay, 1999–2010	59.8	68.2	1.2	46.3	57.2	1.9	48.6	56.6	1.4
Countries measuring poverty based on consumption									
Bangladesh, 2000–10	60.4	65.3	0.8	55.4	58.4	0.5	58.9	63.6	0.8
Cambodia, 2007–10	66.3	68.6	1.1	60.8	61.0	0.1	62.2	64.3	1.1
Ghana, 1998–2005	56.1	60.1	1.0	49.5	51.3	0.5	52.3	54.2	0.5
Moldova, 2001–10	78.8	81.8	0.4	73.1	68.1	−0.8	76.4	73.5	−0.4
Mongolia, 2007–11	72.5	72.9	0.1	64.9	60.4	−1.8	66.0	62.0	−1.5
Nepal, 1996–2003	57.9	61.1	0.8	55.1	55.0	0.0	57.0	58.6	0.4
Peru, 2004–10	68.3	69.2	0.2	51.5	51.2	−0.1	55.0	50.8	−1.3
Philippines, 2006–09	65.4	67.5	1.1	55.1	57.2	1.3	59.7	61.8	1.2
Romania, 2001–09	82.2	84.8	0.4	60.9	—	—	71.9	67.1	−0.9
Sri Lanka, 2002–09	74.2	76.3	0.4	65.3	68.8	0.7	71.3	73.1	0.4
Thailand, 2000–09	74.2	77.8	0.5	56.9	53.6	−0.7	61.4	65.6	0.7
Vietnam, 2004–10	73.4	76.3	0.7	64.6	67.6	0.8	69.6	70.9	0.3

Sources: Data from SEDLAC, various years; FAO n.d.; World Bank East Asia and Pacific regional unit household surveys and national household surveys.
Note: — = not available; PPP = purchasing power parity.

both labor force participation and employment of women increased by about 23 percent between 2000 and 2008 (World Bank 2012).

However, this trend is not homogeneous across countries or within them. Indeed, the share of working adults (15 years of age or older) per household declined (in order of most to least) in Mongolia, Sri Lanka, Ghana, and Honduras across the distribution. Such a change could be positive if the main breadwinners were earning higher incomes, thus enabling the youths to continue in school and the older adults to retire. However, even within countries, the data show some important differences across the distribution in how the share of working adults has changed over time. For example, the share of working adults declined significantly among the poor in Brazil, Chile, and Costa Rica, even though these

Table 3.3 Share of Working Adults per Household, by Poverty Level, in Selected Developing Countries, 2000s

	Average of all households			*Poor households (≤ $1.25-a-day PPP)*			*Poor households (≤ $2.50-a-day PPP)*		
Country and years of data	*Initial Year (%)*	*Final year (%)*	*Annual average change (%)*	*Initial Year (%)*	*Final year (%)*	*Annual average change (%)*	*Initial Year (%)*	*Final year (%)*	*Annual average change (%)*
Countries measuring poverty based on income									
Argentina, 2000–10	48.8	55.7	1.3	26.3	27.0	0.3	32.8	34.7	0.6
Brazil, 2001–09	60.4	62.7	0.5	42.8	34.8	−2.6	50.9	46.7	−1.1
Chile, 2000–09	49.4	49.6	0.1	14.9	6.9	−8.3	27.4	15.7	−6.0
Colombia, 2002–10	55.1	60.5	1.2	40.2	39.1	−0.3	46.0	46.2	0.1
Costa Rica, 2000–08	53.7	56.9	0.7	22.5	16.5	−3.8	31.4	26.3	−2.2
Ecuador, 2003–10	61.5	59.4	−0.5	49.4	50.7	0.4	53.7	51.7	−0.5
Honduras, 1999–2009	63.2	59.6	−0.6	55.1	41.3	−2.8	57.7	50.3	−1.4
Panama, 2001–09	51.7	59.7	1.8	45.7	50.3	1.2	44.6	51.8	1.9
Paraguay, 1999–2010	61.7	64.1	0.3	51.2	49.1	−0.4	53.6	53.8	0.0
Countries measuring poverty based on consumption									
Bangladesh, 2000–10	46.9	48.2	0.3	49.7	50.5	0.2	47.8	49.1	0.3
Cambodia, 2007–10	81.3	85.1	1.5	81.9	84.6	1.1	81.8	85.0	1.3
Ghana, 1998–2005	41.4	39.2	−0.8	38.1	32.0	−2.5	39.3	35.6	−1.4
Moldova, 2001–10	65.3	66.1	0.1	64.7	76.0	1.8	64.1	71.0	1.1
Mongolia, 2007–11	62.8	54.9	−3.3	55.7	45.9	−4.7	61.4	52.7	−3.8
Nepal, 1996–2003	32.7	33.8	0.5	32.7	34.0	0.6	32.7	34.2	0.6
Peru, 2004–10	69.4	72.5	0.7	82.5	78.3	−0.9	79.1	80.1	0.2
Philippines, 2006–09	59.5	58.7	−0.4	64.1	63.6	−0.3	62.1	61.4	−0.4
Romania, 2001–09	83.2	82.1	−0.2	79.5	n.a.	n.a.	83.6	74.1	−1.5
Sri Lanka, 2002–09	53.7	49.6	−1.1	53.1	45.0	−2.3	53.8	49.4	−1.2
Thailand, 2000–09	74.7	74.4	−0.1	60.6	72.0	1.9	78.2	71.3	−1.0
Vietnam, 2004–10	79.1	78.5	−0.1	50.8	52.2	0.5	54.7	54.9	0.1

Sources: Data from SEDLAC, various years; FAO n.d.: World Bank East Asia Pacific regional unit harmonized household surveys and national household surveys.
Note: "Working adults" are defined as household members (aged 15–64 years) who are occupied in work for pay. PPP = purchasing power parity.

countries had a higher share of working adults on average—indicating that the increasing share of working adults was occurring mostly at the top end of the distribution.

In most of the countries, however, the rise of working-adult populations might not only indicate an increase in workers per household but also reflect evidence that labor incomes per adult increased at the bottom of the distribution in many of these countries. Unfortunately, we cannot determine whether the poor are earning more because of higher hourly wages or because of more hours worked. In any case, labor incomes have usually increased among the poor.

Figure 3.4 Change in Subsidies and Other Social Transfers in Selected Developing Countries, 2000s

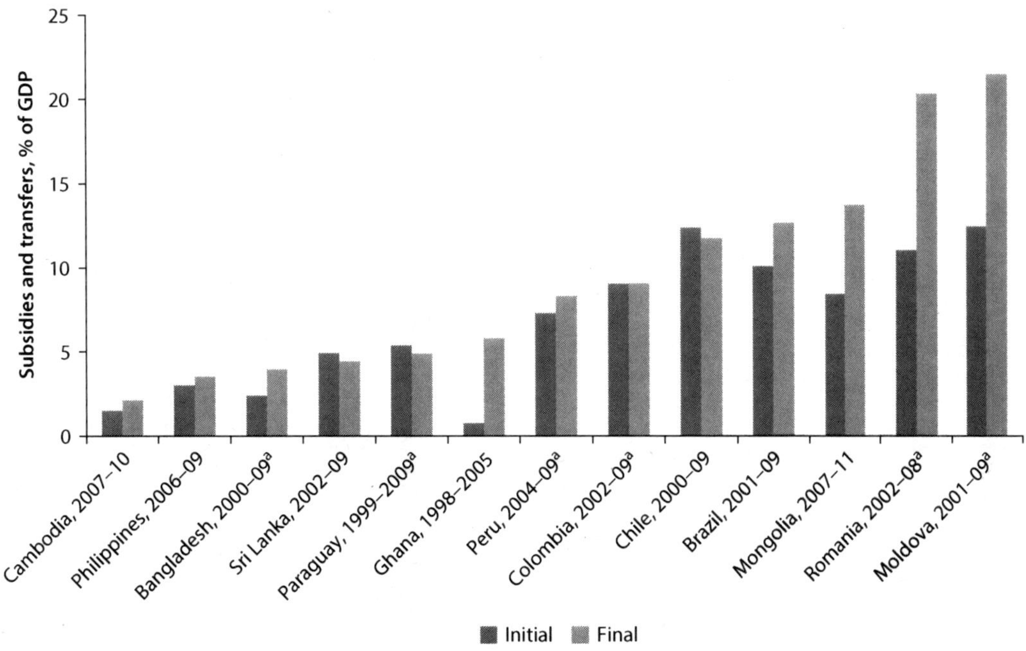

Source: World Bank 2012.
Note: GDP = gross domestic product.
a. The reported subsidy and transfer data are for a year that is one year earlier than the household survey.

Growth in Nonlabor Income

A third major factor in poverty reduction could have been strongly related to growth in nonlabor incomes. For example, for countries where data is readily available, figure 3.4 shows that public subsidies and other social transfers have increased in several countries over the past decade. Government spending for subsidies and transfers increased more than sixfold in Ghana and by more than 60 percent as a share of GDP in Bangladesh, Moldova, Mongolia, and Romania.

In addition to public sources of transfers, private transfers, such as remittances, have grown strongly in many of the countries (figure 3.5), as these cases exemplify:

- *In Nepal,* remittances grew from 1 percent of GDP in 1996 to 12 percent in 2003.
- *In Moldova,* they increased from 14 percent of GDP in 2001 to 22 percent in 2010.
- *In Honduras,* they nearly tripled, going from 6 percent of GDP in 1999 to 17.8 percent in 2009.

How important were these increased transfers—whether public or private—to poverty reduction? For instance, if remittances mostly reached higher-income

Figure 3.5 Change in International Remittances to Selected Developing Countries, 2000s

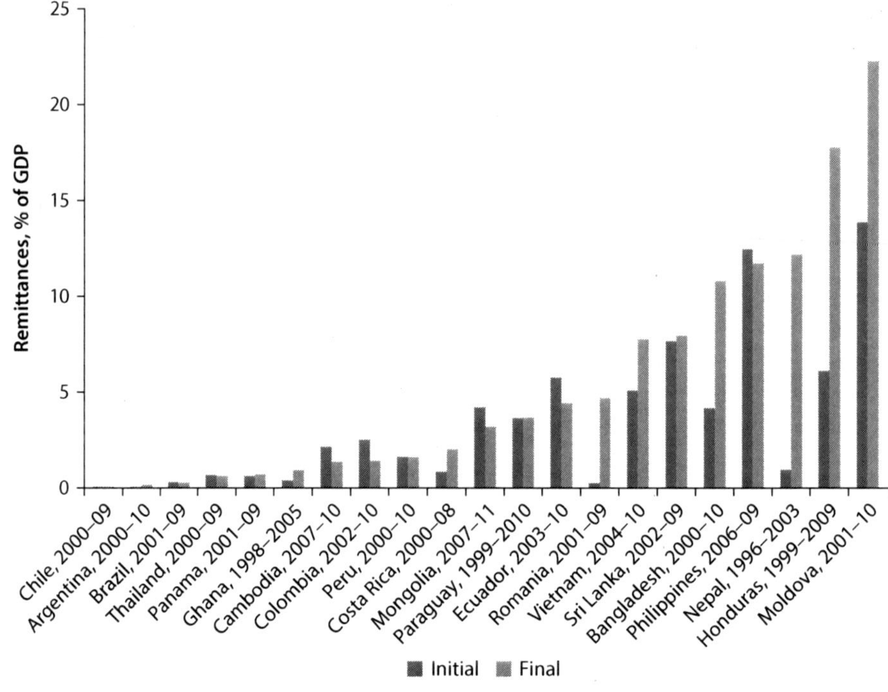

Source: World Bank 2012.
Note: GDP = gross domestic product.

households, one would not expect poverty to decline. As table 3.4 shows, most countries in our sample did see an increase in transfers as a share of total household income, but the impact of these among the poor varied. Transfers were especially important for poor households in Argentina, Brazil, Colombia, Moldova, and Peru. However, the share of transfers in total household income actually declined among poor households in some countries (Cambodia, Ghana, Honduras, and Sri Lanka), partly reflecting relatively weaker public social protection programs, but also highlighting the fact that remittances do not always help the poor (table 3.4).

Changes in Consumption or Savings Patterns

Finally, in the absence of measurement error, changes in consumption-based poverty could also be related to changes in consumption and savings patterns. In the context of growing incomes, households could either increase consumption proportionately or they could increase their savings. However, given measurement errors in income and expenditure aggregates in household surveys, it is difficult to differentiate between household consumption changes resulting from real behavioral shifts and those resulting from measurement errors.

Whatever the cause—or causes—of apparent household consumption changes, table 3.5 shows a full range of patterns.

Table 3.4 Share of Transfers in Total Household Income, by Poverty Level, in Selected Developing Countries, 2000s

	All households			*Poor households (≤ $1.25-a-day PPP)*			*Poor households (≤ $2.50-a-day PPP)*		
Country and years of data	*Initial Year (%)*	*Final year (%)*	*Annual average change (%)*	*Initial Year (%)*	*Final year (%)*	*Annual average change (%)*	*Initial Year (%)*	*Final year (%)*	*Annual average change (%)*
Countries measuring poverty based on income									
Argentina, 2000–10	4.7	6.5	3.3	12.7	48.9	14.4	8.7	32.9	14.3
Brazil, 2001–09	1.2	5.8	21.3	4.9	47.0	32.6	2.8	24.8	31.1
Chile, 2000–09	—	6.4	—	—	42.3	—	—	27.7	—
Colombia, 2002–10	4.7	9.2	8.6	9.2	30.8	16.4	6.8	20.7	14.9
Costa Rica, 2000–08	—	4.5	—	—	28.6	—	—	19.8	—
Ecuador, 2003–10	9.0	10.6	2.3	24.8	35.3	5.1	15.1	24.4	7.1
Honduras, 1999–2009	9.1	7.1	-2.5	11.9	3.7	-11.0	10.1	2.8	-12.0
Panama, 2001–09	10.1	12.3	2.4	26.1	41.2	5.9	21.8	32.3	5.0
Paraguay, 1999–2010	8.4	9.0	0.7	8.3	16.9	6.7	10.4	16.3	4.2
Countries measuring poverty based on consumption									
Bangladesh, 2000–10	2.7	3.5	2.5	1.8	2.0	0.8	2.5	3.1	2.1
Cambodia, 2007–10	2.6	1.7	-12.6	3.2	2.6	-7.4	3.0	2.1	-11.7
Ghana, 1998–2005	5.1	5.1	0.1	3.6	2.8	-3.2	3.8	3.8	-0.2
Moldova, 2001–10	4.5	24.0	20.5	7.2	22.5	13.5	6.2	19.0	13.2
Mongolia, 2007–11	25.7	29.3	3.4	49.4	69.9	9.1	35.4	48.1	8.0
Nepal, 1996–2003	3.0	4.9	7.5	2.7	3.7	4.5	2.9	4.7	7.0
Peru, 2004–10	7.6	5.4	-5.4	4.2	10.4	16.3	3.9	8.5	14.0
Philippines, 2006–09	21.1	22.5	2.2	23.0	25.1	2.9	19.9	21.3	2.3
Romania, 2001–09	8.1	8.7	0.8	29.7	...	—	19.4	33.8	7.2
Sri Lanka, 2002–09	2.2	2.1	-0.2	3.2	1.8	-8.0	2.3	1.8	-3.6
Thailand, 2000–09	9.9	10.7	0.9	18.6	19.1	0.3	11.7	14.3	2.2
Vietnam, 2004–10	11.1	9.6	-2.5	9.8	10.8	1.6	9.7	10.6	1.6

Sources: Data from SEDLAC, various years; FAO n.d.: World Bank's East Asia Pacific regional unit harmonized household surveys and national household surveys.
Note: — = not available; ... = negligible; PPP = purchasing power parity.

- *In Bangladesh, Ghana, and Peru,* the consumption-to-income ratio increased among households at the bottom of the income distribution, while it fell among those at the top.
- *In Nepal, Sri Lanka, and Thailand,* this ratio remained more or less flat across the distribution.
- *In Moldova and Romania,* the consumption-to-income ratio fell more among households at the bottom of the income distribution than it did among those at the top.

Although we cannot differentiate between measurement error and changing behavior as drivers of change in the consumption-to-income ratios, we *can* show

Table 3.5 Change in Household Consumption-to-Income Ratio in Selected Developing Countries, 2000s

	Bangladesh 2000–10			Ghana 1998–2005			Moldova 2001–10			Nepal 1996–2003			Peru 2005–09			Romania 2001–09			Sri Lanka 2002–09			Thailand 2000–09		
Income decile	*Initial year (%)*	*Final year (%)*	*Annual average change (%)*	*Initial year (%)*	*Final year (%)*	*Annual average change (%)*	*Initial year (%)*	*Final year (%)*	*Annual average change (%)*	*Initial year (%)*	*Final year (%)*	*Annual average change (%)*	*Initia year (%)*	*Final year (%)*	*Annual average change (%)*	*Initial year (%)*	*Final year (%)*	*Annual average change (%)*	*Initial year (%)*	*Final year (%)*	*Annual average change (%)*	*Initial year (%)*	*Final year (%)*	*Annual average change (%)*
1	1.8	2.3	3	22.6	34.8	6	15.3	18.4	2	3.3	2.9	−2	1.6	1.9	5	4.51	2.37	−8	3.1	3.0	0	1.5	1.2	−3
2	1.2	1.5	2	5.9	8.3	5	4.0	1.9	−8	1.9	1.6	−2	1.3	1.4	2	1.89	1.16	−6	1.5	1.5	0	1.1	1.0	−2
3	1.0	1.3	2	3.3	4.6	5	2.9	1.5	−7	1.5	1.4	−1	1.2	1.2	1	1.44	0.99	−5	1.3	1.3	0	1.0	0.9	−1
4	1.0	1.1	1	2.5	3.4	5	2.2	1.3	−6	1.2	1.2	0	1.2	1.1	−1	1.26	0.88	−4	1.2	1.2	1	0.9	0.9	−1
5	1.0	1.0	0	2.2	2.5	2	1.8	1.2	−5	1.1	1.1	0	1.1	1.0	−1	1.10	0.82	−4	1.1	1.1	−1	0.9	0.8	−1
6	1.0	0.9	−1	1.7	2.2	3	1.6	1.1	−4	1.0	0.9	−1	1.1	1.0	−2	1.01	0.74	−4	1.0	1.0	0	0.8	0.8	0
7	1.0	0.8	−2	1.5	1.6	0	1.3	1.0	−3	1.0	1.0	0	1.0	0.9	−1	0.92	0.71	−3	1.0	0.9	−1	0.8	0.8	0
8	0.9	0.7	−2	1.5	1.2	−2	1.1	0.9	−2	0.9	0.9	0	0.9	0.9	−2	0.85	0.65	−3	0.9	0.9	−1	0.7	0.7	0
9	0.9	0.6	−4	1.3	1.0	−3	0.9	0.9	−1	0.9	0.8	−1	0.8	0.8	−1	0.77	0.60	−3	0.8	0.8	−1	0.6	0.6	0
10	0.8	0.5	−5	0.8	0.5	−6	0.7	0.7	0	0.8	0.8	−1	0.7	0.7	0	0.64	0.49	−3	0.7	0.5	−3	0.5	0.5	0

Sources: FAO n.d.; national household surveys.

Note: The eight countries measured represent those out of the 21-country sample set that measure poverty by consumption rather than by income.

how changes in this ratio affect overall changes in poverty. In short, each source of change described above could have contributed to the observed reductions in poverty over the past decade. How large of a contribution each of these forces made is the next question.

Results

Main Driver of Poverty Reduction: Labor Income Growth

Which factor—demographics, labor income, public transfers, or remittances—contributed the most to observed reductions in poverty? One key result stands out: the most important contributor to poverty reduction has been the growth in earnings, as a result of higher employment and higher labor incomes.

In 12 of the 21 countries with substantial declines in poverty, the combined effect of higher labor income and higher employment rates explain more than half of the poverty reduction; in another 6 countries, those two factors account for more than 40 percent of the reduction (as shown in figure 3.6 and table 3.6). This result holds true regardless of the decomposition path taken, as these results are an average of every possible decomposition path, as described in chapter 2, following Shapley (1953) and Shorrocks (1999).

Interestingly, in most cases, the greatest poverty reducer throughout the 2000s was labor income growth, rather than an increase in the share of working adults. Indeed, such growth alone cut poverty by more than half in 10 out of the 21 countries. In contrast, growth in the share of employed adults cut poverty by more than 20 percent in only 4 countries.

Importance of Demographic Changes

Although increases in labor income are the main contributors to reductions in poverty in most countries, demographics also mattered. In particular, a higher share of working-age adults in the household made the largest contribution to poverty reduction in Costa Rica, Paraguay, and the Philippines, but it was also important in Bangladesh, Cambodia, Chile, and Honduras.

Changes in the share of adults per household were also relatively important in explaining declines in moderate poverty in Bangladesh, Cambodia, Chile, Costa Rica, Ecuador, Honduras, the Philippines, and Paraguay (as shown in and figure 3.6 and table 3.6). In contrast, in Mongolia, the share of adults per household among the poor decreased, therefore increasing poverty and pointing to an unequalizing force there (table 3.6).

In general, increased percentages of working-age adults contributed positively to poverty reduction. However, the magnitude of this effect is small relative to the effect of labor income growth.

Roles of Employment Growth and Labor Income

Earnings growth, resulting from higher employment and higher labor incomes, was the most important contributor to poverty reduction. However, of these two elements, it was the growth in labor incomes that made most of the difference.

Figure 3.6 Decomposition of Changes in Moderate Poverty, by Level, in Selected Developing Countries, 2000s

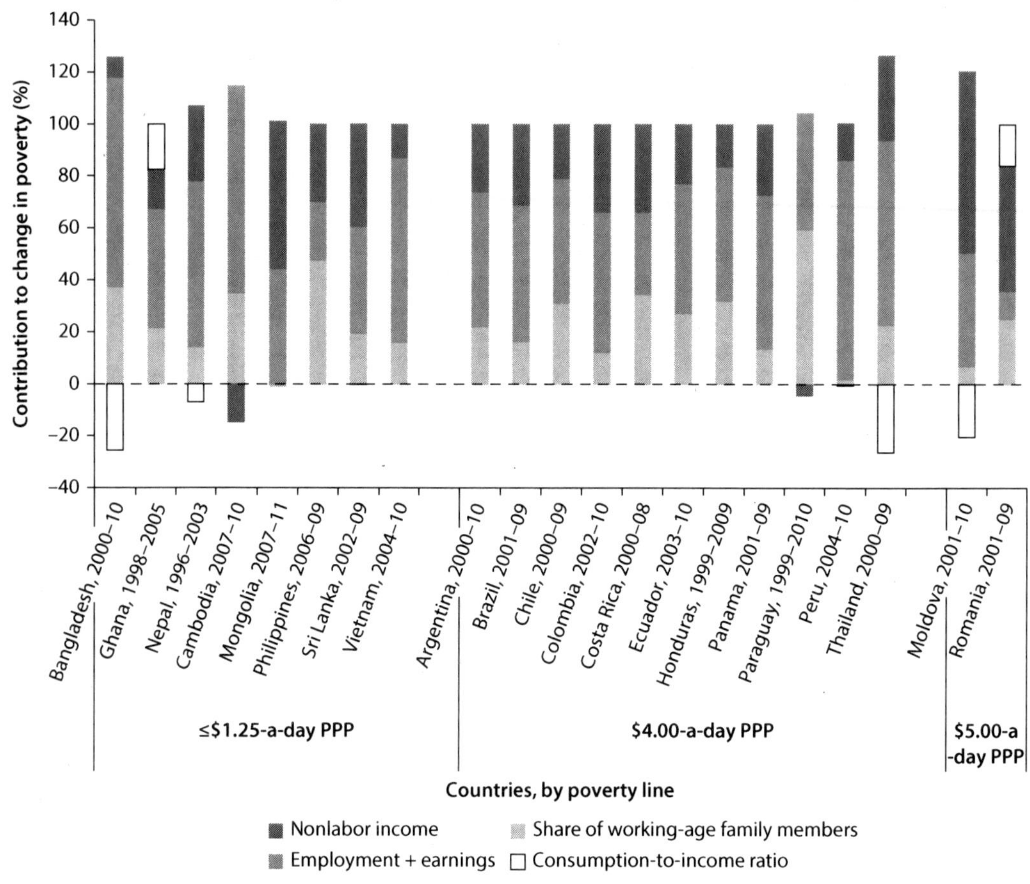

Sources: Data from SEDLAC, various years; FAO n.d.; and national household surveys.
Note: PPP = purchasing power parity. "Nonlabor income" refers to public and private transfers (including remittances), pensions, capital, and other nonlabor income. "Employment + earnings" refers to the combination of increased employment among working-age adults (aged 15–64 years) and increases in their earnings. Consumption-based measures of poverty are used in Bangladesh, Ghana, Nepal, Peru, Thailand, Moldova, and Romania. The remaining countries use income-based measures of poverty.

Although higher employment typically contributed to poverty reduction, lower employment among the poor partially offset poverty reduction in some countries (table 3.6). For instance, as shown in table 3.3, employment declined among the poor in more than one-third of the countries in our sample: Ecuador, Ghana, Honduras, Mongolia, the Philippines, Sri Lanka, Thailand, and Vietnam. It is no wonder that reductions in employment actually offset poverty reduction in these countries (table 3.6).

Overall, the increase in workers' earnings was relatively more important in reducing poverty than the increase in the number of workers or in the number of jobs. Although we cannot disentangle whether earnings increased because of improvements in the quality of jobs, changes in productivity, or simply

Table 3.6 Contributions to Declines in Moderate Poverty, by Level, in Selected Developing Countries, 2000s

	≤ $1.25-a-day PPP								≤$4.00-a-day PPP											≤$5.00-a-day PPP	
	Bangladesh, 2000–10	*Cambodia, 2007–10*	*Ghana, 1998–2005*	*Mongolia, 2007–11*	*Nepal, 1996–2003*	*Philippines, 2006–09*	*Sri Lanka, 2002–09*	*Vietnam, 2004–10*	*Argentina, 2000–10*	*Brazil, 2001–09*	*Chile, 2000–09*	*Colombia, 2002–10*	*Costa Rica, 2000–08*	*Ecuador, 2003–10*	*Honduras, 1999–2009*	*Panama, 2001–09*	*Paraguay, 1999–2010*	*Peru, 2004–10*	*Thailand, 2000–09*	*Moldova, 2001–10*	*Romania, 2001–09*
Poverty rate																					
Initial period (%)	57.7	34.0	38.2	13.1	73.7	31.7	14.8	18.1	27.5	43.1	23.2	61.6	29.2	51.5	66.1	43.4	43.3	45.8	31.4	93.8	75.3
Final period (%)	40.3	29.6	23.5	6.0	53.1	27.6	4.7	8.7	14.6	27.6	11.8	39.5	18.9	33.4	52.1	29.9	32.8	30.0	16.6	58.7	33.2
Total change (ppts)	−17.4	−4.4	−14.7	−7.1	−20.6	−4.1	−10.1	−9.4	−13.0	−15.5	−11.4	−22.1	−10.2	−18.1	−14.1	−13.5	−17.3	−15.8	−14.8	−35.1	−42.2
Contributions to poverty reduction																					
Consumption-to-income ratio (%)	−25.6	n.a.	17.7	n.a.	−6.9	n.a.	−0.19	n.a.	n.a.	n.a.	n.a.	n.a.	n.a.	n.a.	n.a.	n.a.	n.a.	−0.4	−26.4	−20.4	16.0
Share of adults in the household (%)	37.2	34.9	21.4	−1.0	14.2	47.6	19.5	15.9	22.0	16.4	31.0	12.1	34.4	27.1	32.0	13.5	59.5	1.8	22.8	6.9	25.1
Share of occupied (working) adults (%)	20.5	33.3	−3.6	−18.2	13.4	−0.9	−21.8	−4.3	16.7	10.9	−0.1	15.8	14.2	−3.3	−4.1	29.1	11.6	17.0	−9.7	−0.4	21.7
Labor income (earnings) per adult (%)	60.2	46.4	49.6	62.6	50.4	23.2	62.9	75.4	35.2	41.6	48.2	38.3	17.7	53.3	55.8	30.2	33.2	67.5	80.9	44.2	−10.9
Capital (%)	7.8	—	5.0	—	5.9	—	0.0	—	−5.4	−0.7	−4.2	4.3	3.9	−0.7	3.8	−0.2	0.0	3.4	1.5	1.0	21.6
Pension (%)	0.0	−5.2	0.0	3.2	0.0	2.2	1.5	2.9	14.9	17.9	15.8	4.6	23.6	6.2	3.2	10.4	−3.0	16.0	36.8	23.0	6.3
Transfers (%)	15.7	−8.1	10.0	52.2	23.0	27.6	−1.6	8.0	7.3	9.1	41.8	15.6	22.4	13.6	3.4	16.4	−1.0	−0.9	2.3	35.0	9.7
Other nonlabor income (%)	−15.9	−1.5	0.0	1.2	0.0	0.2	39.8	2.1	9.3	4.8	−32.5	9.4	−16.1	3.8	6.0	0.5	−0.3	−4.3	−8.2	10.7	10.6
Total contributions (%)	100.0	100.0	100.0	100.0	100.0	100.0	100.0	100.0	100.0	100.0	100.0	100.0	100.0	100.0	100.0	100.0	100.0	100.0	100.0	100.0	100.0

Sources: SEDLAC, various years; FAO n.d.; World Bank harmonized household surveys for East Asia and Pacific countries and national household surveys.

Note: PPP = purchasing power parity; ppts = percentage points; — = not available; n.a. = not applicable. "Occupied (working) adults" is defined as those 15–64 years of age. Consumption-based measures of poverty are used in Bangladesh, Ghana, Moldova, Nepal, Peru, Romania, and Thailand. Income-based measures of poverty are used in Argentina, Brazil, Cambodia, Chile, Colombia, Costa Rica, Ecuador, Honduras, Mongolia, Panama, Paraguay, the Philippines, and Vietnam.

longer hours, we *can* conclude that it was workers' labor income growth that made the difference rather than higher employment rates.

Roles of Nonlabor Income and Consumption

Although nonlabor income, such as public and private transfers, was also important, its contribution toward declines in moderate poverty in most of the sample countries was relatively small. The exceptions were Moldova, Mongolia, and Romania, where transfers contributed relatively more to reductions in poverty than they did elsewhere. In Romania, this was related to changes in transfers and capital income; in Mongolia, to a significant increase in social transfers with the introduction of the Human Development Fund; and in Moldova, mostly to increased international remittances.

Finally, for countries where poverty is measured by consumption, these decompositions suggest that reductions in the consumption-to-income ratio generally helped to reduce poverty in Ghana and Romania, where the consumption-income ratio increased at the bottom of the distribution. However, in all other instances, decreases in the consumption-to-income ratio during the past decade did not reduce poverty as much as it would have if consumption had remained a constant share of income.[4]

Further Decompositions by Poverty Line

Annex 3B presents more-detailed decompositions of poverty reductions in the sample countries according to different international poverty lines ($1.25 a day, in table 3B.1; $2.50 a day, in table 3B.2; and $4.00–$5.00 a day, in table 3B.3). Moreover, each of the annex 3B tables includes decompositions along three dimensions defined by Foster, Greer, and Thorbecke (1984):

- The poverty headcount rate (the proportion of the population that is poor), represented as FGT0
- The poverty gap (the distance between the incomes of the poor and the poverty line), represented as FGT1[5]
- The poverty severity (a measure that gives greater weight to those furthest away from the poverty line), represented as FGT2[6]

For middle-income countries, the $2.50-a-day poverty line is close to national extreme poverty lines. In such cases, nonlabor incomes are relatively more important (table 3B.1) because transfers play a larger role in poverty reduction.[7] For instance, transfers account for about 87 percent in Chile; 58 percent of poverty reduction in Thailand; 40 percent in the Philippines; and 20–30 percent in Colombia, Costa Rica, Ecuador, Moldova, and Panama.

Regardless of which poverty line is used, transfers play a more important role for those who live the furthest below the poverty line, the extreme poor. Transfers account for a greater share of the declines in both the poverty gap (FGT1) and poverty severity (FGT2), as the data show in tables 3B.1, 3B.2, and 3B.3. Particularly in Argentina, Brazil, Chile, Costa Rica, Moldova, the Philippines, Thailand, and Vietnam, increases in cash transfers and pensions jointly account for a larger share of the decline in poverty severity than do changes in labor income (table 3B.2). This finding is consistent with the improvements those countries have made in their social protection systems, which are typically targeted at the bottom of the distribution and have increased in performance over the past decade (World Bank 2013).[8]

Summary and Conclusions

This chapter has implemented a distinct approach to account for the relative contributions of demographics, labor income, and nonlabor income to the significant poverty reductions observed in 21 countries during the past decade. In contrast to methods that focus on aggregate summary statistics as detailed in chapter 2, the method adopted here generates entire counterfactual distributions, allowing us to identify the contributions of these factors to observed distributional changes. Another contribution is the chapter's application of the best-known remedy for path dependence, which is to calculate the decomposition across all possible paths and then take the average among them.

From Useful Findings, More Questions

For most of the 21 countries in our sample, the most important contributor to reductions in moderate poverty has been the growth in labor income. In particular, among 12 of them with substantial declines in poverty, changes in labor income and employment explain more than half of the change in poverty; in another 6 countries, the same changes account for more than 40 percent of reduced poverty.

Demographic changes had their role: the swelling numbers of working-age adults translated into larger numbers of occupied adults per household, and the increased employment reduced poverty. As the data confirmed, however, it was not so much increased employment but increased earnings per occupied adult that made the largest contribution to poverty reduction. Although we cannot distinguish whether the earnings increased because of higher hourly wages, better-quality jobs, higher productivity, or greater number of hours worked, the point is that higher labor incomes appear to be the key factor behind reductions in poverty observed in the past decade.

Declining dependency ratios also pointed to the importance of demographic changes in alleviating poverty, especially in Bangladesh, Cambodia, Chile, Costa Rica, Honduras, Paraguay, and the Philippines. In most cases, however, these effects were smaller than the effect of labor income growth.

As for employment rates, we find that overall employment gains typically contributed to poverty reduction, but in places where employment decreased specifically among the poor, poverty naturally increased. Even in cases where employment growth helped to reduce poverty, the increase in workers' earnings had relatively more impact on reducing poverty than the increase in the share of employed adults.

Finally, both public and private transfers contributed significantly to reduction of moderate poverty, albeit less so than labor income growth. They became far more important when accounting for changes in extreme poverty. From decomposition of the extreme-poverty headcount, poverty gap, and poverty severity (table 3B.1), we find that transfers and pensions contributed a relatively higher share than labor income growth. These results point to the crucial role that social protection systems play in reaching the extreme poor.

Limitations and Next Steps

The decomposition method applied here is quite useful for distinguishing the main contributors to poverty reduction. Its main limitation is that it cannot shed light on *why* workers' earnings increased. Any number of alternatives arise: Did earnings increase because of changes in the endowments of the population, such as higher educational levels or increases in other productive assets? Did marketplace premiums rise for workers with those endowments? In many developing countries, poverty reduction has coincided with the labor force's increasing education and health—as well as, in some cases, more equitable distribution of land or other productive assets. Therefore, such distinctions as the effects of changing endowments—and the *returns* from those endowments—are important if we are to fully understand changes in poverty and how to further reduce it.

To resolve this issue, we must consider alternative decomposition techniques that impose an underlying labor model and greater structure than the nonparametric approach adopted here (Juhn, Murphy, and Pierce 1993; Bourguignon, Ferreira, and Lustig 2005; Bourguignon, Ferreira, and Leite 2008). It is to this task that the remainder of the book is dedicated.

Annex 3A: Data Sources

For the data on Latin American countries, we use the SEDLAC dataset, which covers all countries in mainland Latin America and four of the largest countries in the Caribbean. Most household surveys included in the sample are nationally representative. For comparability purposes, this dataset computes income using a common method across countries and years. In particular, it constructs a common household income variable that includes all the ordinary sources of income and estimates of the imputed rent from home ownership. (For further methodological details, see the "Methodology" link on the SEDLAC website: http://sedlac.econo.unlp.edu.ar/eng/.) Only the Latin

American countries have available data on hours of work, allowing for further decomposition in the report.

For the data on Bangladesh, Moldova, Peru, Romania, Sri Lanka, and Thailand, we use the national Household Income and Expenditure Survey (HIES) for each year. We make temporal and spatial adjustments for comparability reasons. For Ghana and Nepal, we use the RIGA dataset (FAO n.d.).

Table 3A.1 Survey Sources of Data for Poverty Reduction Analysis in Selected Developing Countries, 2000

Sampled countries	*Initial period and survey*	*Final period and survey*
Countries that use income-based poverty measures		
Argentina	2000 EPH-C	2010 EPH-C
Brazil	2001 PNAD	2009 PNAD
Chile	2000 CASEN	2009 CASEN
Colombia	2002 GEIH	2010 GEIH
Costa Rica	2000 EHPM	2008 EHPM
Ecuador	2003 ENEMDU	2010 ENEMDU
Honduras	1999 EPHPM	2009 EPHPM
Panama	2001 EH	2009 EH
Paraguay	1999 EPH	2010 EPH
Countries that use consumption-based poverty measures		
Bangladesh	2000 HIES	2010 HIES
Cambodia	2007 CSES	2010 CSES
Ghana	1998 RIGA	2005 RIGA
Moldova	2001 HBS	2010 HBS
Mongolia	2007 HSES	2011 HSES
Nepal	1996 RIGA	2003 RIGA
Peru	2004 ENAHO	2010 ENAHO
Romania	2001 HBS	2009 HBS
Sri Lanka	2002 HIES	2009 HIES
Thailand	2000 SES	2009 SES
Philippines	2006 FIES	2009 FIES
Vietnam	2004 VHLSS	2010 VHLSS

Note: EPH-C = Encuesta Permanente de Hogares-Continua (Argentina); PNAD = Pesquisa Nacional por Amostra de Domicilios (Brazil); CASEN = Encuesta de Caracterización Socioeconómica Nacional (Chile); GEIH = Gran Encuesta Integrada de Hogares (Colombia); EHPM = Encuesta de Hogares de Propósitos Múltiples (Costa Rica); ENEMDU = Encuesta de Empleo, Desempleo y Subempleo (Ecuador); EPHPM = Encuesta Permanente de Hogares de Propósitos Múltiples (Honduras); EH = Encuesta de Hogares (Panama); EPH = Encuesta Permanente de Hogares (Paraguay); HIES = Household Income and Expenditure Survey (Bangladesh); CSES = Cambodia Socio-Economic Survey; RIGA = Rural Income Generating Activities (Nepal); HBS = Household Budget Survey (Romania); HSES = Household Socio-Economic Survey (Mongolia); ENAHO = Encuesta Nacional de Hogares (Peru); SES = Household Socio-Economic Survey (Thailand); FIES = Family Income and Expenditure Survey (Philippines); VHLSS = Vietnam Household Living Standards Survey.

Annex 3B: Complementary Tables

Table 3B.1 Contributions to the Decline in the $1.25-a-Day (PPP) Poverty Headcount in Selected Developing Countries, 2000s

	Consumption-based measure of welfare					
	Bangladesh, 2000–10	*Sri Lanka, 2002–09*	*Ghana, 1998–2005*	*Nepal, 1996–2003*	*Peru, 2004–10*	*Moldova, 2001–10*
Poverty headcount rate (FGT0)[a]						
Initial period (%)	57.7	14.8	38.2	73.7	3.5	27.5
Final period (%)	40.3	4.7	23.5	53.1	0.8	0.5
Total change (ppts)	−17.4	−10.1	−14.7	−20.6	−2.6	−27.0
Decomposition of FGT0[a]						
Consumption-to-income ratio (%)	−25.6	−0.2	17.7	−6.9	−9.3	−20.2
Adult population (%)	37.2	19.5	21.4	14.2	−14.9	5.7
Occupation share (%)	20.5	−21.8	−3.6	13.4	−3.1	−1.9
Labor income (%)	60.2	62.9	49.6	50.4	115.7	27.7
Capital (%)	7.8	0.0	5.0	5.9	1.4	0.0
Pension (%)	—	1.5	—	—	−4.7	35.8
Transfers (%)	15.7	−1.6	10.0	23.0	10.8	46.1
Other nonlabor income (%)	−15.9	39.8	—	—	4.1	6.7
Total change (%)	100.0	100.0	100.0	100.0	100.0	100.0
Decomposition in FGT1[b]						
Consumption-to-income ratio (%)	−60.6	−37.4	0.8	−10.7	−44.0	—
Adult population (%)	47.2	24.7	28.0	12.4	−40.5	—
Occupation share (%)	25.3	−76.3	−20.9	17.0	−12.5	—
Labor income (%)	99.1	93.2	70.9	54.0	176.4	—
Capital (%)	4.9	0.0	6.5	4.8	2.4	—
Pension (%)	—	2.7	—	—	−9.6	—
Transfers (%)	16.7	−3.7	14.6	22.5	23.8	—
Other nonlabor income (%)	−32.6	96.8	—	—	4.1	—
Total change (%)	100.0	100.0	100.0	100.0	100.0	—
Decomposition in FGT2[c]						
Consumption-to-income ratio (%)	−107.9	−112.6	−20.7	−17.8	−86.2	—
Adult population (%)	59.8	36.9	36.6	10.3	−64.7	—
Occupation share (%)	30.4	−181.4	−40.2	17.9	−27.7	—
Labor income (%)	151.8	128.1	98.4	60.2	234.1	—
Capital (%)	1.5	0.0	6.0	4.7	4.4	—
Pension (%)	—	6.6	—	—	−14.7	—
Transfers (%)	20.0	−3.2	19.9	24.7	53.5	—
Other nonlabor income (%)	−55.7	225.7	—	—	1.2	—
Total change (%)	100.0	100.0	100.0	100.0	100.0	—

Sources: Data on Ghana and Nepal from FAO n.d. Data on Bangladesh, Moldova, Peru, Romania, Sri Lanka, and Thailand from household surveys. Latin American data from SEDLAC, various years. Data on Cambodia, Mongolia, the Philippines, and Vietnam from World Bank harmonized surveys for the East Asia and Pacific region.

Note: ppts = percentage points; PPP = purchasing power parity; — = not available; n.a. = not applicable.

a. FGT0 refers to the Foster, Greer, and Thorbecke (1984) measure of the poverty headcount index, which measures the proportion of the population that is counted as poor using the $1.25-a-day standard.

b. FGT1 refers to the measure of the poverty gap index, which adds up the extent to which individuals on average fall below the poverty line, expressed as a percentage of the poverty line (Foster, Greer, and Thorbecke 1984).

c. FGT2 refers to the measure of poverty severity, calculated as the poverty gap index squared, which implicitly puts more weight on observations that fall well below the poverty line (Foster, Greer, and Thorbecke 1984).

Income-based measure of welfare											
Argentina, 2000–10	*Brazil, 2001–09*	*Colombia, 2002–10*	*Costa Rica, 2000–08*	*Ecuador, 2003–10*	*Honduras, 1999–2009*	*Panama, 2001–09*	*Paraguay, 1999–2010*	*Cambodia, 2007–10*	*Mongolia, 2007–11*	*Philippines, 2006–09*	*Vietnam, 2004–10*
5.1	11.8	20.7	5.5	12.2	24.9	15.4	14.0	34.0	13.1	31.7	18.1
1.8	6.1	8.2	2.4	4.6	17.8	4.6	7.2	29.6	6.0	27.6	8.7
−3.3	−5.7	−12.6	−3.1	−7.6	−7.1	−10.8	−9.3	−4.4	−7.1	−4.1	−9.4
n.a.	n.a.	n.a.	n.a.	n.a.	n.a.	n.a.	n.a.	n.a.	n.a.	n.a.	n.a.
20.0	11.2	5.2	7.1	19.0	41.4	4.0	34.7	34.9	−1.0	47.6	15.6
−5.7	−3.7	8.7	−2.8	−15.3	3.5	14.1	6.4	33.3	−18.2	−0.9	−4.3
14.3	44.7	48.7	26.7	50.3	51.5	39.9	47.8	46.4	62.6	23.2	75.4
−19.7	−4.4	0.4	10.7	−1.7	7.7	0.5	−1.3	—	—	—	—
29.2	6.2	−2.2	61.3	5.2	6.7	10.4	−1.4	−5.2	3.2	2.2	2.9
37.7	37.3	31.0	55.2	36.0	−20.8	31.8	9.8	−8.1	52.2	27.6	8.0
24.2	8.8	8.2	−58.2	6.5	10.0	−0.7	3.9	−1.5	1.2	0.2	2.1
100.0	100.0	100.0	100.0	100.0	100.0	100.0	100.0	100.0	100.0	100.0	100.0
n.a.	n.a.	n.a.	n.a.	n.a.	n.a.	n.a.	n.a.	n.a.	n.a.	n.a.	n.a.
16.5	7.9	−1.5	−2.0	13.3	52.6	2.3	30.8	16.0	−7.7	44.2	8.5
−7.9	−11.4	5.2	−23.2	−20.2	1.0	8.0	3.3	23.4	−14.0	−5.3	1.9
8.4	28.1	51.0	6.6	41.6	41.9	42.4	43.9	74.9	58.6	23.0	39.0
−26.9	−9.0	−3.3	24.0	−4.4	15.9	−0.8	−0.8	—	—	—	—
24.5	0.6	−6.7	130.3	5.0	16.6	10.9	−0.4	−3.4	2.9	2.8	34.2
54.5	68.1	45.6	114.4	55.0	−42.7	42.0	17.6	−8.5	59.6	33.5	12.0
31.0	15.6	9.7	−150.1	9.7	14.7	−4.8	5.7	−2.4	0.6	1.8	4.4
100.0	100.0	100.0	100.0	100.0	100.0	100.0	100.0	100.0	100.0	100.0	100.0
n.a.	n.a.	n.a.	n.a.	n.a.	n.a.	n.a.	n.a.	n.a.	n.a.	n.a.	n.a.
11.8	6.0	−4.4	−7.4	9.3	78.6	0.7	30.7	10.7	−12.1	39.7	−112.6
−7.2	−14.4	3.0	−39.8	−23.1	−9.6	3.8	−0.5	19.1	−10.3	−7.1	278.4
6.5	14.2	49.5	−12.8	35.0	21.6	42.4	39.1	82.3	52.6	20.6	−696.3
−30.4	−11.2	−5.1	35.5	−7.0	32.2	−1.4	0.3	—	—	—	—
20.0	−2.3	−8.9	188.3	5.0	33.7	11.7	−0.3	−3.1	3.0	3.2	543.6
66.0	88.2	54.4	166.9	68.3	−78.7	50.4	23.7	−7.4	66.7	39.3	60.1
33.2	19.5	11.4	−230.8	12.5	22.2	−7.7	7.0	−1.7	0.1	4.3	26.9
100.0	100.0	100.0	100.0	100.0	100.0	100.0	100.0	100.0	100.0	100.0	100.0

Table 3B.2 Contributions to the Decline in the $2.50-a-Day (PPP) Poverty Headcount in Selected Developing Countries, 2000s

	Consumption-based measure of welfare							
	Bangladesh, 2000–10	*Sri Lanka, 2002–09*	*Ghana, 1998–2005*	*Nepal, 1996–2003*	*Peru, 2004–10*	*Thailand, 2000–09*	*Moldova, 2001–10*	*Romania, 2001–09*
Poverty headcount rate (FGT0)[a]								
Initial period (%)	89.2	61.9	71.8	94.3	22.9	7.9	71.4	23.7
Final period (%)	84.0	45.1	58.3	84.9	11.7	2.5	12.9	4.2
Total change (ppts)	−5.2	−16.8	−13.5	−9.5	−11.2	−5.3	−58.5	−19.5
Decomposition of FGT0[a]								
Consumption-to-income ratio (%)	−56.1	7.4	18.5	−30.9	4.8	−47.0	−2.9	15.3
Adult population (%)	46.4	14.5	21.1	18.7	7.4	35.8	7.2	48.4
Occupation share (%)	23.3	−7.7	−0.9	6.2	5.6	−10.1	6.6	24.8
Labor income (%)	85.6	51.1	52.2	62.3	70.1	61.0	26.2	−33.0
Capital (%)	5.3	0.0	1.6	9.7	1.5	5.9	0.4	38.3
Pension (%)	—	1.9	—	—	−0.4	—	25.5	−20.2
Transfers (%)	24.8	2.0	7.3	34.0	10.0	57.8	30.1	16.2
Other nonlabor income (%)	−29.3	30.9	—	—	1.0	−3.4	7.0	10.2
Total change (%)	100.0	100.0	100.0	100.0	100.0	100.0	100.0	100.0
Decomposition in FGT1[b]								
Consumption-to-income ratio (%)	−46.3	3.4	14.0	−14.0	0.3	−131.5	−15.9	51.3
Adult population (%)	43.9	17.6	22.7	14.9	−0.1	58.2	4.9	138.0
Occupation share (%)	22.4	−14.6	−6.1	13.5	1.8	−39.8	6.0	70.9
Labor income (%)	81.4	54.3	55.1	53.8	85.8	67.8	22.9	−154.8
Capital (%)	6.2	0.0	4.3	6.5	1.4	13.6	0.2	117.1
Pension (%)	—	1.7	—	—	−2.0	—	29.5	−120.9
Transfers (%)	17.9	0.5	10.0	25.3	10.9	126.7	46.8	14.8
Other nonlabor income (%)	−25.6	37.0	—	—	1.8	5.0	5.6	−16.4
Total change (%)	100.0	100.0	100.0	100.0	100.0	100.0	100.0	100.0
Decomposition in FGT2[c]								
Consumption-to-income ratio (%)	−54.5	−4.2	8.2	−12.7	−7.4	−264.8	−31.2	148.6
Adult population (%)	45.8	19.3	25.0	13.4	−8.2	95.2	2.8	320.2
Occupation share (%)	23.9	−26.2	−12.1	15.3	−1.5	−95.6	5.3	175.7
Labor income (%)	91.6	61.0	61.8	54.3	103.2	49.5	16.2	−387.5
Capital (%)	5.5	0.0	5.1	5.6	1.6	28.1	−0.2	280.8
Pension (%)	—	1.9	—	—	−3.4	—	32.7	−336.5
Transfers (%)	17.4	−0.3	12.0	24.0	13.3	253.4	70.1	−14.5
Other nonlabor income (%)	−29.6	48.5	—	—	2.4	34.3	4.3	−86.7
Total change (%)	100.0	100.0	100.0	100.0	100.0	100.0	100.0	100.0

Sources: Data on Ghana and Nepal from FAO n.d. Data on Bangladesh, Moldova, Peru, Romania, Sri Lanka, and Thailand from household surveys. Latin American data from SEDLAC, various years. Data on Cambodia, Mongolia, the Philippines, and Vietnam from World Bank harmonized surveys for the East Asia and Pacific region.

Note: ppts = percentage points; PPP = purchasing power parity; — = not available; n.a. = not applicable.

a. FGT0 refers to the Foster, Greer, and Thorbecke (1984) measure of the headcount index, which measures the proportion of the population that is counted as poor using the $2.50-a-day standard.

b. FGT1 refers to the measure of the poverty gap index, which adds up the extent to which individuals on average fall below the poverty line, and expresses it as a percentage of the poverty line (Foster, Greer, and Thorbecke 1984).

c. FGT2 refers to the measure of poverty severity, calculated as the poverty gap index squared, which implicitly puts more weight on observations that fall well below the poverty line (Foster, Greer, and Thorbecke 1984).

Income-based measure of welfare												
Argentina, 2000–10	*Brazil, 2001–09*	*Chile, 2000–09*	*Colombia, 2002–10*	*Costa Rica, 2000–08*	*Ecuador, 2003–10*	*Honduras, 1999–2009*	*Panama, 2001–09*	*Paraguay, 1999–2010*	*Cambodia, 2007–10*	*Mongolia, 2007–11*	*Philippines, 2006–09*	*Vietnam, 2004–10*
14.2	27.4	9.0	42.3	14.7	31.5	47.9	28.7	26.7	57.3	35.7	62.2	56.4
6.4	15.1	4.3	22.0	7.6	15.9	36.2	16.1	18.4	60.1	22.5	60.3	33.2
−7.8	−12.3	−4.7	−20.3	−7.1	−15.6	−11.6	−12.6	−8.3	2.8	−13.2	−1.9	−23.2
n.a.	n.a.	n.a.	n.a.	n.a.	n.a.	n.a.	n.a.	n.a.	n.a.	n.a.	n.a.	n.a.
20.6	16.5	31.9	10.5	25.3	24.5	37.4	9.2	56.8	53.0	5.4	71.2	16.0
10.4	6.9	−18.4	14.0	9.3	−6.0	−3.1	22.5	6.5	29.0	−22.0	−18.8	3.0
29.5	44.8	46.9	40.7	24.5	53.2	57.8	33.5	43.8	−162.6	75.0	8.1	68.6
−9.1	−1.1	−11.3	3.0	4.7	−1.1	3.8	0.0	−2.4	—	—	—	—
19.9	10.7	31.9	2.7	31.5	4.7	3.7	9.8	−3.8	1.8	3.3	2.7	4.3
16.1	16.7	87.4	20.1	28.3	20.2	−6.9	24.5	−0.5	−18.6	36.4	40.7	5.2
12.7	5.4	−68.4	9.0	−23.6	4.5	7.2	0.5	−0.4	−2.6	1.9	−4.0	2.9
100.0	100.0	100.0	100.0	100.0	100.0	100.0	100.0	100.0	−100.0	100.0	100.0	100.0
n.a.	n.a.	n.a.	n.a.	n.a.	n.a.	n.a.	n.a.	n.a.	n.a.	n.a.	n.a.	n.a.
18.7	12.7	42.6	5.4	15.1	21.5	43.8	5.3	41.0	54.1	0.9	49.1	14.8
1.1	0.4	−50.2	9.5	−0.8	−12.2	−1.5	14.5	6.7	47.6	−18.3	−5.3	0.2
20.9	41.7	17.2	45.9	20.2	50.3	54.3	38.4	44.3	24.9	67.4	21.4	66.7
−15.6	−3.4	−32.2	0.4	10.1	−2.2	7.4	−0.2	−1.5	—	—	—	—
23.6	7.3	72.1	−1.4	61.5	4.7	7.4	10.3	−1.5	−4.5	3.5	2.9	8.0
31.4	32.8	191.6	31.2	53.0	32.0	−20.8	33.3	8.1	−16.9	45.0	32.1	7.4
19.8	8.5	−141.1	9.2	−59.1	6.0	9.3	−1.6	2.9	−5.2	1.5	−0.1	2.8
100.0	100.0	100.0	100.0	100.0	100.0	100.0	100.0	100.0	100.0	100.0	100.0	100.0
n.a.	n.a.	n.a.	n.a.	n.a.	n.a.	n.a.	n.a.	n.a.	n.a.	n.a.	n.a.	n.a.
17.2	10.4	64.2	1.8	7.8	18.1	48.9	3.5	35.7	27.1	−2.6	45.6	8.0
−3.3	−4.5	−95.7	7.0	−10.5	−15.9	−0.9	10.7	5.0	27.8	−16.8	−4.7	12.7
15.0	35.9	−26.9	48.3	14.3	46.8	48.5	40.4	43.8	62.1	63.8	22.1	27.7
−20.9	−5.7	−65.9	−1.5	16.0	−3.2	11.7	−0.5	−1.1	—	—	—	—
24.1	4.4	129.3	−4.2	91.3	4.8	11.8	10.7	−1.0	−3.7	3.2	2.9	36.7
43.0	48.0	348.1	39.1	79.6	41.9	−31.7	38.7	13.1	−10.1	51.2	32.8	10.8
24.9	11.4	−253.2	9.6	−98.5	7.5	11.7	−3.5	4.4	−3.1	1.2	1.2	4.1
100.0	100.0	100.0	100.0	100.0	100.0	100.0	100.0	100.0	100.0	100.0	100.0	100.0

Table 3B.3 Contributions to the Decline in the $4.00–$5.00-a-Day (PPP) Poverty Headcount in Selected Developing Countries, 2000s

	Consumption-based measure of welfare					*Income-based measure of welfare*								
	$4.00-a-day poverty line			*$5.00-a-day poverty line*		*$4.00-a-day poverty line*								
	Peru, 2004–10	*Sri Lanka, 2002–09*	*Thailand, 2000–09*	*Moldova, 2001–10*	*Romania, 2001–09*	*Argentina, 2000–10*	*Brazil, 2001–09*	*Chile, 2000–09*	*Colombia, 2002–10*	*Costa Rica, 2000–08*	*Ecuador, 2003–10*	*Honduras, 1999–2009*	*Panama, 2001–09*	*Paraguay, 1999–2010*
Poverty headcount rate (FGT0)														
Initial period (%)	45.8	84.7	31.4	93.8	75.3	27.5	43.1	23.2	61.6	29.2	51.5	66.1	43.4	50.3
Final period (%)	30.0	78.1	16.6	58.7	33.2	14.6	27.6	11.8	39.5	18.9	33.4	52.1	29.9	33.0
Total change (ppts)	−15.8	−6.6	−14.8	−35.1	−42.2	−13.0	−15.5	−11.4	−22.1	−10.2	−18.1	−14.1	−13.5	−17.3
Decomposition of FGT0 [a]														
Consumption-to-income ratio (%)	5.1	−9.0	−11.8	−20.9	15.8	n.a.	n.a.	n.a.	n.a.	n.a.	n.a.	n.a.	n.a.	n.a.
Adult population (%)	9.0	9.7	24.2	3.5	24.1	22.0	16.4	31.0	12.1	34.4	27.1	32.0	13.5	59.5
Occupation share (%)	10.0	−24.3	4.0	6.5	20.4	16.7	10.9	−0.1	15.8	14.2	−3.3	−4.1	29.1	11.6
Labor income (%)	62.5	75.1	47.5	37.3	1.9	35.2	41.6	48.2	38.3	17.7	53.3	55.8	30.2	33.2
Capital (%)	2.1	0.0	2.8	0.6	21.0	−5.4	−0.7	−4.2	4.3	3.9	−0.7	3.8	−0.2	0.0
Pension (%)	0.6	4.3	—	25.1	−2.8	14.9	17.9	15.8	4.6	23.6	6.2	3.2	10.4	−3.0
Transfers (%)	10.0	6.5	33.1	37.2	8.7	7.3	9.1	41.8	15.6	22.4	13.6	3.4	16.4	−1.0
Other nonlabor income (%)	0.7	37.7	0.3	10.6	11.0	9.3	4.8	−32.5	9.4	−16.1	3.8	6.0	0.5	−0.3
Total change (%)	100.0	100.0	100.0	100.0	100.0	100.0	100.0	100.0	100.0	100.0	100.0	100.0	100.0	100.0

table continues next page

Table 3B.3 Contributions to the Decline in the $4.00–$5.00-a-Day (PPP) Poverty Headcount in Selected Developing Countries, 2000s *(continued)*

	Consumption-based measure of welfare					*Income-based measure of welfare*								
	$4.00-a-day poverty line			*$5.00-a-day poverty line*		*$4.00-a-day poverty line*								
	Peru, 2004–10	*Sri Lanka, 2002–09*	*Thailand, 2000–09*	*Moldova, 2001–10*	*Romania, 2001–09*	*Argentina, 2000–10*	*Brazil, 2001–09*	*Chile, 2000–09*	*Colombia, 2002–10*	*Costa Rica, 2000–08*	*Ecuador, 2003–10*	*Honduras, 1999–2009*	*Panama, 2001–09*	*Paraguay, 1999–2010*
Decomposition in FGT1 [b]														
Consumption-to-income ratio (%)	3.4	2.8	−35.9	−10.8	20.0	n.a.	n.a.	n.a.	n.a.	n.a.	n.a.	n.a.	n.a.	n.a.
Adult population (%)	5.9	15.0	31.8	5.6	44.0	20.5	14.8	33.9	8.7	25.8	24.2	38.0	8.0	49.8
Occupation share (%)	6.0	−14.3	−5.8	6.6	27.0	9.3	5.5	−15.8	12.3	7.9	−7.7	−2.1	19.9	8.1
Labor income (%)	72.3	56.9	53.7	27.5	−25.6	28.3	42.4	41.7	42.2	19.2	52.1	55.6	35.2	41.2
Capital (%)	1.7	0.0	4.9	0.3	36.5	−9.9	−2.0	−11.9	2.1	6.5	−1.5	5.2	−0.1	−1.3
Pension (%)	−0.5	2.3	—	26.5	−20.7	19.2	11.7	31.6	1.4	40.1	5.1	5.1	10.3	−2.6
Transfers (%)	10.1	2.1	51.5	36.9	11.7	18.4	20.9	85.7	24.0	35.6	22.9	−9.5	27.3	3.8
Other nonlabor income (%)	1.2	35.1	−0.2	7.5	7.1	14.3	6.8	−65.1	9.3	−35.0	5.0	7.7	−0.7	1.1
Total change (%)	100.0	100.0	100.0	100.0	100.0	100.0	100.0	100.0	100.0	100.0	100.0	100.0	100.0	100.0
Decomposition in FGT2 [c]														
Consumption-to-income ratio (%)	0.9	1.9	−68.4	−13.0	30.5	n.a.	n.a.	n.a.	n.a.	n.a.	n.a.	n.a.	n.a.	n.a.
Adult population (%)	2.1	16.8	41.1	5.4	72.8	19.1	13.2	39.5	5.9	18.6	22.0	42.3	5.8	43.3
Occupation share (%)	3.6	−16.5	−18.2	6.3	40.6	4.0	1.6	−34.3	10.0	1.5	−10.9	−1.6	15.4	6.6
Labor income (%)	80.8	56.4	57.1	24.6	−64.3	23.1	40.9	28.2	44.9	18.6	50.4	53.7	37.8	43.1
Capital (%)	1.6	0.0	8.1	0.2	61.1	−14.1	−3.3	−23.3	0.6	9.5	−2.1	7.3	−0.2	−1.3
Pension (%)	−1.4	2.0	—	27.8	−51.5	21.7	8.5	53.2	−1.0	57.1	4.8	7.3	10.4	−1.9
Transfers (%)	10.8	1.1	78.0	42.3	11.6	27.8	30.7	143.6	30.2	49.8	29.9	−18.1	32.7	7.6
Other nonlabor income (%)	1.6	38.3	2.4	6.5	−0.8	18.3	8.3	−106.9	9.4	−55.2	5.9	9.1	−1.8	2.5
Total change (%)	100.0	100.0	100.0	100.0	100.0	100.0	100.0	100.0	100.0	100.0	100.0	100.0	100.0	100.0

Sources: Data on Ghana and Nepal from FAO n.d. Data on Bangladesh, Moldova, Peru, Romania, Sri Lanka, and Thailand from household surveys. Latin American data from SEDLAC, various years. Data on Cambodia, Mongolia, the Philippines, and Vietnam from World Bank harmonized surveys for the East Asia and Pacific region.

Note: ppts = percentage points; PPP = purchasing power parity; — = not available; n.a. = not applicable.

a. FGT0 refers to the Foster, Greer, and Thorbecke (1984) measure of the headcount index, which measures the proportion of the population that is counted as poor.

b. FGT1 refers to the measure of the poverty gap index, which adds up the extent to which individuals on average fall below the poverty line and expresses it as a percentage of the poverty line (Foster, Greer, and Thorbecke 1984).

c. FGT2 refers to the measure of poverty severity, calculated as the poverty gap index squared, which implicitly puts more weight on observations that fall well below the poverty line (Foster, Greer, and Thorbecke 1984).

Notes

1. SEDLAC is a joint effort of the Centro de Estudios Distributivos Laborales y Sociales (CEDLAS) of the Universidad Nacional de La Plata in Buenos Aires and the World Bank's Latin American Poverty and Gender Group. For more information about SEDLAC, see its website: http://sedlac.econo.unlp.edu.ar/eng/.
2. For more information about RIGA, see its page on the FAO website: http://www.fao.org/economic/riga/riga-database/en/.
3. For a more comprehensive treatment of how global poverty measures have developed historically, see Chen and Ravallion (2010). The World Bank's interactive website, PovcalNet (developed by the Bank's Development Research Group), also allows users to replicate calculations made by World Bank researchers to estimate the extent of absolute poverty in the world as well as "to calculate poverty measures under different assumptions" (PovcalNet online poverty analysis tool, http://iresearch.worldbank.org/PovcalNet/index.htm).
4. Note that the consumption-to-income ratio is the ratio of measured consumption to measured income. To the extent that there is measurement error in both of these, interpretations about changes in this ratio must be treated with caution.
5. FGT1 refers to the Foster, Greer, and Thorbecke (1984) measure of the poverty gap index, which adds up the extent to which individuals on average fall below the poverty line, and expresses it as a percentage of the poverty line.
6. FGT2 refers to the Foster, Greer, and Thorbecke (1984) measure of poverty severity, calculated as the poverty gap index squared, which implicitly puts more weight on observations that fall well below the poverty line.
7. We do not report decompositions for Chile and Thailand using the $1.25-a-day poverty line because only 1 percent or less of the population in those countries experiences poverty at that level.
8. Also, see Fiszbein et al. (2009) for a review of conditional cash transfer programs.

Bibliography

Bourguignon, François, Francisco H. G. Ferreira, and Nora Lustig, eds. 2005. *The Microeconomics of Income Distribution Dynamics in East Asia and Latin America.* Washington, DC: World Bank.

Bourguignon François, Francisco H. G. Ferreira., and Phillippe G. Leite 2008. "Beyond Oaxaca-Blinder: Accounting for Differences in Household Income Distributions." *Journal of Economic Inequality* 6 (2): 117–48.

Chen, Shaohua and Martin Ravallion. 2010. "The Developing World Is Poorer Than We Thought, but No Less Successful in the Fight Against Poverty." *Quarterly Journal of Economics* 125 (4): 1577–625.

Datt, Gaurav, and Martin Ravallion. 1992. "Growth and Redistribution Components of Changes in Poverty Measures: A Decomposition with Applications to Brazil and India in the 1980s." *Journal of Development Economics* 38: 275–96.

FAO (Food and Agriculture Organization of the United Nations). n.d. Rural Income Generating Activities (RIGA). Database, FAO, Rome; World Bank and American University, Washington, DC, http://www.fao.org/economic/riga/riga-database/en/.

Ferreira, Francisco H. G. 2012. "Distributions in Motion: Economic Growth, Inequality, and Poverty Dynamics." In *The Oxford Handbook of the Economics of Poverty*, edited by Philip N. Jefferson, 427–62. New York: Oxford University Press.

Fiszbein, Ariel, Norbert Schady, Francisco H. G. Ferreira, Margaret Grosh, Pedro Olinto, and E. Skoufias. 2009. *Conditional Cash Transfers: Reducing Present and Future Poverty*. Washington, DC: World Bank.

Foster, James, Joel Greer, and Erik Thorbecke. 1984. "A Class of Decomposable Poverty Measures." *Econometrica* 52 (3): 761–65.

Juhn, Chinhui, Kevin M. Murphy, and Brooks Pierce. 1993. "Wage Inequality and the Rise of Returns to Skill." *Journal of Political Economy* 101 (3): 410–42.

Ravallion, Martin, and Shaohua Chen. 2007. "China's (Uneven) Progress against Poverty." *Journal of Development Economics* 82 (1): 1–42.

SEDLAC (Socio-Economic Database for Latin America and the Caribbean). Various years. Statistical database produced by CEDLAS (Center for Distributional, Labor and Social Studies) of the Universidad Nacional de la Plata, Buenos Aires; and World Bank, Washington, DC. http://sedlac.econo.unlp.edu.ar/eng/.

Shapley, Lloyd. 1953. "A Value for *n*-Person Games." In *Contributions to the Theory of Games*, Vol. 2, edited by H. W. Kuhn and A. W. Tucker, 307–17. Princeton, NJ: Princeton University Press.

Shorrocks, Anthony F. 1999. "Decomposition Procedures for Distributional Analysis: A Unified Framework Based on Shapley Value." Unpublished manuscript, University of Essex and Institute for Fiscal Studies.

World Bank. 2005. *World Development Report 2006: Equity and Development*. Washington, DC: World Bank and Oxford University Press.

———. 2012. *World Development Indicators 2012*. Washington, DC: World Bank. http://data.worldbank.org/data-catalog/world-development-indicators. Online database.

———. 2013. *World Development Indicators 2013*. Washington, DC: World Bank. http://data.worldbank.org/data-catalog/world-development-indicators. Online database.

CHAPTER 4

Counterfactual Decomposition of Changes in Poverty Outcomes

Introduction

This chapter reviews decomposition methods commonly used to identify key factors that drive changes in the observed poverty outcomes. The review focuses on a variety of microeconometric methods and delves into the identification strategy underlying each of these methods. Macro-decomposition methods, such as those discussed in chapter 2, explain changes in poverty in terms of changes in aggregate statistics (such as the mean), relative inequality, subgroup population shares, and within-group poverty.

The usefulness of such macro methods in policy making is severely limited because these methods identify determining factors that are hard to target with policy instruments. Ravallion (2001) explains that a better understanding of the heterogeneity of policy impact requires a deeper empirical analysis of distributional change at the micro level. Micro-decomposition methods thus go beyond the summary statistics that are the focus of macro methods and attempt to link distributional changes to fundamental elements that drive these changes, such as individual or household characteristics that facilitate policy targeting.

The logic underpinning all these methods (including the macro ones discussed in chapter 2) can be organized around the following terms:

- *Domain*: the distributional change a method seeks to decompose on the basis of a model that links the outcome of interest to its determining factors.
- *Outcome model*: the assumed relationship between the outcome of interest and its determining factors, the specification of which determines the potential scope of the decomposition.
- *Scope*: the set of explanatory factors that decomposition methods seek to identify.

This chapter adapts a previous work by the same author (Essama-Nssah 2012).

- *Identification*: the assumptions needed to recover, in a meaningful way, the terms of the decomposition that affect the outcome.
- *Estimation*: the computation of the relevant parameters on the basis of sample data.

The point of departure for micro-decomposition methods is the fact that a poverty measure is a functional[1] of a distribution of living standards. An individual's living standard is an outcome of interaction between opportunities offered by society and the individual's ability to identify and exploit such opportunities. In other words, an individual's living standard is a payoff from participation in the life of society.

One can thus think of life in society as a game defined by a set of rules governing various interactions of the parties involved (players). These rules spell out what the concerned parties are allowed to do and how these allowable actions determine outcomes. An environment within which a game is played consists of three basic elements: a set of potential participants, a set of possible outcomes, and a set of possible participant types (players). Player types are characterized by their preferences, capabilities, information, and beliefs (Milgrom 2004). The operation of a game can be represented by a function that maps environments to potential outcomes. Thus an individual *payoff* is a function of *participation* and *type*.

This paradigm leads us to consider an individual's living standard to be a function of *endowments, behavior*, and the *circumstances* that determine the *returns* to these endowments from any social transaction. These elements span the scope of most micro-decomposition methods and represent some of the deep structural drivers of the distributional changes underlying the observed variations in poverty outcomes.

Although macro- and micro-decomposition methods differ in their scope, they share the same fundamental *identification strategy* based on the notion of *ceteris paribus* variation. Attribution of outcomes to policy is the hallmark of policy impact evaluation. Variations in individual outcomes associated with a policy's implementation are not necessarily the result of the policy in question. These variations could be driven by changes in *confounding* factors in the socio-economic environment. At the most fundamental level, all identification strategies seek to isolate an independent source of variation in policy and link it to the outcome of interest to ascertain impact.

Similarly, macro- and micro-decomposition methods also identify the determinants of differences across living-standard distributions by comparing counterfactual distributions with the observed ones. Counterfactual distributions are obtained by changing one determining factor at a time while holding all the other factors fixed (a straight application of *ceteris paribus* identification strategy).

The linchpin of the whole process is the estimation of credible counterfactuals. In the context of micro-decomposition methods, for instance, one must carefully estimate a key counterfactual: the distribution of outcomes in the base state ($t = 0$) assuming the distribution of individual characteristics prevailing in the end state ($t = 1$). Put another way, such a counterfactual represents the distribution of outcomes that would prevail in the end state if the characteristics in that state had been treated according to the outcome structure prevailing in initial state. Depending on the chosen functional form for the outcome equation, there are both parametric and nonparametric ways of estimating this counterfactual.

The rest of the chapter is divided into three sections. The next section reviews methods to identify and estimate the *composition* (or endowment) *effect* and *structural* (or price) *effect* associated with variation in a general distributional statistic. Both aggregate and detailed decompositions are considered. This is followed by a section that focuses on proposed methods to account for behavioral responses to changes in the socioeconomic environment. These methods rely on the specification and estimation of a microeconometric model based on some theory of individual (or household) behavior and social interaction. The final section summarizes the chapter's findings.

As the chapter proceeds, the methods first reviewed are considered statistical, while those covered in the later section accounting for behavioral responses are structural in nature. One particular advantage of the statistical approach is that it gives the analyst semi- and nonparametric ways to identify the aggregate effects without having to impose a functional form on the relationship between the outcome and its determinants. However, the statistical framework cannot shed light on the mechanism underlying that relationship. The decomposition results therefore lack any causal interpretation. Because these methods are based on statistical models of conditional distributions, it is conceivable that the behavioral effect is mixed up with the price effect identified by these methods.

Structural methods go a step further toward identifying factors associated with structural elements underpinning the observed changes in poverty outcomes. Both the statistical and structural approaches seek to model conditional outcome distributions. A key distinction between the two approaches is that the former relies entirely on statistics while the latter combines economics and statistics.

The Composition and Structural Effects

As noted earlier, an individual's living standard is an outcome of participation in the life of society. This outcome is a function of the individual's endowments, behavior, and the circumstances that determine the returns to these endowments from any socioeconomic transaction. In this section, we focus on the role of endowments and the returns to those endowments in driving the distributional changes[2] that underlie changes in poverty outcomes. We consider changes in both distributional statistics and entire distributions. We also discuss the contribution of unobservable characteristics.

All methods reviewed in this section are consistent with the logic of the basic Oaxaca-Blinder decomposition (Blinder 1973; Oaxaca 1973). The methods differ mainly in the ability to account for (a) heterogeneity in the composition and structural effects along the entire outcome distribution and (b) the contribution of observable or unobservable characteristics to both types of effects.

In particular, using a linear regression model to link the outcome variable to individual or household characteristics allows one to perform both aggregate and detailed decompositions of changes in distributional statistics. Decomposing differences in density functions or across quantiles reveals how the composition and structural effects vary along the outcome distribution. Under some specifications of the outcome model (Juhn, Murphy, and Pierce 1993), it is possible to explicitly account for the contribution of unobservables to the structural effect. Finally, it is important to keep in mind the analogy between the Oaxaca-Blinder decomposition and treatment effect analysis. This analogy underlies the development of flexible methods for estimating the endowment and structural effects.

Changes in Distributional Statistics

In the context of assessing variations in individual and social outcomes, the composition or endowment effect indicates the change in outcome that is due only to changes in the distribution of observable characteristics of agents. The structural or price effect is the result of changes in the returns to those characteristics. Although we focus on changes in poverty outcomes, it is instructive to consider the more general approach that applies to all distributional statistics, including poverty and inequality measures.

We frame the analysis of the underlying distributional changes within the logic of the standard Oaxaca-Blinder decomposition based on an outcome model that considers both individual and social outcomes (Blinder 1973; Oaxaca 1973). We discuss, in turn, the outcome model, the identification, and the estimation of the relevant effects. Our presentation relies heavily on Fortin, Lemieux, and Firpo (2011).

Outcome Model

Let θ stand for the social outcome of interest. This is a distributional statistic that we view as a functional of the distribution of individual outcomes, F_y. As noted above, an individual outcome y is a function of endowments, behavior, and returns to endowments. We are interested in decomposing a change in the social outcome from the base period $t = 0$ to the end period $t = 1$. Let $F_{y_0|t=0}$ stand for the outcome distribution observed in the initial period and $F_{y_1|t=1}$ for that observed in the final period. We can express distributional change between states 0 and 1 by the following variation in $\theta(F_y)$:

$$\Delta_O^\theta = \theta\left(F_{y_1|t=1}\right) - \theta\left(F_{y_0|t=0}\right). \tag{4.1}$$

Equation (4.1) characterizes the domain of the decomposition methods considered in this chapter. As far as the scope is concerned, most micro-decomposition methods seek to decompose this overall difference on the basis of the relationship between the outcome variable and individual or household characteristics. The following equation represents a general expression of that relationship:

$$y_t = \varphi_t\,(x_t, \varepsilon_t),\ t = 0,1. \tag{4.2}$$

Equation (4.2) suggests that conditional on the observable characteristics, x, the outcome distribution depends only on the function $\varphi_t(\cdot)$ and the distribution of the unobservable characteristics ε. Thus there are four potential terms in the scope of micro-decomposition methods based on this model. Differences in outcome distributions between the two periods may be the result of (a) differences in the returns to observable characteristics given the functions defining the outcome structure; (b) differences in the returns to unobservable characteristics also defined by the structural functions; (c) differences in the distribution of observable characteristics; and (d) differences in the distribution of unobservable characteristics.

The classic Oaxaca-Blinder method seeks to decompose the overall difference in unconditional mean outcome between two groups or time periods. In this case, $\theta(F_y) = \mu(F_y) = E(y)$. The overall difference in the mean outcome between the two periods can therefore be written as $\Delta_O^{\mu} = [E(y_1) - E(y_0)]$. This framework assumes an additive linear relationship between the outcome variable y and its determinants. The equivalent of equation (4.2) can therefore be written as $y_t = x_t\beta_t + \epsilon_t; t = 0, 1$.

Identification

Given the potential scope implied by the outcome model (equation [4.2]), the next step is to impose enough restrictions to identify the factors of interest. In general, these restrictions are imposed on the form of the outcome functions, $\varphi_t(\cdot)$, and on the joint distribution of the observable and unobservable characteristics, x and ε. On the basis of the general outcome model represented by the definition of the distributional statistic θ, along with equation (4.2), it is impossible to distinguish the contribution of the returns to observables from that of unobservables. These two terms can therefore be lumped into a single term: the structural effect, also called the price effect, noted Δ_S^{θ}. Let Δ_X^{θ} stand for the composition effect and $\Delta_{\varepsilon}^{\theta}$ for the effect associated with differences in the distribution of unobservables. The issue now is to identify these three effects so that they account for the overall difference described by equation (4.1).

Just as in the case of the size and redistribution effects discussed in chapter 2, we rely on counterfactual decomposition to identify the composition and structural effects. Let $y_{0|t=1}$ be the outcomes that would have prevailed in period 1 if individual characteristics in that period had been rewarded according to the reward regime prevailing in period 0, that is, according to $\varphi_0(\cdot)$. Let $F_{y_0|t=1}$ stand for the corresponding distribution and $\theta(F_{y_0|t=1})$ for the corresponding value of the statistic of interest. By definition, the composition effect is given by the following expression: $\Delta_X^{\theta} = \left[\theta(F_{y_0|t=1}) - \theta(F_{y_0|t=0})\right]$.

This term is meaningful and identifiable only if it emerges from a *ceteris paribus* variation of the distribution of observable characteristics. Given the scope of the decomposition implied by the underlying outcome model and the fact that we are lumping together the returns to both observables and unobservables, we must restrict movements in the conditional distribution of unobservable characteristics (given observables) and the structure of individual outcomes.

We therefore assume that the conditional distribution of unobservables is the same in both states of the world. This is the so-called *ignorability* assumption usually made in the context of observational studies of treatment effect.

We further assume that the outcome structure, $\varphi()$, remains stable as we adjust the distribution of observables to obtain the relevant counterfactual outcome. This assumption is sometimes referred to as simple treatment assumption or the assumption of *no general equilibrium effects*. Ignorability implies that $\Delta_{\varepsilon}^{\theta} = 0$. Combining the assumption of ignorability with that of no general equilibrium effects secures the identification of both the composition and structural effects. The structural effect is identified by $\Delta_S^{\theta} = \left[\theta\left(F_{y_1|t=1}\right) - \theta\left(F_{y_0|t=1}\right)\right]$. The overall difference in equation (4.1) can therefore be expressed as

$$\Delta_O^{\theta} = \left[\theta\left(F_{y_0|t=1}\right) - \theta\left(F_{y_0|t=0}\right)\right] + \left[\theta\left(F_{y_1|t=1}\right) - \theta\left(F_{y_0|t=1}\right)\right], \tag{4.3}$$

where the first term on the right-hand side is the endowment effect and the second is the structural effect. In the context of poverty analysis, if P stands for the poverty measure of interest, then equation (4.3) implies that observed changes in poverty can be decomposed as follows:

$$\Delta_O^{P} = \left[P\left(F_{y_0|t=1}\right) - P\left(F_{y_0|t=0}\right)\right] + \left[P\left(F_{y_1|t=1}\right) - P\left(F_{y_0|t=1}\right)\right]. \tag{4.4}$$

In addition to assuming a linear model for the individual outcome, the classic Oaxaca-Blinder decomposition assumes that the conditional mean of ε given the observables is equal to zero. This assumption, which is stronger than ignorability, implies that the conditional mean outcome can be written as follows: $E(y|x) = x\beta$. Therefore β is a measure of the effect of x on the conditional mean outcome. By the law of iterated expectations, we know that the unconditional mean outcome is $E(y) = E_x[E(y|x)] = E(x)\beta$. This result means that β also measures the effect of changing the mean value of x on the unconditional mean value of y. This is the interpretation underlying the original Oaxaca-Blinder decomposition.

The domain of the standard Oaxaca-Blinder decomposition can therefore be written as $\Delta_O^{\mu} = \left[E(x_1)\beta_1 - E(x_0)\beta_0\right]$. This overall difference in means is subject to counterfactual decomposition as follows: The average outcome for period 1 valued on the basis of the reward parameters for period 0 is equal to $E(x_1)\beta_0$. This is a counterfactual outcome for period 1. We can subtract it from, and add it back to, the above overall mean difference to get the following expression: $\Delta_O^{\mu} = \left[E(x_1) - E(x_0)\right]\beta_0 + \left[E(x_1)(\beta_1 - \beta_0)\right]$.[3] Looking at the regression coefficients β as characterizing the returns to (or reward for) observable characteristics, this *aggregate decomposition* reveals that under the identifying assumptions, the overall mean difference can be expressed as $\Delta_O^{\mu} = \Delta_X^{\mu} + \Delta_S^{\mu}$, where Δ_X^{μ} is the composition (endowment) effect, and Δ_S^{μ} is the structural (price) effect.

Estimation

Parametric and Nonparametric Approaches. There are both parametric and non-parametric approaches to estimating the counterfactuals involved in the identification and hence estimation of the composition and structural effects. DiNardo, Fortin, and Lemieux (1996) show that the counterfactual distribution, $F_{y_0|t=1}$, can be estimated by properly reweighing the distribution of covariates in period 0. One can express the resulting counterfactual distribution as follows:[4]

$$F_{y_0|t=1}(y) = \int F_{y_0|x_0}(y|x)\,w(x)\,dF_{x_0}(x), \tag{4.5}$$

where the reweighing factor is equal to $w(x) = \frac{dF_{x_1}(x)}{dF_{x_0}(x)} = \frac{P(t=1|x)}{1-P(t=1|x)} \cdot \frac{1-\pi}{\pi}$.

These weights are proportional to the conditional odds of being observed in state 1. The proportionality factor depends on π, which is the proportion of cases observed in state 1. One can easily compute the reweighing factor on the basis of a probability model, such as logit or probit. Furthermore, if one is interested only in the aggregate decomposition of the variation in a distributional statistic, then the only needs are an estimate of the relevant counterfactual distribution and the corresponding value of the statistic in question.

The decomposition presented in equation (4.3) suggests a nonparametric identification strategy and can be estimated by the inverse probability weighting (IPW) method implied by equation (4.5). Nonparametric methods allow analysts to decompose changes in distributional statistics into endowment and structural effects without having to assume a functional form for the outcome model. The downside is that one cannot separate the respective contributions of the observable and unobservable factors into the structural effect, nor can one account for changes in agents' behavior. Later on, we consider a way of separating the contribution of unobservables from that of observables, and in the concluding section we review proposed methods to account for behavioral responses.

A parametric approach to the estimation of the composition and structural effect requires a more explicit link between the distributional statistic of interest and individual or household characteristics (depending on the unit of analysis). This approach entails imposing more structure on the individual outcome equation (4.2) and finding a way of expressing the distributional statistic, θ, as an explicit function of the covariates of interest. Given the assumption that the function $\varphi(\cdot)$ in equation (4.2) is linear and separable in observable covariates x and unobservable factors ε, the classic Oaxaca-Blinder decomposition relies on the law of iterated expectations to establish a direct link between the unconditional mean of y (the distributional statistic of interest) and individual characteristics. The assumption that the conditional mean of the error term given the observables is zero ensures that the ordinary least squares (OLS) method of estimation will produce unbiased and consistent estimates of key parameters.

Use of Influence Functions. Things are not so simple for general distributional statistics such as quantiles, poverty, and inequality measures. For instance, if one is interested in understanding changes in welfare distribution from one period to another, it is necessary to deal with the entire distribution. However, one can use influence functions to establish a direct link between the distributional statistic of interest and individual (or household) characteristics and make suitable assumptions that allow counterfactual decomposition *à la* Oaxaca-Blinder.

The influence function of a functional $\theta(F)$ is basically its first-order directional derivative (Hampel 1974). Let $G(b)$ be a mixture of two distributions F and H such that $G(b) = bH + (1 - b)F$. This expression says that an observation under $G(\cdot)$ is randomly sampled from H with probability b or from F with probability $(1 - b)$. The directional derivative of θ at F in the direction of H tells us how the functional θ changes as G gets closer and closer to F. Formally, we write

$$\nabla\theta_{G\to F} = \lim_{b\to 0}\frac{\theta(G(b)) - \theta(F)}{b} = \frac{\partial}{\partial b}\theta(bH + (1-b)F)\,|_{b=0}. \tag{4.6}$$

Let $H = \Delta_y$, the distribution function for a probability measure that assigns mass 1 to y in the domain of F. In other words, $\Delta_y(v)$ is equal to one if $y \le v$; otherwise it is equal to zero.[5] In this case, $G(b) = b\Delta_y + (1 - b)F$, and the influence function of the functional $\theta(F)$ can be written as[6]

$$IF(y;\theta,F) = \nabla\theta_{F\to\Delta_y}. \tag{4.7}$$

This is an indicator of the relative effect of a small perturbation in F on $\theta(F)$. In that sense, it is a measure of robustness.[7] The influence function defined in equation (4.7) measures the effect that a single observation has on a functional.

It is useful at this stage to note that the directional derivative of the mean of F in the direction of H is equal to

$$\frac{\partial}{\partial b}\left[\int v\big(bh(v) + (1-b)f(v)\big)dv\right]_{b=0} = \int vh(v)dv - \int vf(v)dv. \tag{4.8}$$

In other words, the directional derivative of the mean of F at F in the direction of H is equal to $\nabla\mu_{F\to H} = \mu_H - \mu_F$. Hence, the influence function of the mean of F is equal to

$$IF(y;\mu,F) = \nabla\mu_{F\to\Delta_y} = y - \mu_F. \tag{4.9}$$

The expected value of the influence function of a distributional statistic is equal to zero in all cases in which the frequencies and the range of the y-values are bounded. Firpo, Fortin, and Lemieux (2009) define the recentered or rescaled influence function (RIF) as the leading two terms of a von Mises (1947) linear approximation of the associated functional.[8] It is equal to the functional plus the corresponding influence function. Let $IF(y;\theta)$ stand for the influence function of $\theta(F_y)$, then $RIF(y;\theta) = \theta(F_y) + IF(y;\theta)$. The fact that the expected value of the influence function is equal to zero implies that the expected value of the RIF is equal to the corresponding distributional statistic. In other words, $\theta(F_y) = E[RIF(y;\theta)]$. By the law of iterated expectations, the distributional statistic of interest can be written as the conditional expectation of the recentered influence function (given the observable covariates, x). This is the RIF regression that for $\theta(F_y)$ can be expressed as $E[RIF(y;\ \theta)|x]$. The distributional statistic $\theta(F_y)$ can therefore be expressed in terms of this conditional expectation as follows:

$$\theta(F_y) = \int E\left[RIF(y;\ \theta)|x\right]dF(x). \qquad (4.10)$$

This expression suggests that to assess the impact of covariates on $\theta(F_y)$, one needs to integrate over the conditional expectation $E[RIF(y;\ \theta)|x]$. This can be easily done using regression methods. At this point, one has a choice between linear and nonlinear models.

Linear and Nonlinear Specifications. If one assumes linearity, the conditional expectation of the RIF can be written as a linear function of observable covariates as follows: $E[RIF(y;\theta)|x] = x\beta$. One can then apply OLS to the following equation:

$$RIF(y;\theta) = x\beta + \varepsilon. \qquad (4.11)$$

Fortin, Lemieux, and Firpo (2011) explain that the expected value of the linear approximation of the RIF regression is equal to the expected value of the true conditional expectation because the expected value of the approximation error is zero. This fact makes the extension of the standard Oaxaca-Blinder decomposition to RIF regressions both simple and meaningful. Interestingly, the influence function for the mean presented in equation (4.9) implies that the corresponding recentered influence function is $RIF(y;\ \mu,\ F) = y$. Hence, the ordinary linear regression of y on a set of covariates x is indeed an RIF regression. So the standard Oaxaca-Blinder decomposition is in fact based on RIF regression.

Based on equation (4.11), we find that the endowment effect identified on the basis of an RIF regression can be written as follows:

$$\Delta_X^\theta = \left[E(x|t=1) - E(x|t=0)\right]\cdot\beta_0. \qquad (4.12)$$

The corresponding structural effect is

$$\Delta_S^\theta = E(x|t=1)\cdot(\beta_1 - \beta_0). \qquad (4.13)$$

This decomposition may involve a bias, because the linear specification is only a local approximation that may not hold in the case of large changes in covariates.[9] The solution to this problem is to combine the reweighing method described earlier with RIF regression.[10]

Given the analogy between the mean and the class of additively separable poverty measures, equation (4.9) implies that the influence function of any member of that class is

$$IF(y;\ P,\ F) = I(y \le z)\psi(y|z) - P(F;\ z), \qquad (4.14)$$

where $I(y \leq z)$ is an indicator function and $P(F; z)$ is the poverty measure written in a way emphasizing that this distributional statistic is a functional of F (Cowell and Victoria-Feser 1996; Essama-Nssah and Lambert 2012). The corresponding recentered influence function is

$$RIF(y; P, F) = I(y \leq z)\psi(y|z). \tag{4.15}$$

For these poverty measures, one can in fact use nonlinear specifications of the RIF regression (for example, logit or probit for the headcount index and tobit for the other poverty measures).[11] Fairlie (2005) proposes an extension of the Oaxaca-Blinder decomposition to logit and probit models, while Sinning, Hahn, and Bauer (2008) explain how to extend this method to nonlinear models in general.[12]

There is also an indirect way of identifying (and hence estimating) the composition and structural effects that account for the variation in poverty measures that are members of the additively separable class. As noted in chapter 2, variation in poverty over time can be expressed as a weighted sum of points on the growth incidence curve (GIC). Since the GIC describes outcome variation across quantiles, one can use RIF regression to perform decompositions of differences across quantiles and thus decompose growth incidence into the composition and structural effects. One would need RIFs for the quantiles under consideration. Firpo, Fortin, and Lemieux (2009) note that the RIF of the τth quantile of the distribution of y is the following:[13]

$$RIF(y; q_\tau) = q_\tau + IF(y; q_\tau) = q_\tau + \frac{\left[\tau - I(y \leq q_\tau)\right]}{f_y(q_\tau)}, \tag{4.16}$$

where $I(\cdot)$ is an indicator function for whether the outcome variable y is less than or equal to the τth quantile and $f_y(q_\tau)$ is the density function of y evaluated at the τth quantile.

One can use equation (4.16) repeatedly to decompose, for instance, the first 99 quantiles (percentiles) of the outcome distribution of interest. This means that we can decompose the GIC into a component associated with the composition (or endowment) effect and a second one related to the structural (or the price) effect. Formally, we express this decomposition as follows:

$$g(y) = g_x(y) + g_s(y). \tag{4.17}$$

Equation (4.17) implies that the elasticity of poverty with respect to the mean outcome ($\zeta_P(g) = \frac{1}{\gamma P}\int_0^z y\psi'(y|z)g(y)f(y)dy$) can also be decomposed into a composition and a structural effect as follows:

$$\zeta_P(g) = \frac{1}{\gamma P}\int_0^z y\psi'(y|z)g_X(y)f(y)dy + \frac{1}{\gamma P}\int_0^z y\psi'(y|z)g_S(y)f(y)dy. \tag{4.18}$$

The first term on the right-hand side of equation (4.18) represents the endowment effect based on the corresponding effect for the GIC. Similarly, the second term is the structural effect based on the corresponding effect for the GIC.

It is important to note that this indirect decomposition applies not only to this class of poverty measures but also to all additively separable social evaluation functions such as the Atkinson (1970) and the S-Gini welfare functions.[14] This fact implies that the rate of growth of *per capita* income, γ, can also be decomposed into two components reflecting the composition and structural effects. It can be shown that when there is no aversion to inequality, the Atkinson welfare function ranks social states on the basis of the average outcome (such as average income or expenditure).

Thus, the rate of change in social welfare induced by a distributional change is captured by the per capita rate of growth, which can be expressed as a weighted sum of points along the GIC. Indeed, $\gamma = \frac{\Delta\mu}{\mu} = \int_0^{m_y} \frac{y}{\mu} g(y) dF(y)$, where m_y stands for the maximum income or expenditure, and each point on the GIC is weighted by the slope of the Lorenz curve at that point. Clearly, this rate of growth can be decomposed on the basis of equation (4.17) into an endowment effect and a structural effect. Given that the level and pattern of growth depend on factor accumulation and productivity, we can interpret the endowment effect as an indicator of changes in factor accumulation and the structural effect as an indicator of changes in productivity.

Some Advantages of Linearity. As noted earlier, one has the choice between nonlinear and linear specifications of the RIF regression model. Linearity has the added advantage of making it possible to perform a detailed decomposition that can further decompose each of these effects in terms of the contributions of the relevant covariates. Fortin, Lemieux, and Firpo (2011) explain that a decomposition approach provides a detailed decomposition when it allows one to apportion the composition effect or the structural effect into components attributable to each explanatory variable. The contribution of each explanatory variable to the composition effect is analogous to what Rothe (2010) calls a "partial composition effect."[15]

Assuming a linear RIF regression model, let x_k and β_k stand, respectively, for the kth element of x and β. Then the endowment and price effects can be written in terms of sums over the explanatory variables. For the endowment effect, we have

$$\Delta_X^{\theta} = \sum_{k=1}^{m} \left[E(x_k | t = 1) - E(x_k | t = 0) \right] \beta_{0k}. \tag{4.19}$$

Similarly, for the structural effect, we have the following expression:

$$\Delta_S^{\theta} = \sum_{k=1}^{m} E(x_k | t = 1)(\beta_{1k} - \beta_{0k}). \tag{4.20}$$

Expressions (4.19) and (4.20) provide a simple way of dividing the endowment and price effects into the contribution of a single covariate or a group of covariates as needed.[16] Such detailed decompositions are not easy to obtain for nonlinear models.

Changes along the Entire Outcome Distribution

The decomposition of changes in distributional statistics generally produces information about the aggregate composition and structural effects. Although the linearity assumption can help identify the contribution of various covariates to these aggregate effects, it does not tell us how these effects vary along the entire outcome distribution.

To obtain this information, we now consider the decomposition of differences in density functions and across quantiles. The decomposition of changes in density functions relies on nonparametric methods. In the case of quantiles, we focus on the use of quantile regression (a parametric method). All the methods reviewed in this section are purely statistical in the sense that they all rely on models of the conditional distribution of outcomes given the covariates.

Differences in Density Functions

For decomposition purposes, one needs a model that links the outcome of interest to household characteristics. To focus on differences in density functions, we maintain that the outcome variable y has a joint distribution with characteristics, x. This distribution is characterized by the following joint density function: $J_t(y, x)$, $t = 0, 1$. For instance, poverty analysis relies on household consumption expenditure (y) as a measure of welfare. Thus data from a household income and expenditure survey characterize the joint distribution of expenditure and household characteristics (x).

Just as the standard Oaxaca-Blinder decomposition is based on the unconditional mean, the generalization of that method considered here requires the marginal distribution of y noted as $f_t(y)$. This marginal density function can be obtained by integrating the covariates x out of the joint density. Furthermore, the factorization principle allows one to write the joint density as a product of the distribution of y conditional on x, $g_t(y|x)$, and the joint distribution of characteristics, $h_t(x)$. These are the two factors underpinning the decomposition. Any change in the marginal outcome distribution induced by a variation in the distribution of observed characteristics (*ceteris paribus*) represents the *endowment effect*, while any change in the distribution associated with a (*ceteris paribus*) variation in the conditional distribution is interpreted as the *price-behavioral effect* (Bourguignon and Ferreira 2005).

To see clearly what is involved,[17] we express the joint density function as a product of the two underlying functions: $J_t(y, x) = g_t(y|x)h_t(x)$, $t = 0, 1$. On the basis of this factorization, we can write the marginal density of y in a way that facilitates the expression and interpretation of the decomposition results, that is,

$f_t(y) \equiv f_{gt}^{ht}(y)$. Thus the observed change in the outcome distribution between the two periods can be stated as follows:

$$\Delta f = f_1(y) - f_0(y) \equiv f_{g1}^{h1}(y) - f_{g0}^{h0}(y). \tag{4.21}$$

We can add to and subtract from the difference defined in (4.21) the following counterfactual:[18] $f_{g0}^{h1}(y)$. This is the marginal density function that would obtain if the conditional distribution were that of period 0 and if the joint distribution of characteristics were that prevailing in period 1. This transformation leads us to the following generalized decomposition of changes in the marginal density of y:

$$\Delta f = \left[f_{g0}^{h1}(y) - f_{g0}^{h0}(y)\right] + \left[f_{g1}^{h1}(y) - f_{g0}^{h1}(y)\right]. \tag{4.22}$$

The configuration of the indices (subscripts and superscripts) for the marginal distributions involved in (4.22) suggests an interpretation of the various components of the decomposition. The first component on the right-hand side is the *endowment effect* (based on changes in the joint distribution of observed characteristics). The second component measures the *price-behavioral effect* (linked to the change in the conditional distribution of y, which, in fact, also includes the effect of unobservables).

Kernel Density Approaches. In their study of the role of institutional factors in accounting for changes in the distribution of wages in the United States, DiNardo, Fortin, and Lemieux (1996) demonstrate how to implement empirically the above decomposition using kernel density methods to estimate the relevant density functions. The *histogram* is the oldest and most common density estimator (Silverman 1986), and kernel methods may be viewed as ways of smoothing a histogram.[19]

The basic idea is to estimate the density $f(y)$ by the proportion of the sample that is near y. One way of proceeding is to choose some interval or "band" and to count the points in the band around each y and normalize the count by the sample size multiplied by the bandwidth. The whole procedure can be viewed as sliding the band (or window) along the range of y, calculating the fraction of the sample per unit within the band, and plotting the result as an estimate of the density at the midpoint of the band (Deaton 1997).[20]

The kernel estimate of the density function $f_t(y)$ can be written as follows:

$$\hat{f}_t(y) = \frac{1}{hn_t}\sum_{i=1}^{n_t} K\left(\frac{y_{it} - y}{h}\right),\ t = 0, 1, \tag{4.23}$$

where h is the bandwidth representing the smoothing parameter, n_t is the sample size for period t, y is the focal point where the density is estimated, and $K(\cdot)$ is the kernel function. A kernel function is essentially a weighting function chosen to give more weight to points near y and less weight to those far away. In particular, it will assign a weight of zero to points just outside and just inside the band.

As a weighting function, the kernel function should satisfy four basic properties: (a) positive, (b) integrate to unity over the band, (c) symmetric around zero so that points below y get the same weight as those an equal distance above, and (d) decreasing in the absolute value of its argument. The most common kernel functions used in empirical work are the Gaussian and Epanechnikov kernels.[21]

The counterfactual density function that is the linchpin of the decomposition presented in equation (4.22) can be written in a manner analogous to the distribution functions underlying the decomposition presented in equation (4.3).[22] In other words, $f_{g0}^{h1}(y) = f_{y_0|t=1}$. This density can be estimated by reweighing the kernel estimate for period 0 using the same function as the one underlying the counterfactual distribution defined in equation (4.5). The resulting expression is

$$\hat{f}_{y_0|t=1}(y) = \frac{1}{hn_0}\sum_{i=1}^{n_0} w(x)K\left(\frac{y_{i0}-y}{h}\right). \tag{4.24}$$

A Semiparametric Approach. Machado and Mata (2005) propose a semiparametric approach to estimating the density functions needed in the above decomposition. Their approach is based on a two-step procedure to derive marginal density functions from the conditional quantile process that fully characterizes the conditional distribution of y given the covariates x. Specifically, these authors model the conditional distribution of y given x by a linear conditional quantile function as follows:

$$q_\tau(y_t|x_t) = x_t\beta_t(\tau),\ \tau \in (0, 1), t = 0, 1. \tag{4.25}$$

The second step entails estimating the marginal density function of y that is consistent with the conditional quantile process defined by equation (4.25). This is achieved by running the following algorithm:

1. Draw a random sample of size m from a uniform distribution on [0, 1] to get τ_j for $j = 1, 2, \ldots, m$.
2. For each τ_j, use available data to estimate the quantile regression model and get m estimates of coefficients $\hat{\beta}_t(\tau_j)$, $j = 1, 2, \ldots, m$.
3. Given that x_t is a $(n_t\ x\ k)$ matrix of data on covariates, draw a random sample of size m from the rows of x_t and denote each such sample by x_{jt}^s.
4. The corresponding values of the outcome variable are given by $y_{jt}^s \equiv x_{jt}^s\hat{\beta}_t(\tau_j)$, $j = 1, 2, \ldots, m$.

The validity of this procedure stems from the *probability integral transformation theorem*, which states that if u is a random variable uniformly distributed over [0, 1], then $y = F^{-1}(u)$ is distributed like F. Here τ_j is assumed to be a realization of $F_{y_t|x_t}$. Given model (4.25), the corresponding conditional quantile regression model can be written as

$$q_{\tau_j}\left(y_t|x_t\right) = F^{-1}_{y_t|x_t}\left(\tau_j, x_t\right) = x_t\beta_t\left(\tau_j\right),\ t = 0, 1 \tag{4.26}$$

A modified version of the above algorithm leads to the critical counterfactual upon which the decomposition is based. Recall that the counterfactual of interest is the density function of the outcome in period 1, assuming that the characteristics of that period had been rewarded according to the system prevailing in period 0. This counterfactual can be estimated by applying the above algorithm to the data for period 0, except that at stage 3, covariates must be drawn from data for period 1. On the basis of equation (4.26), the conditional regression model associated with this counterfactual is the following:

$$q_{\tau_j}\left(y_0|x_1\right) = F^{-1}_{y_0|x_0}\left(\tau_j, x_1\right) = x_1\beta_0\left(\tau_j\right). \tag{4.27}$$

As noted by Fortin, Lemieux, and Firpo (2011), this approach is computationally demanding. They suggest a simplification based on the estimation of a large number of quantile regressions (say, 99) instead of using the random process. The conditional quantile function can then be inverted to obtain the conditional cumulative distribution that must be averaged over the empirical distribution of the covariates to yield the unconditional distribution function. In fact, Machado and Mata (2005) acknowledge that this is a viable alternative to their method.

Differences across Quantiles

As discussed earlier in the context of RIF regression analysis, one can also work with quantiles, which are easier for detailed decompositions, instead of density functions to decompose changes along the entire outcome distribution. Because the decomposition must be based on marginal distributions, one needs to work with marginal quantiles, not conditional ones. There are multiple ways to go about it. An alternative to using RIF regression is to derive marginal quantiles from equations (4.25) and (4.26)—based on the Machado and Mata (2005) procedure—or by numerical integration as proposed by Melly (2005).

To link conditional quantiles to marginal quantiles, Angrist and Pischke (2009) start from the observation that the proportion of the population below q_τ conditional on x is equal to the proportion of conditional quantiles that are below q_τ. Let $I(\cdot)$ be the indicator function that takes a value of one if its argument is true and zero otherwise. Again, let $F_{y|x}()$ stand for the conditional cumulative distribution function (CDF) of y given x. Thus the proportion of the population for whom the outcome y is less than q_τ is equal to $F_{y|x}\left(q_\tau|x\right) = \int_0^1 I\left[F^{-1}_{y|x}\left(\tau\,|\,x\right) < q_\tau\right]d\tau$, where the term on the right-hand side is equal to the proportion of conditional quantiles that are below q_τ.

On the basis of equation (4.25), we can rewrite this proportion as $F_{y|x}(q_\tau|x) = \int_0^1 I[x\beta(\tau) < q_\tau]d\tau$. The marginal distribution of y, $F_y()$, from which one derives marginal quantiles, is obtained by integrating the conditional distribution over the whole range of the distribution of the covariates (Melly 2005). The resulting expression is $F_y(q_\tau) = \int\left(\int_0^1 I[x\beta(\tau) < q_\tau]d\tau\right)dF_x$. The sample analog of this expression—based on an estimation of quantile regressions at every percentile for a sample of size n—is given by the following expression (Angrist and Pischke 2009):

$$\hat{F}_Y(q_\tau) = \frac{1}{n}\sum_{i=1}^{n}\left(\frac{1}{100}\sum_{\tau=0}^{1} I(x_i\beta_\tau < q_\tau)\right). \tag{4.28}$$

The marginal quantile corresponding to the above estimator of the marginal distribution of the response variable is obtained by inverting equation (4.28). We note these marginal quantiles as $q_\tau\left(x_t, \hat{\beta}_t(\tau)\right) = inf\left\{q\text{: } \hat{F}_Y(q_\tau)\right\}$.

The generalized Oaxaca-Blinder decomposition described by equation (4.3) can equivalently be stated in terms of these marginal quantiles. The observed change in the marginal distribution of the response variable is now written as $\Delta q_\tau = q_\tau\left(x_1, \hat{\beta}_1(\tau)\right) - q_\tau\left(x_0, \hat{\beta}_0(\tau)\right)$. To distinguish the endowment effect from the price effect, we subtract from and add to this expression the following counterfactual outcome: $q_\tau\left(x_1, \hat{\beta}_0(\tau)\right)$. This counterfactual involves the characteristics of period 1 evaluated with the prices (coefficients) of period 0. The corresponding decomposition analogous to expression (4.3) is the following:

$$\Delta q_\tau = \left[q_\tau\left(x_1, \hat{\beta}_0(\tau)\right) - q_\tau\left(x_0, \hat{\beta}_0(\tau)\right)\right] + \left[q_\tau\left(x_1, \hat{\beta}_1(\tau)\right) - q_\tau\left(x_1, \hat{\beta}_0(\tau)\right)\right]. \tag{4.29}$$

Consistent with equation (4.3), the first term on the right-hand side of equation (4.29) is the endowment effect at the τth quantile, while the second term measures the price effect at the same location. Again, changes along the entire outcome distribution are obtained by performing this decomposition for the first 99 percentiles.

Accounting for the Contribution of Unobservables

Recall that based on equation (4.2), the contribution of unobservable characteristics into changes in the outcome distribution has at least two potential components: the first relates to changes in the returns to unobservables and the second to the distribution of these characteristics. All the decomposition methods discussed so far lump the first component together with the returns to observables in the structural effect. Furthermore, the contribution of changes in the distribution of unobservable characteristics is ruled out by either the ignorability assumption or the zero-conditional-mean assumption. The issue now is this: Under what conditions can we identify these effects that up to now have been swept under the rug, so to speak?

Further Decomposition of the Structural Effect

Juhn, Murphy, and Pierce (1993) assume *additive linearity* for the outcome model and *conditional rank preservation* to decompose differences in outcome distributions in a way that accounts for the contribution of unobservables.[23] Under additive linearity, the function defining the outcome variable is separable in x and ε. We can therefore write the outcome model as follows:

$$y_t = x_t\beta_t + \upsilon_t,\ t = 0, 1, \tag{4.30}$$

where $\upsilon_t = \zeta_t(\varepsilon)$, some function of unobservable characteristics.

The assumption of conditional rank preservation means that a given individual has the same rank in the distribution of υ_0 as in the distribution of υ_1, conditional on observable characteristics. To see this formally, let $F_{\upsilon|x}(\upsilon_t|x_t)$ stand for the distribution of υ_t conditional on x_t. Also, let $\tau_{i0}(x_i) = F_{\upsilon|x}(\upsilon_{i0}|x_i)$ be the rank of individual i with observed characteristics x_i in the conditional distribution of υ_0 given x, and let $\tau_{i1}(x_i) = F_{\upsilon|x}(\upsilon_{i1}|x_i)$ be individual i's rank in the conditional distribution of υ_1 given x. Conditional rank preservation says that $\tau_{i0}(x_i) = \tau_{i1}(x_i)$. Fortin, Lemieux, and Firpo (2011) explain that one can secure conditional rank invariance by assuming ignorability and that the functions υ_t are strictly increasing in ε. In other words, these functions are *monotonic*.[24]

As expected, separability allows the analyst to construct counterfactuals separately for observables and unobservables. To see what is involved, consider the case of a particular individual, i, with outcome $y_{i1} = x_{i1}\beta_1 + \upsilon_{i1}$ in period 1. Let υ^c_{i0} represent what the residual part of the outcome would have been had the unobservable characteristics of this individual been treated as in the initial period, *ceteris paribus*. The corresponding counterfactual for the full outcome is $y^c_{i0} = x_{i1}\beta_1 + \upsilon^c_{i0}$. Comparing this counterfactual with the observed outcome reveals the contribution of changes in the returns to unobservable characteristics of individual i to the overall change in the individual's outcome. We denote this as $\Delta^y_{S,\sigma} = \left(y_{i1} - y^c_{i0}\right) = \left(\upsilon_{i1} - \upsilon^c_{i0}\right)$. Next, we replace β_1 with β_0 in the expression for y^c_{i0}. This operation yields the following counterfactual: $y^b_{i0} = x_{i1}\beta_0 + \upsilon^c_{i0}$. Let $\Delta^y_{S,\beta} = \left(y^c_{i0} - y^b_{i0}\right)$. This term is equivalent to $\Delta^y_{S,\beta} = x_{i1}\left(\beta_1 - \beta_0\right)$ and clearly shows the contribution of changes in the returns to observable characteristics.

Thus, separability along with ignorability and monotonicity make it possible to split the structural effect into (a) one component resulting from changes in the returns to observables and (b) another linked solely to changes in returns to unobservables. In other words, the total structural effect[25] is equal to $\Delta^y_S = \Delta^y_{S,\beta} + \Delta^y_{S,}$.

The composition effect Δ^y_X can be identified residually from the following expression: $\Delta^y_O - \Delta^y_S = \Delta^y_X + \Delta^y_\varepsilon$, where $\Delta^y_O = (y_{i1} - y_{i0})$. The assumption of conditional independence implies, however, that $\Delta^y_\varepsilon = 0$. Recall that this assumption implies that the conditional distribution of unobservables does not vary across groups (periods). Therefore, under the prevailing identifying assumptions, the difference between the overall outcome difference and the structural effect identifies the observable composition effect.

The question now is, how does one identify v_{i0}^c? This is where rank preservation comes in. This assumption leads to the following *imputation rule*:

$$v_{i0}^c = F_{v_0|x}^{-1}\left(\tau_{i1}\left(x_i\right)\right). \tag{4.31}$$

This imputation rule says that for individual i in the end period, the counterfactual for the residual outcome is equal to the residual outcome associated with the individual located at the same rank in the conditional distribution of residual outcomes in the base period. In practice, one would estimate β_0 and β_1 using OLS. Bourguignon and Ferreira (2005) explain that empirical implementation of a *rank-preserving transformation* is complicated by the fact that both samples do not necessarily have the same number of observations. However, if one is willing to assume that both distributions are the same up to some proportional transformation, then the rank-preserving transformation can be approximated by multiplying residuals in the base period by the ratio of the standard deviation in the end period to the one in the initial period.

Fortin, Lemieux, and Firpo (2011) point out that assuming constant returns to unobservables and homoskedasticity allows one to write the unobserved component of the outcome as $v_t = \sigma_t \varepsilon$. Homoskedasticity implies that the conditional variance of ε is constant (and can be normalized to one). Equation (4.30) can therefore be written as follows:

$$y_t = x_t\beta_t + \sigma_t\varepsilon, t = 0, 1. \tag{4.32}$$

Applications and Limitations of Juhn-Murphy-Pierce Model

As it turns out, this is the version of the model used by Juhn, Murphy, and Pierce (1991) in their study of the evolution of the wage differential between blacks and whites in the United States. In that context, the standard deviation of the residuals in the wage equation stands both for within-group inequality in the wage distribution and for the price of unobserved skills (Yun 2009).

The outcome model specified in equation (4.32) has also been used to study the gender pay gap. In that context, $t = 1$ is taken to represent males while $t = 0$ stands for females, and the wage regime for males is considered the nondiscriminatory one. The counterfactual used in the decomposition is the outcome that female workers would have experienced if they had been paid like their male counterparts. Care must be taken when applying this version of the model to decompose differences in mean outcome using OLS, because the OLS residuals sum up to zero. To see this, consider the following expression of standard Oaxaca-Blinder decomposition that explicitly shows the residuals:

$$\begin{aligned} \Delta_O^{\mu} = & \left[E(x_1) - E(x_0)\right]\beta_1 + E(x_0)(\beta_1 - \beta_0) \\ & + \left[E(\epsilon_1) - E(\varepsilon_0)\right]\sigma_1 + E(\varepsilon_0)(\sigma_1 - \sigma_0). \end{aligned} \tag{4.33}$$

The terms associated with the unobservables in the right-hand side of equation (4.33) will disappear if the decomposition is based on OLS applied to each equation separately.

To get around this issue, Juhn, Murphy, and Pierce (1991) assume that the returns to observable characteristics are the same for both groups and apply OLS to only one group, constructing an auxiliary equation for the other group. In the context of gender wage gap studies, OLS is applied to the equation for males only. The equation for female workers is constructed as follows: $y_0 = x_0\beta_1 + \upsilon_0$. The implied decomposition is

$$\Delta_O^{\mu} = \left[E(x_1) - E(x_0)\right]\beta_1 - E(\upsilon_0) = \left[E(x_1) - E(x_0)\right]\beta_1 - \sigma_1 E(\eta_0), \qquad (4.34)$$

where $\eta_0 = \dfrac{\upsilon_0}{\sigma_1}$. The above expression is computed on the basis of the sample analogs of the parameters of interest. The first term in the twofold decomposition presented in equation (4.34) represents the predicted gap, while the second stands for the residual gap.

As Yun (2009) points out, the residual gap is equal to the structural effect in the standard Oaxaca-Blinder decomposition. Yet, this structural effect represents returns to observable characteristics. It is therefore hard to see how the Juhn, Murphy, and Pierce (1991) procedure helps to identify the contribution of unobservables. Yun (2009) proposes instead the decomposition defined by equation (4.33), under the assumption that the expected value of unobservable terms is not equal to zero. However, that author does not provide an implementation procedure corresponding to this situation.

Relationship to Treatment Effect Analysis

As Fortin, Lemieux, and Firpo (2011) point out, there is a powerful analogy between the classic Oaxaca-Blinder decomposition method and treatment effect analysis.[26] Treatment impact analysis seeks to identify and estimate the average effect of treatment (intervention) on the treated (those exposed to an intervention) on the basis of the difference in average outcomes between the treated and a comparison group.

In that context, *t* indicates treatment status. It is equal to one for the treated and zero for the untreated (the comparison or control group). The expression, $\Delta_O^{\mu} = \left[E(y_1) - E(y_0)\right]$, can therefore be interpreted as the difference in average outcomes between the treated and untreated. Under the assumptions underlying the basic Oaxaca-Blinder method,[27] this difference is clearly the result of differences in observable characteristics (the composition effect) and in treatment status. The part resulting from the difference in treatment status is known as the average treatment effect on the treated (ATET) and is in fact equal to the structural or price effect.

Countering Selection Bias

Note that the conventional approach to impact evaluation also relies on *ceteris paribus* variation of treatment to identify its average effect on the treated. Within that logic, the composition effect is equivalent to *selection bias* that must be driven to zero by the use of randomization, propensity score matching, or similar methods.

Randomization. To ensure that the distribution of observed and unobserved characteristics is the same for both the treated and the control groups, randomization is employed. By balancing observed and unobserved characteristics between the groups before the administration of treatment, randomization guarantees that the average difference in outcome between the two groups is the result of treatment alone, hence the causal interpretation given to this parameter under those circumstances. In other words, the first term on the right-hand side of equation (4.3) (that is, the endowment effect or selection bias) is equal to zero under random assignment to treatment and full compliance.[28] Clearly, randomization is designed to implement a *ceteris paribus* variation in treatment.

Conditioning by Stratification. In the context of observational studies where the investigator does not have control over the assignment of subjects to treatment, the determination of the causal effect of treatment hinges critically on the understanding of the underlying *treatment assignment or selection mechanism*, which must explain how people end up in alternative treatment states. The assumption of selection on observables (also known as *ignorability*) is often invoked to implement *ceteris paribus* identification of ATET through conditioning by stratification.

Propensity Score Matching. Basically, conditioning by stratification entails comparing only those subjects with the same value of covariates x across the two groups (treated and untreated). This type of selection of individuals from the two groups is known as *matching.* A potential dimension problem is associated with matching when there are many observable characteristics taking many values. Insisting on conditioning based on exact values can lead to too few observations in each subgroup characterized by these observables. This dimensionality problem can be resolved by matching on the *propensity score*, that is, the conditional probability of receiving treatment given observable characteristics (Rosenbaum and Rubin 1983).

Usefulness of Treatment Effect Analysis

The analogy between treatment effect analysis and the Oaxaca-Blinder decomposition method has been extremely useful for the development of flexible estimation methods for endowment and structural effects. As noted earlier, selection on observables implies that the conditional distribution of unobservable factors is the same in both groups (treated and comparison). Although this assumption is weaker than the zero-conditional-mean assumption[29] used in the standard Oaxaca-Blinder decomposition, it is enough to secure identification and consistent estimation of the ATET and hence the structural effect, Δ_S^{μ} (in the Oaxaca-Blinder framework).

Fortin, Lemieux, and Firpo (2011) give the example of education and unobservable ability. They explain that if education and ability are correlated, this creates an endogeneity problem that prevents a linear regression of earnings on education to produce consistent estimates of the structural parameters measuring the return to education. Yet the aggregate decomposition remains valid as long as the correlation between ability and education is the same in both groups.

A major implication of the difference in identification assumptions between the traditional Oaxaca-Blinder approach and treatment effect analysis is that consistent estimators of the ATET such as IPW and matching can be used to estimate the structural effect (Δ_S^{μ}) even if the underlying relationship between the outcome and covariates is not linear. Given such an estimate, the composition effect can be calculated as a residual from the overall mean difference as follows: $\Delta_X^{\mu} = \Delta_O^{\mu} - \Delta_S^{\mu}$. In particular, decomposition methods based on this weighting procedure are known to be efficient. It is also worth noting that the generalization of the Oaxaca-Blinder decomposition to variation in other distributional statistics such as quantiles, poverty, and inequality measures enables an analyst to study the distributional and poverty impacts of an assigned intervention.

Limitations of the Analogy with Treatment Effect Analysis

Although treatment effect analysis can help with the identification and estimation of the structural effect, it is notable that this effect does not necessarily inherit the causal interpretation generally enjoyed by the ATET for two basic reasons: (a) In many cases, group membership is not the result of a choice or an exogenous assignment but is rather a consequence of an intrinsic characteristic, such as gender or race, and (b) many of the observable covariates are not equivalent to the pretreatment variables that are not supposed to be affected by the treatment.

The standard Oaxaca-Blinder decomposition method has two other important limitations: First, each covariate's contribution to the structural effect is highly sensitive to the choice of the omitted group when the explanatory variables include a categorical variable. (Jann [2008] discusses possible solutions to this problem.)

Second, the decomposition provides consistent estimates only under the assumption that the conditional expectation is linear. Under the linearity assumption, the counterfactual average when $t = 1$ is simply equal to $E(x_1|t = 1)\cdot\beta_0$. This is estimated by the cross product of sample means of characteristics for $t = 1$ with the relevant OLS coefficients from $t = 0$. The corresponding estimate is $\bar{x}_1\hat{\beta}_0$. The counterfactual mean outcome will not be equal to this term when linearity does not hold.

One possible solution is to reweigh the sample for $t = 0$ using the inverse probability method discussed earlier and to compute the counterfactual mean outcome on the basis of statistics from the reweighed counterfactual sample. Let $\bar{x}_0^c$ be the vector of the means of adjusted covariates in $t = 0$ and $\hat{\beta}_0^c$ the corresponding least squares coefficients. Then the correct counterfactual mean outcome when the linearity assumption does not hold is $\bar{x}_0^c\hat{\beta}_0^c$. This is the term to add to and subtract from the empirical version of the overall difference in mean outcome to get the appropriate estimates of the endowment and structural effects when the linearity assumption fails.

Accounting for Behavior

A key limitation of the decomposition methods discussed so far is that they do not account for changes in agents' behavior in response to changes in their socioeconomic environments—whether those changes are the result of economic shocks, policy reform, or other causes. Given the maintained hypothesis—that the living standard of individuals in a given society depends crucially on what they do with their assets (innate and external) subject to the opportunities offered by that society—this section focuses on modeling agents' behavior to account for their reactions to changes in their socioeconomic environment.

Standard economic theory explains behavior in terms of the principles of *optimization* and *market interaction*. Modeling behavior entails the specification of the following elements (Varian 1984):

- The actions a socioeconomic agent can take.
- The constraints the agent faces.
- The objective function used to evaluate feasible actions.

The assumption that the agent seeks to maximize the objective function subject to constraints implies that the outcome variables used to represent the consequences of behavior can be expressed as functions of parameters of the socioeconomic environment, embedded in the constraints facing the agent. We consider the Roy (1951) model of choice and consequences along with its interpretation in the context of modeling the determinants of the living standard. This model stems from the optimization principle and applies to discrete choice problems. We also discuss key considerations in simulating counterfactual distributions underlying any decomposition exercise.

The Roy Model of Choice and Consequences

Heckman and Honoré (1990) explain that the original Roy (1951) model was designed for the study of occupational choice and its implications for the distribution of earnings in an economy where agents are endowed with different sets of *occupation-specific skills*. In the two-skill Roy model, each income-maximizing agent has one skill usable only in one sector and a second skill usable in only another sector (Heckman and Honoré 1990). Therefore, the two-skilled agent can freely choose to work in only one of two activities (in this case, either fishing or hunting) on the basis of their productivity in each.

Under this scenario, an agent with a given skill endowment will choose to work in the sector where the potential income is higher. There are no investment opportunities to augment sector-specific skills, nor are there costs associated with changing sectors. These authors also show that self-selection implies a lower level of inequality in earnings compared with a benchmark case where workers are randomly assigned to jobs. The fact that occupational choice has significant implications for earnings distribution makes the Roy model a relevant framework for analyzing agents' behavioral responses to changes in their socioeconomic environment.

Heckman and Sedlacek (1985) discuss an extension of the basic framework by including nonmarket activity as an option in the choice set facing socioeconomic agents who are now assumed to *maximize utility* instead of income. The utility of participating in each of the sectors depends on both sector-specific attributes (such as the wage rate, employment risk, or job status) and individual characteristics. That we observe only sectoral choices and not the underlying utility function means it is possible to identify only parameters associated with differences in utility across sectors. These authors also consider the contribution of self-selection to income inequality and find that in this general model, self-selection can increase both between- and within-sector inequality compared with a random allocation of workers to sectors.

At the most fundamental level, the Roy model is characterized by two components: a selection mechanism and the associated potential outcomes. These outcomes are possible consequences of the choice made through the selection mechanism. The extended version of the Roy model is consistent with discrete choice models to the extent that utility-maximizing agents face a discrete choice set.

Discrete Choice Modeling

Train (2009) characterizes a discrete choice model in terms of two fundamental elements: the *choice set* and the *decision process* (or the decision rule). The choice set is the collection of alternatives from which the decision maker chooses one. This set must be *exhaustive* in the sense that it must include all possible alternatives, the latter being *mutually exclusive* from the perspective of the decision maker. Finally, the number of alternatives must be *finite*. In the case of discrete models of labor supply, for instance, the choice set can be represented by a few options, such as not working, working part time, and working full time.

Just as in the case of the *consumption-leisure paradigm*, the decision process assumes utility-maximizing behavior (Essama-Nssah 2012). It is therefore assumed that the decision maker chooses the alternative that provides the greatest net benefit or utility. Let u_{hj}, $j = 1, 2, \ldots m$ be the utility that agent h gets from alternative j. The decision rule implies that the agent chooses alternative k if and only if $u_{hk} > u_{hj}\ \forall j \neq k$.

This decision-making process is usually framed within the logic of the random utility model, in which utility has two parts: The first, known as the *representative utility*, is a function of some observable characteristics of the decision maker and of the alternatives (Train 2009). The second component is a set of unobservable random factors. Formally, the utility function is written as $u_{hj} = v_{hj} + \varepsilon_{hj}$, where v is the representative utility and ε represents the unobserved portion of utility that is treated as random.

Now, the statement that alternative k is chosen if, and only if $u_{hk} > u_{hj}$ $\forall j \neq k$ can be equivalently expressed as follows: k is chosen if and only if $(\varepsilon_{hj} - \varepsilon_{hk}) < (v_{hk} - v_{hj})$ $\forall j \neq k$. Because of the uncertainty implied by the random part of the utility function, one can make only probabilistic statements about the decision maker's choice. The probability that agent h chooses option k is defined by the following expression:[30]

$$P_{hk} = Pr[(\varepsilon_{hj} - \varepsilon_{hk}) < (v_{hk} - v_{hj})\ \forall j \neq k]. \tag{4.35}$$

The type of discrete choice model derived from the above probability statement is determined by the assumptions made about the distribution of the unobserved portion of the utility function. For instance, the common logit model assumes that the random factors are independently and identically distributed (iid) extreme value variables for all options. In other words, each choice is independent from the others.[31]

An Interpretation of the Roy Model

Coulombe and McKay (1996) provide an interesting interpretation of the Roy model that is consistent with our maintained hypothesis that an individual's living standard is a payoff from participation in the life of society. Using the household as the unit of analysis, these authors argue that a household's living standard depends fundamentally on the socioeconomic group to which it belongs (or its economic activity status). To frame this view within the logic of the Roy model, the authors further argue that one needs to explain the selection mechanism leading to the observed socioeconomic group and, conditional on that choice, the determinants of the living standard in that group. This logic leads to a two-equation model—one representing the selection mechanism and the second modeling the living standard conditional on the choice of a particular socioeconomic group.

Modeling the Selection Mechanism. Modeling the selection mechanism boils down to modeling the probability defined in equation (4.35). Consistent with the random utility framework underlying this expression, and assuming that the random elements are generated independently by an extreme value distribution, the multinomial logit model can be used to explain the probability of choosing an option. Formally, we express that probability as

$$P_{hk} = \frac{\exp(z_{hk}\gamma_k)}{\left[1+\sum_{j=2}^{m}\exp(z_{hj}\gamma_j)\right]}, \tag{4.36}$$

where z_{hj} is the set of relevant explanatory variables, and m is the total number of socioeconomic groups. The probability defined in (4.36) is essentially the propensity score.

The specification of the explanatory variables requires a good understanding of the determinants of the choice of a socioeconomic group. Three technological factors affect this choice in the context of the general Roy model (Autor 2009):

- The distribution of skills and abilities;
- The correlations among these skills in the population; and
- The technologies for applying these skills.

Coulombe and McKay (1996) make a similar point in a case study of Mauritania. They define socioeconomic groups in terms of the income-generating opportunities available to households and their members. In particular, they consider four mutually exclusive and exhaustive groups of households: (a) households working predominantly as employees (whether in the public or private sector); (b) those engaged mostly in agricultural self-employment; (c) those engaged mainly in nonfarm self-employment; and (d) those not in the labor force. In essence, socioeconomic groups are determined on the basis of the household's main economic activity or source of income.

As to the determinants of the choice of socioeconomic group, these authors argue that the choice depends on variables (such as education, wages, or profit rates) that affect relative returns from economic activities and consumption preferences. In particular, they make the point that the extent to which household members choose either self-employment over wage employment or to stay out of the labor market depends on the interaction between (a) total household labor supply within and outside the household (a consumption decision) and (b) its total labor demand (a production decision) for both household members and hired labor. In other words, the household's socioeconomic classification reflects both consumption parameters (such as its demographic composition and the characteristics of the head of household) and production parameters relevant to self-employment (such as fixed inputs and variable costs).

Modeling the Living Standards. Equation (4.36) models the selection mechanism. We need an outcome equation to complete the model—the living standard conditional on the choice of socioeconomic group—within the logic of the Roy framework. Following Coulombe and McKay (1996), we let y_{hk} stand for the log of per capita expenditure for household h in socioeconomic group k, and η_{hk} for a random disturbance. The outcome equation associated with equation (4.36) can be written by analogy to the standard Mincer equation (in labor economics) as follows:

$$y_{hk} = x_h\beta_k + \eta_{hk}. \tag{4.37}$$

Equations (4.36) and (4.37) constitute a system designed to explain household-level living standards. In their case study, Coulombe and McKay (1996) distinguish two categories of determinants: household-level demographic factors and group-level demographic factors. These demographic variables include household size, household composition, and characteristics of the economic head of the household (such as educational level, marital status, gender, and ethnicity). Group-specific factors include those affecting total household income. For those engaged in wage employment, such factors would include level of education, sector of employment, and numbers of hours worked in a year to account for seasonal work.

Given that such variables are difficult to measure at the household level (the unit of analysis), one could either (a) define and measure these variables only for the economic head of household or (b) adopt some form of aggregation over household members. Naturally, this would entail some loss of the heterogeneity found at the individual level. In the case of agricultural self-employment, specific factors include land size and quality, tenure status, use of fertilizer, insecticides, hired labor, access to extension services, and commercialization. Similar considerations apply to nonagricultural self-employment. For households outside the labor market, possible sources of livelihood include asset holdings, borrowing, and public and private transfers.

Another important consideration here is the classification of variables as exogenous or endogenous. This classification hinges on the time horizon chosen. For instance, in the long run, the living standard can affect demographic variables, such as household size and composition (Coulombe and McKay 1996). But in the short run, it is reasonable to think of the direction of influence as running from demographic variables to the living standard. The Coulombe-McKay study adopts a short-to-medium time frame so that most of the variables listed above are considered exogenous with respect to the model described by equations (4.36) and (4.37).

Further Extensions of the Roy Model

The model presented in Inchauste *et al.* (2012) and later in chapter 6 of this volume expands this framework by modeling educational and sectoral choice as endogenous. For nonfarm workers, employment type is modeled endogenously, as individuals could be salaried, daily workers, nonfarm self-employed, farm workers, or not working at all. Similarly, because farm households are likely to be diversified, a separate model for employment type is specified for farm workers who engage in a secondary occupation.

Bourguignon, Ferreira, and Leite (2008) go one step further and model changes in household demographics as endogenous. In that framework, socioeconomic group, per capita consumption, education, and household composition are endogenous. Variations in education and in household composition are modeled within the discrete choice framework portrayed by equation (4.36). In that particular application, the demand for education is modeled on the basis of six alternatives: 0 years of schooling, 1–4 years, 5–6 years, 7–8 years, 9–12 years, and 13 or more. The highest level of education is the excluded category. The authors considered the following variables to be purely exogenous: number of adults in the household, region of residence, age, race, and gender. For household demographics, the options are 0, 1, 2, 3, 4, and 5 or more children. The last category is omitted in the estimation.

Note that education is an explanatory variable in the demographic multilogit model.

Leite, Sanchez, and Laderchi (2009) apply this extended framework to analyze the evolution of urban inequality in Ethiopia. They, too, focus on the household as the unit of analysis and use per capita household expenditure as the outcome variable.

Cogneau and Robilliard (2008) use the extended Roy model to study the implications of three targeted poverty reduction policies in Madagascar: (a) a direct subsidy on agricultural production prices, (b) a workfare program, and (c) a uniform untargeted per capita transfer program. While using the household as the unit of analysis and considering consumption as the ultimate welfare indicator, these authors model first the income-generating process at the level of individual household members and then link consumption to household income. Working-age individuals (aged 15–64 years) faced a choice set with three alternatives: family work, self-employment, and wage work. Household composition and location are exogenously given. For self-employment and wage work, an individual's potential earnings are equal to a task price multiplied by a given idiosyncratic amount of efficient labor. "Efficient labor" is assumed to be a function of some observable characteristics (such as age, experience, and location) and unobservable skills. Family work is rewarded by a reservation wage that is a function of individual and household characteristics.[32]

In the absence of labor market segmentation, the simple selection rule of the basic Roy (1951) model would base sector choice on a comparison of the reservation wage and potential wages in the other two sectors. To account for labor market segmentation, Cogneau and Robilliard (2008) define a segmentation variable in terms of the relative cost of entry between self-employment and wage work, and adjust the selection rule accordingly.

For policy evaluation, these authors embed the occupational choice model into a broader microeconomic module that includes the demand system for consumption goods. To keep things simple, they assume that consumption or saving decisions are separable from labor supply decisions. They also assume a fixed common savings rate of 5.2 percent so that aggregate consumption is equal to the implied consumption propensity multiplied by disposable income. The latter is the sum of farm profits, labor income, earnings from self-employment, and nonlabor income, such as capital income and transfers. Total consumption is allocated to three composite goods (agricultural, informal, and formal) according to budget shares derived from available data.

The three policies considered—subsidized agricultural production prices, the workfare program, and the uniform untargeted per capita transfer program—have the potential of inducing large macroeconomic effects because their collective cost represents about 5 percent of Madagascar's gross domestic product. To account for this, the authors link the micro module to a small three-sector (agriculture, informal, and formal) computable general equilibrium model. The integrated framework makes it possible to consider the macroeconomic impact of the policy options along with their impact on inequality and poverty.

Adding a general equilibrium model removes a key limitation of the decomposition methods discussed up to this point. These methods rely on either a purely statistical or a microeconomic model of behavior that cannot account for general equilibrium effects.

Simulating Counterfactual Distributions

The simulation of counterfactual distributions needed for the decomposition of distributional changes requires estimation of some version of the Roy system (composed of a selection equation and an outcome equation) for the initial and end periods. Counterfactual distributions can then be simulated by switching parameters and variables between these two estimated models one element at a time, holding all the other factors constant.

In general, parameters of sample selection models can be estimated with two-stage methods or the maximum-likelihood approach. We summarize here the basic ideas underlying two-step procedures that are also known as control function methods or generalized residual methods (Todd 2008). These methods are commonly used in the context of an explicit model of the outcome process involving a selection mechanism as well as an outcome equation. The selection mechanism is usually modeled within a random utility framework, and identifying assumptions are based on functional form restrictions or exclusion restrictions (analogous to the instrumental variable [IV] approach).

In particular, the control function approach seeks to model conditional expectations of potential outcomes (given observable characteristics and occupational or socioeconomic status) in a way that relates unobservable determinants of outcomes to the observables, including the choice of a socioeconomic group. This is consistent with the view that the underlying endogeneity problem is the result of omitted variables. The control functions represent the omitted variables. The key assumption in this method is that the observable determinants of both selection and outcomes are independent of the unobservable determinants (Heckman and Navarro-Lozano 2004).

Combining Parametric and Nonparametric Techniques

Once the model has been estimated, counterfactual decompositions are performed. Building on the statistical approaches previously discussed in "The Composition and Structural Effects" section, Bourguignon, Ferreira, and Leite (2008) propose the combination of parametric and nonparametric techniques in constructing the desired counterfactuals.

To see clearly what is involved, recall that the density function characterizing the joint distribution of the outcomes and covariates can be written as a product of the two underlying density functions—one characterizing the conditional distribution of outcomes given the covariates, and the other the joint distribution of covariates. Earlier, we expressed this relation as $J_t\,(y, x) = g_t(y|x)h_t(x)$, $t = 0, 1$. As noted earlier, this factorization suggests that counterfactual distributions can be obtained by combining the conditional outcome distribution from one period (such as the initial period) with the joint distribution of covariates from the other period (such as the end period). An example of this type of combination would be the following:

$$J_{g_0}^{h_1}(y,x) = g_0(y|x)h_1(x). \tag{4.38}$$

A key distinction between the methods discussed in the section on composition and structural effects and those reviewed in this section is that the methods in section 3 are based on statistical models of the conditional outcome distribution, while the methods discussed here rely on economic modeling of this conditional distribution. Thus, equations (4.36) and (4.37) characterizing the basic Roy model must be seen as modeling the conditional outcome distribution, $g_t(y|x)$.

The method of Bourguignon, Ferreira, and Leite (2008) as well as the model adopted in chapter 6 use the *parametric approach* to generate counterfactuals for the conditional outcome distribution and *nonparametric sample-reweighting techniques* to construct counterfactuals for the joint distribution of exogenous covariates. These authors argue that the parametric approach for the conditional distribution has the advantage of providing a clear economic interpretation of the parameter estimates along with great flexibility in exchanging parameters from one period to another (that is, from one state of the world to another).

Application in Context of the Roy Framework

To see how this works in the context of the Roy framework, use the estimated model to write the approximation to the conditional outcome distribution as follows:

$$y_t = s\left(x_t,\ z_t;\ \widehat{\gamma}_t,\ \widehat{\beta}_t,\ \widehat{\varepsilon}_t,\ \widehat{\eta}_t\right). \tag{4.39}$$

Thus a change in the conditional outcome distribution as a result of a ceteris paribus change in the parameters of the multinomial logit model of selection can be computed easily as follows:

$$\Delta y = s\left(x_0,\ z_0;\ \widehat{\gamma}_1,\ \widehat{\beta}_0,\ \widehat{\varepsilon}_0,\widehat{\eta}_0\right) - s\left(x_0,\ z_0;\ \widehat{\gamma}_0,\ \widehat{\beta}_0,\ \widehat{\varepsilon}_0,\ \widehat{\eta}_0\right). \tag{4.40}$$

When a counterfactual requires a normalization of exogenous covariates for both periods, we can simply apply the DiNardo, Fortin, and Lemieux (1996) approach described earlier. The handling of the residuals in this process requires some care. In the case of the residuals associated with the outcome equations, for instance, one can resort to the *rank-preserving transformation* described earlier.

Concluding Summary and Remarks

The design and implementation of effective strategies for poverty reduction require relevant and reliable analytical input. The bedrock of this input is certainly a rich and reliable dataset (both qualitative and quantitative) to be used in poverty measurement and analysis. In this context, there is a need for a sound understanding of the fundamental factors that account for observed variations in poverty either across space or over time.

This chapter has reviewed some of the basic decomposition methods that are commonly used to identify sources of variation in poverty outcomes at both the macro and micro levels. It has focused on micro-decomposition approaches because aggregate methods fail to account for the heterogeneity of the factors that drive the observed changes in aggregate poverty.

Decomposition as Social Impact Evaluation

The decomposition of changes in poverty is an exercise in social impact evaluation that assesses changes in *individual* and *social* outcomes attributable to socioeconomic shocks or policy implementation. Outcome models that underlie micro-decomposition methods are consistent with the view that an individual's living standard is a payoff from one's participation in the life of society.

Accordingly, that payoff is a function of *endowments, behavior*, and the *circumstances* that determine the *returns* to these endowments from any social transaction. These elements drive the distributional changes that define the potential scope of micro-decomposition methods. In general, the *scope* of a decomposition method is the set of explanatory factors the method tries to uncover by decomposition. The specification of an *outcome model* thus determines the potential scope of the corresponding decomposition method.

Statistical and Structural Methods

Micro-decomposition methods fall into two basic categories: *statistical* and *structural*. All seek to model the joint distribution of the outcome variable and its determining factors. This joint distribution can be factorized into a product of (a) the conditional outcome distribution and (b) the marginal distribution of exogenous (independent) variables.

Statistical methods rely uniquely on statistical principles to model the conditional outcome distribution, while *structural methods* rely on both economics and statistics to model this object. In particular, the structural methods considered here use utility maximization in a partial equilibrium setting to characterize individual behavior and social interaction. Statistical methods therefore are purely *descriptive*, while structural ones are considered *predictive*.

Identification through Counterfactual Comparison

Identification concerns the assumptions needed to recover, in a meaningful way, the factors of interest at the population level. These assumptions involve both the functional form of the outcome model and the joint distribution of factors that determine the outcome. Although macro- and micro-decomposition methods differ in their scope, they share the same fundamental *identification strategy* based on the notion of *ceteris paribus* variation. The implementation of this idea entails the comparison of an observed outcome distribution with a *counterfactual* obtained by changing one factor at a time while holding all the other factors constant.

A key counterfactual used in the identification of endowment and structural effects is the outcome distribution that would have prevailed in one state of the world had individual characteristics been rewarded according to the system applicable in the alternative state. The construction of this counterfactual relies critically on ignorability and the absence of general equilibrium effects. When the outcome model is separable in observables and unobservables, one can assume *rank preservation* to further split the structural effect into a component due to observables and another due to unobservables.

An Analogy: Decomposition, Estimation, and Treatment Effect Analysis

Estimation involves the computation of the relevant parameters on the basis of sample data. There is a powerful analogy between the decomposition methods reviewed here and treatment effect analysis. Both fields of inquiry rely on the same fundamental identification strategy, and the *structural effect* is known to be equivalent to the *treatment effect on the treated.*

This analogy has led to the development of flexible estimation methods for endowment and structural effects. Nonparametric estimation methods, such as IPW, allow an analyst to decompose distributional changes without having to assume a functional form for the outcome model. The downside, however, is the inability to further decompose the structural effect and to account for behavior. Parametric methods are more suitable for these two tasks.

Toward Fuller Causal Interpretations of Decomposition Results

Although the analogy between decomposition methods and treatment effect analysis has helped with the development of estimation methods, it does not necessarily confer a *causal interpretation* to decomposition results. As noted by Ferreira (2010), such an interpretation requires the construction of counterfactual outcome distributions that are fully consistent with a general equilibrium of the economy. One way of achieving this consistency is to base decomposition on a full structural model of *behavior* and *social interaction*. Such a model can be built by embedding a behavioral model, such as the Roy (1951) model of choice and consequences, in a general equilibrium framework.

Finally, we note that the generalization of the Oaxaca-Blinder decomposition to the analysis of variation in other distributional statistics such as quantiles, poverty, and inequality measures enables an analyst to study the distributional and poverty impacts of an assigned intervention.

Notes

1. Roughly speaking, a functional is a function of a function. In this particular context, it is a rule that maps every outcome distribution in its domain into a real number (Wilcox 2005).
2. In particular, Bourguignon and Ferreira (2005) argue that the configuration of income distribution at one point in time is determined by the following factors: (a) the distribution of factor endowments and sociodemographic characteristics among the

population; (b) the returns to these assets and characteristics; and (c) the behavior of socioeconomic agents with respect to resource allocation subject to prevailing institutional arrangements.

3. An alternative expression is based on this counterfactual: $E(x_0)\beta_1$. The corresponding decomposition is $\Delta_O^{\mu} = \left[E(x_1) - E(x_0)\right]\beta_1 + E(x_0)\left[\beta_1 - \beta_0\right]$.
4. To further appreciate the importance of the identifying assumptions, note that the process of reweighing adjusts the distribution of the covariates x in period $t = 0$ so that it becomes similar to that in period $t = 1$. For this adjustment to help us identify the terms of the decomposition, it must be a *ceteris paribus* adjustment. Because $y_0 = \varphi_0(x, \varepsilon)$, the *ceteris paribus* condition would be violated if changing the distribution of x also changed either the function $\varphi_0(\cdot)$ or the conditional distribution of ε given x. This would confound the impact of the adjustment, and the decomposition would be meaningless. Changes in the structural function are ruled out by the simple treatment assumption (no general equilibrium effects), while those in the conditional distribution of ε are ruled out by the ignorability assumption. Under these circumstances, we expect the conditional distribution of y_0 given x to be invariant with respect to adjustments in the distribution of the observable factors x. See Fortin, Lemieux, and Firpo (2011) for a more formal presentation of this argument.
5. This can be expressed with an indicator function as follows: $\Delta_y(v) = I(y < v)$. Recall that an indicator function is equal to one when its argument is true and equal to zero otherwise. In particular, $\int_0^{\infty} \Delta_y(v) f(y)dy = \int_0^{\infty} I(y \leq v) f(y)dy = \int_0^{v} f(y)dy = F(v)$.
6. Essama-Nssah and Lambert (2012) show how to derive the influence function of a functional from the associated directional derivative. They present a collection of influence functions for social evaluation functions commonly used in assessing the social impact of public policy.
7. Wilcox (2005) explains that continuity alone confers only qualitative robustness to the statistic under consideration. A continuous function is relatively unaffected by small shifts in its argument. Similarly, differentiability is related to infinitesimal robustness in the sense that if a function is differentiable and its derivative is bounded, then small variations in the argument will not result in large changes in the function. Thus a search for robust statistics can focus on functionals with bounded derivatives.
8. This is analogous to the approximation of a differentiable function at a point by a Taylor's polynomial.
9. In particular, β_1 and β_0 may differ just because their estimation is based on different distributions of the covariates x, even if the outcome structure remains unchanged (Firpo, Fortin, and Lemieux 2009).
10. For details, see Fortin, Lemieux, and Firpo (2011).
11. Essama-Nssah, Saumik, and Bassolé (2013) use both linear and nonlinear RIF regression models in their study of growth incidence in Cameroon. They find that linear models lead to results that are qualitatively similar to nonlinear specifications. This is a significant methodological finding that should comfort analysts who might worry about the quality of the linear approximation underlying the simple RIF regression approach.
12. To see what is involved, write the conditional mean outcome as $E(y_t|x_t;\beta_t)$, $t = 0,1$. The counterfactual mean outcome when endowments in period 1 are valued under the (reward) regime of period 0 is equal to the following: $E\left(y_1^c|x_1;\beta_0\right)$. The observed

difference in mean outcomes can therefore be decomposed as follows: $\Delta_O^\mu = \left[E\left(y_1^c|x_1;\beta_0\right) - E\left(y_0|x_0;\beta_0\right)\right] + \left[E\left(y_1|x_1;\beta_1\right) - E\left(y_1^c|x_1;\beta_0\right)\right]$. This expression is analogous to equation (4.3). The first term on the right-hand side is the composition effect, and the second term is the structural effect. This is an aggregate decomposition.

13. To see where this expression comes from, let q_τ be the τth quantile of F. Also, let $q_\tau(b)$ stand for the τth quantile of the mixed distribution G so that $G = bH(q_\tau(b)) + (1 - b) F(q_\tau(b)) = \tau$ and $q_\tau(0) = q_\tau$. The first-order derivative of G with respect to b, evaluated at $b = 0$, yields the following expression: $H(q_\tau) - F(q_\tau) + f(q_\tau)q_\tau'(0) = 0$. Hence the directional derivative of this quantile in the direction of H is equal to $q_\tau'(0) = \frac{F(q_\tau) - H(q_\tau)}{f(q_\tau)} = \frac{\tau - H(q_\tau)}{f(q_\tau)}$. Setting $H(q_\tau) = \Delta_y(q_\tau) = I(y \leq q_\tau)$ implies that the influence function of the τth quantile of F is equal to $IF(y;q_\tau, F) = \frac{\tau - I(y \leq q_\tau)}{f(q_\tau)}$.

    For more details, see Essama-Nssah and Lambert (2012).

14. See Essama-Nssah, Saumik, and Bassolé (2013) for an application.
15. This is the effect of a counterfactual change in the marginal distribution of a single covariate on the unconditional distribution of an outcome variable, *ceteris paribus*. Rothe (2010) interprets the *ceteris paribus* condition in terms of rank invariance. In other words, the counterfactual change in the marginal distribution of the relevant covariate is constructed in such a way that the joint distribution of ranks is unaffected.
16. The components of a detailed decomposition are easily computed by replacing (a) the expected values with the corresponding sample means, and (b) the coefficients associated with the covariates with their OLS estimates. An estimate of the endowment effect is $\hat{\Delta}_X^\theta = (\bar{x}_1 - \bar{x}_0)\hat{\beta}_0 = \sum_{k=1}^{m}(\bar{x}_{1k} - \bar{x}_{0k})\hat{\beta}_{0k}$. Similarly, for the structural effect, we have the following expression: $\hat{\Delta}_S^\theta = \bar{x}_1\left(\hat{\beta}_1 - \hat{\beta}_0\right) = \left(\hat{\beta}_{11} - \hat{\beta}_{01}\right) + \sum_{k=2}^{m}\bar{x}_{1k}\left(\hat{\beta}_{1k} - \hat{\beta}_{0k}\right)$.
17. This account draws on Essama-Nssah and Bassolé (2010).
18. To clarify our notation, we consider the simplest case where x represents a single characteristic. No loss of generality is involved. The marginal distribution of y is equal to $f_t(y) = \int_0^{mx} J_t(y,x)dx$, where mx stands for the maximum value of x. Equivalently, $f_t(y) = f_{gt}^{ht}(y) = \int_0^{mx} g_t(y|x)h_t(x)dx$. The counterfactual used in equation (4.22) is therefore defined as follows: $f_{g0}^{h1} = \int_0^{mx} g_0(y|x)h_1(x)dx$. This expression can be derived from the marginal outcome distribution in the initial period, $f_0(y) = \int_0^{mx} g_0(y|x)h_0(x)dx$, by replacing $h_0(x)$ with $h_1(x)$. For this operation to lead to a meaningful counterfactual, two invariance conditions must be met. The conditional distributions $g_t(y|x)$ must be invariant with respect to changes in the marginal distribution of observables, $h_t(x)$. This would be the case if there are no general equilibrium effects. The distribution of unobservables must be at least conditionally independent of that of observables. Ignorability guarantees this.

19. A histogram is "a representation of a frequency distribution by means of rectangles whose widths represent class intervals and whose areas are proportional to the corresponding frequencies" (online version of the Merriam-Webster Unabridged, http://unabridged.merriam-webster.com/).
20. Deaton (1997) further explains that the size of the bandwidth is inversely related to the sample size. The larger the sample size, the smaller the bandwidth. To obtain a consistent estimate of the density at each point, the bandwidth must become smaller at a slower rate than the rate at which the sample size is increasing. However, with only a few points, we need large bands to be able to get any points in each. By widening the bands, we run the risk of biasing the estimate by bringing into the count data that belong to other parts of the distribution. Hence, the increase in the sample size does two things: It allows the analyst to reduce the bandwidth and hence the bias in estimation (due to increased mass at the point of interest). It also ensures that the variance will shrink as the number of points within each band increases.
21. Deaton (1997) argues that the choice of the bandwidth or the smoothing parameter is more important than that of the kernel function. Essentially, estimating densities by kernel methods is an exercise in smoothing the sample observations into an estimated density. The bandwidth controls the amount of smoothing achieved. Oversmoothed estimates are biased, while undersmoothed ones are too variable.
22. The equivalent expression for the decomposition is $\Delta f = \left[f_{y_0|t=1} - f_{y_0|t=0} \right] + \left[f_{y_1|t=1} - f_{y_0|t=1} \right]$.
23. In the context of treatment effect analysis, the assumption of *rank preservation*, also known as *rank invariance*, is used to identify quantile treatment effects (QTE). The assumption implies that given two mutually exclusive states of the world, the outcome at the τth quantile of the outcome distribution in one state has its counterpart at the same quantile of the outcome distribution in the alternative state. Bitler, Gelbach, and Hoynes (2006) explain that when this assumption fails, the QTE approach identifies and estimates the difference between the quantiles and not the quantiles of the difference in outcome distributions. Rank preservation is akin to *anonymity* or *symmetry* used to base growth incidence analysis on cross-section data instead of on panel data. Anonymity implies that when comparing two outcome distributions, the identity of the individual experiencing a particular outcome is irrelevant (Carneiro, Hansen, and Heckman 2002). Thus, a permutation of outcomes between any two individuals in any of the two distributions being compared has no effect on the comparison. One might as well then compare such distributions across quantiles.
24. Recall that ignorability means that the conditional distribution of ε is the same across groups (or periods). Thus individuals with the same set of observable characteristics find themselves at the same rank in both (conditional) distributions. It is well known that a monotonic transformation preserves order. In fact, Rapoport (1999) defines a monotone transformation as "a formula that changes the numbers of one set to the numbers of another set while preserving their relative positions on the axis of real numbers." Since υ_t is obtained from ε through a monotonic transformation $\zeta_t(\cdot)$, rank preservation must therefore follow.
25. Note that the structural effect can also be expressed as $\Delta_S^y = \left(y_{i1} - y_{i0}^b \right)$. In the notation associated with equation (4.2), linearity and rank preservation imply that y_{i0}^b corresponds to the counterfactual outcome obtained by replacing the outcome structure $\varphi_1(\cdot)$ with $\varphi_0(\cdot)$. In other words, y_{i0}^b is the same as $y_{0|t=1}$. This suggests that the

Juhn-Murphy-Pierce (1993) decomposition can be performed in two steps as follows: Start with the overall difference $\Delta_O^y = (y_{i1} - y_{i0})$ and then add to and subtract from this difference the counterfactual outcome y_{i0}^b. This yields a twofold decomposition of the overall difference into the composition and structural effects. Finally add to and subtract from the structural effect the counterfactual outcome y_{i0}^c. This step leads to the final threefold decomposition. Ignorability guarantees that the composition effect is due solely to changes in the distribution of observables.

26. Indeed, Fortin, Lemieux, and Firpo (2011) provide a systematic interpretation of decomposition methods within the logic of program impact evaluation.

27. According to Fortin, Lemieux, and Firpo (2011), these assumptions include the following: (a) The groups are mutually exclusive. (b) The outcome structure is an additively separable function of characteristics. (c) The conditional mean for unobservables given observed characteristics is equal to zero. (d) There is common support for the distributions of characteristics across groups (to rule out cases where arguments of the outcome function may differ across groups. (e) There is simple counterfactual treatment, meaning that the outcome structure of one group is assumed to be a counterfactual for the other group. This last assumption rules out general equilibrium effects so that observed outcomes for one group or time period can be reasonably used to construct counterfactuals for the other group or time period. The Oaxaca-Blinder method therefore follows a partial equilibrium approach.

28. Heckman and Smith (1995) explain that the mean outcome of the control group provides an acceptable estimate of the counterfactual mean if (a) randomization does not alter the pool of participants or their behavior and (b) no close substitutes for the experimental program are readily available. These authors further note that randomization does not eliminate selection bias, but rather balances it between the two samples (participants and nonparticipants) so that it cancels out when computing mean impact. There would be randomization bias if those who participate in an experiment differ from those who would have participated in the absence of randomization. Furthermore, substitution bias would occur if members of the control group can easily obtain elsewhere close substitutes for the treatment.

29. Recall that the identification of the two components of the aggregate Oaxaca-Blinder decomposition relies on the zero-conditional-mean assumption for the unobservable factors stated as $E(\epsilon|x) = 0$. This condition is what allows the analyst to claim that on average, variation in x is unrelated to variation in the unobservables, a manifestation of *ceteris paribus* variation.

30. The expression of this probability can be made more precise by considering an indicator function for the decision rule. The indicator is equal to one when option k is chosen and zero otherwise. The probability that the agent chooses option k is then equal to the expected value of this indicator function over all possible values of the unobserved factors. In other words, $P_{hk} = \int I\left[\left(\varepsilon_{hj} - \varepsilon_{hk}\right) < \left(v_{hk} - v_{hj}\right) \; \forall j \neq k\right] f\left(\varepsilon_h\right) d\varepsilon_h$.

This is in fact a multidimensional integral over the joint density of the random vector, the elements of which represent unobserved factors associated with each alternative. This probability can be interpreted as the proportion of people within the population who face the same observable utility as h for each alternative and choose k (Train 2009).

31. The generalized extreme value model (GEV) allows correlation among unobserved factors. The standard multinomial logit assumes that the random factors are iid with a double exponential distribution. The probit model assumes that the random factors

are jointly distributed normal variables. Train (2009) points out that the identification of discrete choice models relies heavily on the fact that only differences in utility matter and the scale of utility is irrelevant. Hence, only parameters that capture differences across alternatives are identifiable and therefore estimable. This also implies that characteristics of the decision maker that do not vary across alternatives will have no effect unless they are specified in a way that induces differences in utility over alternatives. Glick and Sahn (2006) handle this problem by indexing the coefficients of sociodemographic variables in the representative utility function.

32. For agricultural households, earnings are computed on the basis of a reduced farm profit function (based on the Cobb-Douglas production function) that includes self-consumption and accounts for hired labor. For family members participating in farm work, the reservation wage (a measure of the value of family work) is assumed to depend on their contribution to farm profits.

Bibliography

Angrist, Joshua D., and Jörn-Steffen Pischke. 2009. *Mostly Harmless Econometrics: An Empiricist's Companion*. Princeton, NJ: Princeton University Press.

Atkinson, Anthony B. 1970. "On the Measurement of Inequality." *Journal of Economic Theory* 2 (3): 244–63.

Autor, David H. 2009. "Lecture Note: Self-Selection — The Roy Model." Department of Economics, Massachusetts Institute of Technology, Cambridge, MA. http://econ-www.mit.edu/files/4092.

Bitler, Marianne P., Jonah B. Gelbach, and Hilary W. Hoynes. 2006. "What Mean Impacts Miss: Distributional Effects of Welfare Reform Experiments." *American Economic Review* 96 (4): 988–1012.

Blinder, Alan S. 1973. "Wage Discrimination: Reduced Form and Structural Estimates." *Journal of Human Resources* 8 (4): 436–55.

Bourguignon, François, and Francisco H. G. Ferreira. 2005. "Decomposing Changes in the Distribution of Household Incomes: Methodological Aspects." In *The Microeconomics of Income Distribution Dynamics in East Asia and Latin America*, edited by François Bourguignon, Francisco H. G. Ferreira, and Nora Lustig, 17–46. Washington, DC: World Bank.

Bourguignon, François, Francisco H. G. Ferreira, and Phillippe G. Leite. 2008. "Beyond Oaxaca-Blinder: Accounting for Differences in Household Income Distributions." *Journal of Economic Inequality* 6 (2): 117–48.

Carneiro, Pedro, Karsten T. Hansen, and James J. Heckman. 2002. "Removing the Veil of Ignorance in Assessing the Distributional Impacts of Social Policies." Discussion Paper 453, Institute for the Study of Labor (IZA), Bonn, Germany.

Cogneau, Denis, and Anne-Sophie Robilliard. 2008. "Simulating Targeted Policies with Macro Impacts: Poverty Alleviation Policies in Madagascar." In *The Impact of Macroeconomic Policies on Poverty and Income Distribution: Macro-Micro Evaluation Techniques and Tools*, edited by François Bourguignon, Maurizio Bussolo, and Luiz A. Pereira da Silva, 213–45. Washington, DC: World Bank.

Coulombe, Harold, and Andrew McKay. 1996. "Modeling Determinants of Poverty in Mauritania." *World Development* 24 (6): 1015–31.

Cowell, Frank A., and Maria-Pia Victoria-Feser. 1996. "Poverty Measurement with Contaminated Data: A Robust Approach." *European Economic Review* 40 (9): 1761–71.

Deaton, Angus. 1997. *The Analysis of Household Surveys: A Microeconometric Approach to Development Policy*. Baltimore, MD: Johns Hopkins University Press.

DiNardo, John, Nicole Fortin, and Thomas Lemieux. 1996. "Labor Market Institutions and the Distribution of Wages, 1973–1992: A Semiparametric Approach." *Econometrica* 64 (5): 1001–44.

Essama-Nssah, B. 2012. "Identification of Sources of Variation in Poverty Outcomes." Policy Research Working Paper 5954, World Bank, Washington, DC.

Essama-Nssah, B., and Léandre Bassolé. 2010. "A Counterfactual Analysis of the Poverty Impact of Economic Growth in Cameroon." Policy Research Working Paper 5249, World Bank, Washington, DC.

Essama-Nssah, B., and Peter J. Lambert. 2012. "Influence Functions for Policy Impact Analysis." In *Inequality, Mobility and Segregation: Essays in Honor of Jacques Silber*, Vol. 20, edited by John A. Bishop and Rafael Salas, 135–59. Research on Economic Inequality Series. Bradford, UK: Emerald Group Publishing.

Essama-Nssah, B., Paul Saumik, and Léandre Bassolé. 2013. "Accounting for Heterogeneity in Growth Incidence in Cameroon Using Recentered Influence Function Regression." *Journal of African Economies* 22 (5): 757–95. doi: 10.1093/jae/ejt009.

Fairlie, Robert W. 2005. "An Extension of the Blinder-Oaxaca Decomposition Technique to Logit and Probit Models." *Journal of Economic and Social Measurement* 30 (4): 305–16.

Ferreira, Francisco H. G. 2010. "Distributions in Motion: Economic Growth, Inequality and Poverty Dynamics." Policy Research Paper 5424, World Bank, Washington, DC.

Firpo, Sergio, Nicole Fortin, and Thomas Lemieux. 2009. "Unconditional Quantile Regressions." *Econometrica* 77 (3): 953–73.

Fortin, Nicole, Thomas Lemieux, and Sergio Firpo. 2011. "Decomposition Methods in Economics." In *Handbook of Labor Economics*, Vol. 4A, edited by Orley Ashenfelter and Card David, 1–102. Amsterdam, the Netherlands: North-Holland.

Foster, James, Joel Greer, and Erik Thorbecke. 1984. "A Class of Decomposable Poverty Measures." *Econometrica* 52 (3): 761–66.

Glick, Peter, and David Sahn. 2006. "The Demand for Primary Schooling in Madagascar: Price, Quality and the Choice between Public and Private Providers." *Journal of Development Economics* 79 (1): 118–45.

Hampel, Frank R. 1974. "The Influence Curve and Its Role in Robust Estimation." *Journal of the American Statistical Association* 69 (346): 383–93.

Heckman, James J., and Bo E. Honoré. 1990. "The Empirical Content of the Roy Model." *Econometrica* 58 (5): 1121–49.

Heckman, James J., and Guilherme Sedlacek. 1985. "Heterogeneity, Aggregation, and Market Wage Functions: An Empirical Model of Self-Selection in the Labor Market." *Journal of Political Economy* 93 (6): 1077–125.

Heckman, James J., and Jeffrey A. Smith. 1995. "Assessing the Case of Social Experiments." *Journal of Economic Perspectives* 9 (2): 85–110.

Heckman, James J., and Salvador Navarro-Lozano. 2004. "Using Matching, Instrumental Variables, and Control Functions to Estimate Economic Choice Models." *Review of Economics and Statistics* 86 (1): 30–57.

Inchauste, Gabriela, Sergio Olivieri, Jaime Saavedra, and Hernan Winkler. 2012. "What Is Behind the Decline in Poverty Since 2000? Evidence from Bangladesh, Peru, and Thailand." Policy Research Working Paper 6199, World Bank, Washington, DC.

Jann, Ben. 2008. "The Blinder-Oaxaca Decomposition for Linear Models." *Stata Journal* 8 (4): 453–79.

Juhn, Chinhui, Kevin M. Murphy, and Brooks Pierce. 1991. "Accounting for the Slowdown in Black-White Wage Convergence." In *Workers and Their Wages: Changing Patterns in the United States*, edited by Marvin H. Kosters. Washington, DC: American Enterprise Institute.

———. 1993. "Wage Inequality and the Rise of Returns to Skill." *Journal of Political Economy* 101 (3): 410–42.

Leite, Phillippe G., Alan Sanchez, and Caterina R. Laderchi. 2009. "The Evolution in Urban Inequality in Ethiopia." Paper presented at the Centre for the Study of African Economies 2009 Annual Conference, "Economic Development in Africa," St. Catherine's College, Oxford, March 22–24.

Machado, Jose A. F., and Jose Mata. 2005. "Counterfactual Decomposition of Changes in Wage Distributions Using Quantile Regression." *Journal of Applied Econometrics* 20 (4): 445–65.

Melly, Blaise. 2005. "Decomposition of Differences in Distribution Using Quantile Regression." *Labour Economics* 12 (4): 577–90.

Milgrom, Paul. 2004. *Putting Auction Theory to Work*. Cambridge: Cambridge University Press.

Oaxaca, Ronald L. 1973. "Male-Female Wage Differentials in Urban Labor Markets." *International Economic Review* 14 (3): 693–709.

Rapoport, Anatol. 1999. *Two-Person Game Theory*. Mineola, NY: Dover Publications.

Ravallion, Martin. 2001. "Growth, Inequality and Poverty: Looking Beyond Averages." *World Development* 29 (11): 1803–15.

Rosenbaum, Paul, and Donald Rubin. 1983. "The Central Role of the Propensity Score in Observational Studies for Causal Effects." *Biometrika* 70 (1): 41–55.

Rothe, Christoph. 2010. "Decomposing Counterfactual Distributions." Unpublished manuscript, Toulouse School of Economics, University of Toulouse, France.

Roy, Arthur D. 1951. "Some Thoughts on the Distribution of Earnings." *Oxford Economic Papers* 3 (2): 135–46.

Silverman, Bernard W. 1986. *Density Estimation for Statistics and Data Analysis*. London: Chapman and Hall.

Sinning, Mathias, Markus Hahn, and Thomas K. Bauer. 2008. "The Blinder-Oaxaca Decomposition for Nonlinear Models." *Stata Journal* 8 (4): 480–92.

Todd, Petra E. 2008. "Evaluating Social Programs with Endogenous Program Placement and Selection of the Treated." In *Handbook of Development Economics*, Vol. 4, edited by T. Paul Schultz and John Strauss, 3847–94. Amsterdam, the Netherlands: North-Holland.

Train, Kenneth E. 2009. *Discrete Choice Methods with Simulation*. 2nd ed. Cambridge: Cambridge University Press.

Varian, Hal R. 1984. *Microeconomic Analysis*. 2nd ed. New York: Norton.

von Mises, Richard. 1947. "On the Asymptotic Distribution of Differentiable Statistical Functions." *Annals of Mathematical Statistics* 18 (3): 309–48.

Wilcox, Rand R. 2005. *Introduction to Robust Estimation and Hypothesis Testing*. 2nd ed. Amsterdam, the Netherlands: Elsevier.

Yun, Myeong-Su. 2009. "Wage Differentials, Discrimination and Inequality: A Cautionary Note on the Juhn, Murphy and Pierce Decomposition Method." *Scottish Journal of Political Economy* 56 (1): 114–22.

CHAPTER 5

Why Has Labor Income Increased? An In-Depth Approach to Understanding Poverty Reduction

Introduction

As chapter 3 found, labor market outcomes (in particular, labor income increases per working adult) were the main contributors to poverty reduction in a set of countries where poverty declined substantially during the past decade. A simple micro-decomposition methodology showed this to be true for moderate poverty lines and even extreme poverty lines in some cases. The next logical question is this: Why did total labor income increase—from improved human capital characteristics or from higher *returns* to those characteristics? To answer this question, an underlying model with additional structure is needed.

A broad literature on micro-decomposition methodologies (which chapter 4 described in detail) aims to identify and estimate two effects associated with distributional changes: the composition (or endowment) effect and structural (or price) effect. Either statistical or structural approaches can account for the contributions of these effects. Statistical approaches use semiparametric and nonparametric methods to identify the contributors to distributional changes without having to impose a functional form on the relationship between these changes and their determinants. However, the statistical framework cannot shed light on the mechanism underlying that relationship. In contrast, structural methods further identify the factors underpinning observed changes in poverty outcomes by specifying an economic model and using statistical analysis. In particular, these models *account for behavior*: how agents respond to changes in their socioeconomic environment, whether due to shocks or policy reform.

The structural approach is followed below and in the next chapter (which will apply it in depth to three countries). In particular, this chapter presents a structure for modeling distributional changes over time. The approach rests on the typical economic assumption that agents seek to maximize their utility subject to constraints. That assumption implies that the outcome variables of interest chosen to represent the consequences of behavior (such as educational or sectoral choice) can be expressed as functions of parameters of the socioeconomic environment, embedded in the constraints facing the agent. In particular, throughout this chapter, we consider the Roy (1951) model of choice and consequences (which stems from the optimization principle and applies to discrete choice problems), using it to model individuals' educational levels, sectors, and activity choices.[1]

We then adapt the Bourguignon, Ferreira, and Leite (2008) methodology to distinguish between distributional changes on account of (a) changes in endowments and the returns to those endowments; (b) changes in occupational and sectoral choice; (c) changes in geographical, age, and gender structure of the population; and (d) the nonlabor dimensions such as public transfers (the latter previously explored further in chapter 3).

Therefore, the proposed model formulates an educational choice model, a sectoral choice model, an activity choice model, and individual and household earnings equations. Once all of these models are estimated for individuals and households in each time period, the estimated coefficients from one year can be replaced with the estimates from another year to simulate the impact of changes in each element at a time. For each change, we can construct a counterfactual income distribution and estimate a counterfactual poverty measure for comparison with the observed outcome while holding everything else constant. By changing one element at a time, these decompositions allow us to account for the observed changes in poverty.

Innovations in Cumulative Counterfactual Estimates

In addition, we present an enhanced method to estimate these counterfactuals cumulatively, thereby accounting for the impact of concurrent changes. Although the method presented here draws heavily from Bourguignon and Ferreira (2005) and Bourguignon, Ferreira, and Leite (2008), it also offers some innovations:

- It models farm household income at the household level and models the earnings of individuals in those farm households who have a secondary occupation, thus recognizing not only that farm households typically make labor decisions as a unit but also that these households can be highly diversified.
- It assumes that welfare is measured using a consumption aggregate and accounts for the contribution of changes in the consumption-to-income ratio.
- It ensures that changes in the composition of activities, sectors, and education of the work force are consistent with the counterfactual choices.

As covered in chapters 2 and 3, such decompositions do not identify causal effects, but they are useful to focus attention on the elements that are quantitatively more important in describing changes in poverty. In particular, they can capture the heterogeneity of impacts throughout the distribution and account for the contributions of demographic, sectoral, occupational, and other labor and nonlabor dimensions toward poverty reduction.

After the next section presents the underlying model, the chapter describes the decomposition approach adopted here and concludes with a summary of the proposed model and its innovations. We implement this methodology in three countries around the world, the results for which we report in chapter 6.

Modeling Strategy

Following Bourguignon, Ferreira, and Leite (2008), our approach postulates a model in which characteristics such as age, gender, and geographic location are exogenously determined (and are taken as given), while education, employment activity, sector, and earnings are endogenous (determined within the model), as illustrated in figure 5.1. Therefore, the modeling strategy consists of six stages, each of which influences the next stage in the sequence:

1. Educational choice models
2. Sectoral and activity choice models
3. Farm and nonfarm earnings
4. Total household income, based largely on earnings
5. Household consumption, determined by total household income
6. A consumption-based calculation of the poverty rate

Educational Choice

First, individuals are distributed across educational levels and, further, as a function of age, gender, area (urban versus rural), and region (defined as districts or provinces). This is done for all working-age individuals, following the Roy (1951) model, whereby individuals choose their educational level to maximize their utility. The allocation of individuals across levels of education is estimated with a multinomial logit model (McFadden 1974a, 1974b), specified as follows:

$$I_{hi}^{k} = 1 \text{ if } Z_{hi}\psi^{k} + v_{i}^{k} > Max\left(0, Z_{hi}\psi^{m} + v_{i}^{m}\right),\ j = 1,\ldots,\mathrm{K},\ \forall m \neq k \qquad (5.1)$$

$$I_{hi}^{k} = 0 \text{ for all } k = 1,\ldots,\mathrm{K} \text{ if } Z_{hi}\psi^{k} + v_{i}^{k} \leq 0 \text{ for all } k = 1,\ldots,K,$$

where Z_{hi} is a vector of characteristics specific to individual i and household h; ψ^k is a matrix with vectors of coefficients for each educational level, m; and v_i^k is a vector of random variables identically and independently distributed across individuals and activities according to the law of extreme values. Within a discrete utility-maximizing framework, $Z_{hi}\psi^{k} + v_{i}^{k}$ is interpreted as the utility associated with educational level k, with v_i^k being the unobserved utility determinants of educational level k and the utility of no education being arbitrarily set to zero.

We estimate the conditional distributions of educational levels for each survey year based on age group, gender, region, and area. They are estimated separately for household heads, spouses, and other working-age members. The result of this exercise is a model that estimates the probability of individuals obtaining a certain level of education.

Figure 5.1 Model of Contributors to Poverty Reduction, by Stage Sequence

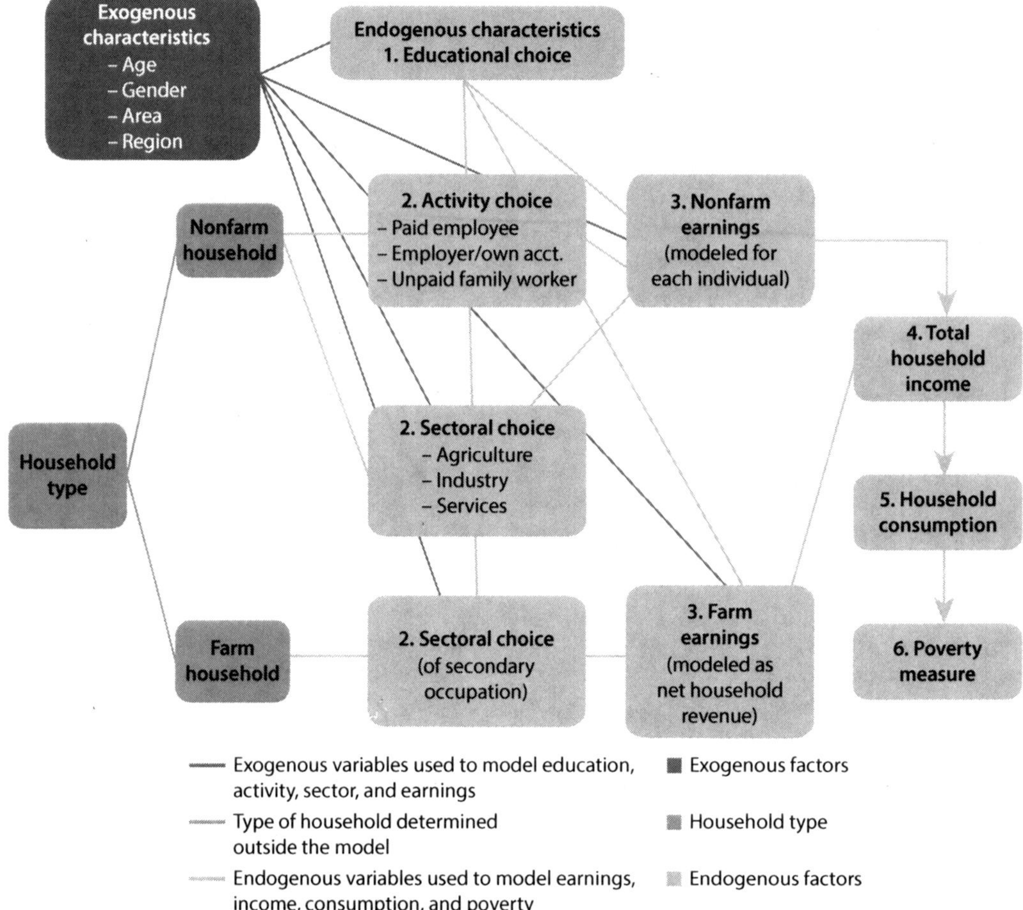

Note: The green boxes are numbered according to the typically sequential stages by which contributors to poverty are determined: 1. Educational choice; 2. Sectoral and activity choice; 3. Farm and nonfarm earnings; 4. Total household income; 5. Household consumption; and 6. Consumption-based poverty rate. Farm households are those whose heads are self-employed in agriculture. "Area" refers to whether the household is urban or rural. "Region" refers to districts or provinces. "Activity choice" refers to an individual's occupational status, which may include paid employment (by hourly wages or salaried); self-employment; unpaid labor (typically for family needs); or unemployment.

Sectoral and Activity Choices

The second stage of the model structure begins with the separation of households into farm and nonfarm categories, as shown in figure 5.1. Farm households are defined as those whose household heads are self-employed in agriculture. All other households are considered to be nonfarm households. This distinction allows us to model the nonfarm sector at the individual level, where workers choose the sector of work. Meanwhile, the farm sector is modeled at the household level because farm households are likely to operate as a single unit of production, thus making labor decisions at the household level.

In developing countries, people commonly engage in nonfarm microenterprises and informal small-scale activities. Although these nonfarm businesses are often modeled at the household level (Haggblade, Hazell, and Reardon 2007, 2010), this modeling implies a trade-off: In particular, if earnings are modeled at the household level, accounting for the contribution to poverty reduction of changes in the population's sectoral or occupational structure is impossible because such changes can be observed only at the individual level.

Once households are divided between farm and nonfarm households, the second stage in the model is the allocation of individuals across work-activity types. In particular, following Roy (1951), individuals choose the sector and type of activity they are engaged in to maximize their utility. As above, this is estimated with a multinomial logit model, where j = {salaried, nonfarm self-employed, unpaid family worker, not employed}. Sectoral choice is also estimated this way, where j = {agriculture, industry, services}—modeled as a function of age, gender, area, region, and educational attainment.

Recognizing that farm households often include members who work on nonfarm activities (Davis et al. 2010), we model those individuals' decisions to undertake secondary activities in order to capture this diversification into nonfarm activities. We assume that the residuals are independently and identically distributed according to a logistic function (a logit model being the estimator of the diversification choice to have a secondary occupation or not) for all household heads who are self-employed in agriculture. The probability of undertaking a secondary activity is modeled as a function of a vector of characteristics that includes individual and household variables such as age, gender, educational level, region, and areas, among others. Random terms are drawn conditional on the initial choice.

Because both the sectoral and activity choices depend on individuals' educational levels, any simulated change in education will imply a change in the activity and sectoral composition of the work force. Although the choice of sector and activity are likely simultaneous decisions, here they are modeled independently for tractability of the model.

Earnings Models

The third portion of the model structure is a set of earnings equations that serve to construct a counterfactual income distribution. For nonfarm households, we model the heterogeneity in individual earnings in each activity j by a log-linear Mincer model:

$$\log(y^j_{hi}) = QX_{hi}\Omega^j + \varepsilon^j_{hi}, \tag{5.2}$$

for $i = 1, \ldots, n_h$, and j = {salaried, nonfarm self-employed, not employed}. Q_{hi} is a vector of individual characteristics, including (a) those determined outside the model (such as gender, area, and region), which we call Z_{hi}, and (b) those determined within the model (including education and sector), which we call X_{hi}. Ω^j is a matrix of coefficients, and ε^j_{hi} are random variables assumed to be distributed identically and independently across individuals according to the standard normal law.[2]

Individual earnings equations for nonfarm workers are estimated separately for household heads, spouses, and other members who are self-employed and salaried. The set of characteristics considered in the specification include age, gender, and education (among others) as well as characteristics of other household members. For instance, in the case of spouses and other members, the specifications include characteristics of the household head (educational level, whether employed, and so on). Similarly, for members of farm households at the individual level, earnings from secondary occupations are estimated as a function of the members' individual characteristics (such as age, gender, educational level, and economic sector where they perform their secondary job).

In both cases, changes in income (y^j_{hi}) could be due to changes in observable endowments (X_{hi}) or changes in the returns to those endowments (Ω^j). However, they could also occur because of changes in unobservables that are captured in the residual term. To capture these changes, we rely on the assumption that the residual terms are drawn from a standard normal distribution.

Earnings of farm households are modeled as the net revenue at the household level:

$$\log \pi^F_h = W_h \Omega^F + \varepsilon^F_h, \tag{5.3}$$

where $W_h = (K_h, X_h)$ includes endowments and household characteristics, Ω^F is a vector of coefficients, and ε^F_h are random variables distributed as a standard normal.

Farm households' net revenues are estimated using ordinary least squares. The vector of characteristics includes endowments such as land and irrigation as well as the household head's individual and household characteristics, including educational level, gender, civil status, and number of members involved in the farm activity, among other characteristics. To capture changes in unobservables, we rely on the assumption that the residual terms are drawn from a standard normal distribution.

Total Income

Finally (and as in chapter 2), the conditional distribution of nonlabor income is estimated nonparametrically—both as a total and by its different components such as remittances, public transfers, and other private transfers. For this purpose, we create cells of household heads of the same educational level, gender, and area (urban or rural). Inside of each cell, we create quantiles of nonlabor income, to which we then ascribe the mean value of each nonlabor income component in each quantile-cell in period s to its counterpart in period t.

Given the labor and nonlabor incomes described above, total household income can be written as

$$Y_h = \left[y^w_h + \mathrm{y}^{\mathrm{se}}_{\mathrm{h}} + \pi^F_h + y^{NL}_h \right], \tag{5.4}$$

where Y is household income per capita; y^w_h and y^{SE}_h are total incomes from salaried labor and self-employed nonfarm labor, respectively; π^F_h is the farm household net revenue function; and y^{NL}_h is household nonlabor income.

Given the choice models described above, this becomes

$$y_h = \left[\sum_{i=1}^{n} I_{hi}^{w} y_{hi}^{w} \left(Q_{hi}, \Omega^{w} \right) + \sum_{i=1}^{n} I_{hi}^{se} y_{hi}^{se} \left(Q_{hi}, \Omega^{se} \right) + \pi_h^F \left(W_h, \Omega^F \right) + y_h^{NL} \right], \quad (5.5)$$

where I_{hi}^{w} and I_{hi}^{se} are indicator variables that are equal to one if individual i in household h is a salaried or self-employed worker. y_{hi}^{w} and y_{hi}^{se} are the corresponding earnings of individual i in household h that depend on individual and household endowments (Q_{hi}) and the returns to those endowments (Ω), which vary across types of activity. Individuals with earnings y_h^w and y_h^{SE} are in the "nonfarm" sector, although this category comprises all salaried workers—including those in agriculture—plus the nonfarm self-employed. For those in the "farm" sector, π_h^F is household net revenue in farm activities, which depends on household endowments (W_{hi}) and the returns to those endowments (Ω^F).

Household Consumption

Since household welfare is typically measured by consumption expenditures, we can write

$$C_h = \frac{\vartheta_h}{n} \left[y_h^w + y_h^{se} + \pi_h^F + y_h^{NL} \right], \quad (5.6)$$

where C_h is household consumption per capita, n is the number of household members, and ϑ_h is the consumption-to-income ratio. Note that once we have defined a way to construct household consumption per capita at the household level, we can construct a distribution of consumption across households and then measure the poverty headcount rate or any other distributional measure.

Poverty Headcount Rate

The poverty headcount index measures the proportion of the population whose consumption falls below the poverty line. Formally,

$$P_0 = \frac{1}{N} \sum_{h=1}^{N} I(C_h < z), \quad (5.7)$$

where N is the total population and $I(\cdot)$ is an indicator function that takes on a value of 1 if the bracketed expression is true and 0 otherwise. If consumption expenditure (C_h) is less than the poverty line (z), then $I(\cdot)$ equals 1 and the household would be counted as poor. Whenever any of the elements in the models described above changes, a new consumption distribution can be generated, and therefore a new poverty rate can be calculated. Similarly, any other distributional statistic can be calculated, including measures of inequality, such as the Gini or the Theil index, as well as other poverty measures, such as the poverty gap and the severity of poverty.

Therefore, equations (5.1)–(5.6) fully characterize the underlying reduced-form models that will allow for the micro-decompositions of poverty. Next, there are two important steps. The first is the estimation strategy, and the second is the construction of counterfactual distributions. We turn to each of these steps in turn.

Decomposition Approach

Estimation Strategy

After each of these reduced-form models has been estimated for years s and t, we decompose the distributional changes by substituting each of the parameters estimated for one year with the parameters of the other year and then by formulating the appropriate counterfactual distribution of income and consumption. Specifically, from equation (5.5) above, we estimate the components of household income for times s and t:

$$\log(y_h)^t = \sum_{i=1}^{n_h} I_{hi}^{w}\left(Q_{hi}\widehat{\Omega}^{w} + \hat{\varepsilon}_{hi}^{w}\right) + \sum_{i=1}^{n_h} I_{hi}^{se}\left(Q_{hi}\widehat{\Omega}^{se} + \hat{\varepsilon}_{hi}^{se}\right) + (W_h\widehat{\Omega}^{F} + \hat{\varepsilon}_h^{F}) + \log(\widehat{y}_h^{NL}), \quad (5.8)$$

which, for simplicity, we express as follows:

$$\log(y_h)^t = f\left(NF\left(\widehat{\Omega}_{NF}^{t}, Z_{hi}^{t}, H_{hi}^{t}, \hat{\varepsilon}_{hi}^{t}\right), O\left(\widehat{\Psi}^{t}, Z_{hi}^{t}, X2_{hi}^{t}, \hat{\upsilon}_{hi}^{t}\right), F\left(\widehat{\Omega}_{F}^{t}, W_{h}^{t}, H_{h}^{t}, \hat{\varepsilon}_{h}^{t}\right), \hat{y}_h^{NL}|^{t}\right), \quad (5.9)$$

where $NF(\cdot)$ = nonfarm earning equations, and $\widehat{\Omega}_{NF}^{t}$ refers to the set of estimated parameters;

Z_{hi}^{t} = exogenous variables such as age, gender, region, and area that are used for the earnings and choice models estimated at the individual level;

$O(\cdot)$ = activity choice equations, and $\widehat{\Psi}^{t}$ refers to the set of estimated parameters;

$H\left(X_{hi}^{t}, \widehat{\theta}_{hi}^{t}, \widehat{\phi}_{hi}^{t}\right)$ = the underlying models for the sectoral and educational structure, where X_{hi}^{t} is a vector of endogenous variables including sector $(X1_{hi}^{t})$ and education $(X2_{hi}^{t})$, which are estimated at the individual level and then used in the activity choice model, with $\widehat{\theta 1}_{hi}^{t}$ and $\widehat{\theta 2}_{hi}^{t}$ being the respective set of estimated parameters;

$F(\cdot)$ = net farm revenue equations, and $\widehat{\Omega}_{F}^{t}$ are the set of estimated parameters;

W_{h}^{t} = exogenous variables such as age, gender, region, and area for the farm net revenue model estimated at the household level;

$\hat{\varepsilon}_{hi}^{t}, \hat{\varepsilon}_{h}^{t}, \hat{\upsilon}_{hi}^{t}, \hat{\phi}_{hi}^{t}$ = error terms for earning equations for nonfarm and farm sectors and endogenous variables such as educational structure, activity choice, and economic sector; and

$y_h^{NL}|^{t}$ = nonlabor income.

From here, we can perform marginal decompositions that consist of changing one component at a time, keeping everything else constant. After describing how this is done for each element, we briefly discuss the cumulative approach, which changes each additional component and adds to the total effect until all components are accounted for. It is important to note that all decompositions are performed considering s as the initial year and then considering t as the initial year. The average of these decompositions is the final result reported in the analysis.[3]

Construction of Counterfactual Distributions

Changes in Poverty as a Result of Changes in Demographics

The first decomposition consists of altering the joint distribution of exogenous household characteristics such as age, gender, region, and area of each individual in the household. Because these variables do not depend on any other variables in the model, one can think of this simulation as the one assuming the greatest degree of exogeneity.

The simulation is performed simply by recalibrating the population of one year by the weights corresponding to the joint distribution of these attributes in the target year. In other words, the demographic characteristics of year t are weighted such that their structure replicates the demographic characteristics of year s. For example, if the share of women in year s is higher than in year t, then the weights in year t are modified so that in the simulation they replicate the structure observed in year s.

Because demographic variables are determinants of the activity, sector, and educational choice models, the reweighed structure of these variables have direct and indirect effects on household income. The indirect effects are calculated by substituting the reweighed demographic variables into the estimated multinomial logit equations to forecast a counterfactual activity, sector, and educational composition of the work force. These new sectors, educational levels, and activities are then fed into the estimated earnings equations, along with the direct effect of changes in the demographic variables. Formally, the vector of variables Z_{hi} in equation (5.9) for year t is substituted for that of year s as follows:[4]

$$\log(y_h)^{s \to t}_{X.Z,W}$$
$$= f\left(NF\left(\widehat{\Omega}^t_{NF}, Z^s_{hi}, H^t_{hi}, \hat{\varepsilon}^t_{hi}\right), O\left(\widehat{\psi}^t, Z^s_{hi}, X2^t_{hi}, \hat{\upsilon}^t_{hi}\right), F\left(\widehat{\Omega}^t_F, W^s_h, H^t_h, \hat{\varepsilon}^t_h\right), y^{NL}_h \mid^t\right) \quad (5.10)$$

The resulting income distribution is then transformed to a new distribution of consumption using equation (5.6) above, where the consumption-to-income ratio is kept constant. Given this new counterfactual distribution of consumption, any new distributional statistic can be computed.

In this case, because we are interested in the contributions to poverty reduction, we apply the poverty line for period t and calculate the counterfactual headcount poverty rate, $P\left\{(y_h)^{s \to t}_{X.Z,W}\right\}_h$. The contribution of demographic changes to the observed change in poverty will be the difference between the poverty rate for year t and the counterfactual generated by equation (5.10), which can be expressed as $\Delta P_{X,Z,W}^{s\to t} = P\{y_h^t\}_h - P\{(y_h)_{X.Z,W}^{s\to t}\}_h$.

Changes in Poverty as a Result of Changes in Structure of Activity

Next, to account for changes in the structure of activity, the coefficients of the activity multinomial logit models for year t are replaced with those of year s. As a result, individuals are reallocated into different activities to conform to the structure observed in year s. To allow for individuals to change activities in the simulation, we must estimate the residual terms of the multinomial logit model (v_i^s) in equation (5.1), which are unobserved. As annex 5A describes in detail, these residuals must be drawn from an extreme value distribution in a way that is consistent with observed choices. In contrast to previous papers (Bourguignon, Ferreira, and Lustig 2005), we use the analytical solution to this problem derived by Train and Wilson (2008).

With the new simulated structure of activity in year t, labor income is projected using the estimated earnings equations for year t and the residuals drawn from a standard normal distribution. Specifically, the set of parameters estimated at time t, $\widehat{\psi}^t$, are substituted by those estimated at time s, $\widehat{\psi}^s$, maintaining everything else constant. This new structure of activities is then used to obtain a counterfactual distribution of income as follows:

$$\log(y_h)_{\psi}^{s\to t} = f\Big(NF\big(\widehat{\Omega}_{NF}^t, Z_{hi}^t, H_{hi}^t, \hat{\varepsilon}_{hi}^t\big), O\big(\widehat{\Psi}^S, Z_{hi}^t, X2_{hi}^t, \hat{v}_{hi}^t\big),$$
$$F\big(\widehat{\Omega}_F^t, W_h^t, H_h^t, \hat{\varepsilon}_h^{NL}\big), y_h^{NL} \mid^t\Big). \qquad (5.11)$$

The resulting counterfactual total household income distribution can then be transformed to a new distribution of consumption using equation (5.6) above, where the consumption-to-income ratio is kept constant. This counterfactual distribution of consumption can be compared with the actual distribution in (5.9). We calculate the counterfactual poverty rate and take the difference from the poverty rate found in period t to obtain the contribution to poverty reduction: $\Delta P_{\psi}^{s\to t} = P\{y_h^t\}_h - P\{(y_h)_{\psi}^{s\to t})\}_h$.

Changes in Poverty as a Result of Changes in Education and Sectoral Composition

Similarly, to account for changes in the educational structure or in the sectoral composition of employment, we use the coefficients from the estimated multinomial logit models. For instance, to account for changes in poverty due to changes in the sectoral composition of the work force, we substitute the $\widehat{\theta 1}_{hi}^t$ parameters in the sectoral equation for time t, with $\widehat{\theta 1}_{hi}^s$. To allow for individuals to change sectors in the simulation, the residual terms in the sectoral multinomial logit model are taken from an extreme value distribution, as described in annex 5A. This will produce a simulated sectoral structure, which will in turn affect nonfarm incomes as well as farm incomes given that we allow for individual choice in secondary occupation. We obtain the counterfactual income distribution as follows:

$$\log(y_h)_{\Theta 1}^{s\to t} = f\Big(NF\big(\hat{\Omega}_{NF}^{t}, Z_{hi}^{t}, H_{hi}^{S}\big(\widehat{\Theta 1_{hi}^{S}}\big), \hat{\varepsilon}_{hi}^{t}\big), O\big(\hat{\Psi}^{S}, Z_{hi}^{t}, X2_{hi}^{t}, \hat{v}_{hi}^{t}\big), \\ F\big(\hat{\Omega}_{F}^{t}, W_{h}^{t}, H_{h}^{S}\big(\widehat{\Theta 1_{h}^{s}}\big), \hat{\varepsilon}_{h}^{t}\big), y_{h}^{NL} \mid^{t}\Big), \quad (5.12)$$

which can be transformed to a new distribution of consumption using equation (5.6) above, as before, thus generating a new poverty rate that can be compared with the actual.

To account for changes in poverty due to changes in education, the process is slightly more complicated because education affects both occupational structure and earnings. As a result, we substitute the parameters for the educational choice equation estimated in time s, $\widehat{\theta 2}_{hi}^{s}$, with those estimated for time t, $\widehat{\theta 2}_{hi}^{t}$, in the H function. As before, to allow for individuals to change educational levels in the simulation, the residual terms in the educational multinomial logit model are taken from an extreme value distribution, as described in annex 5A. Because education affects the choice of activity, the composition of activity across the distribution needs to be simulated. The resulting new distribution of activities is then introduced into the earnings functions, along with the new educational structure, and we obtain the following income counterfactual distribution:

$$\log(y_h)_{\Theta 2}^{s\to t} = f\Big(NF\big(\hat{\Omega}_{NF}^{t}, Z_{hi}^{t}, H_{hi}^{S}\big(\widehat{\Theta 2_{hi}^{S}}\big), \hat{\varepsilon}_{hi}^{t}\big), O\big(\hat{\Psi}^{S}, Z_{hi}^{t}, X2_{hi}^{S}, \big(\widehat{\Theta 2_{hi}^{S}}\big)\hat{v}_{hi}^{t}\big), \\ F\big(\hat{\Omega}_{F}^{t}, W_{h}^{t}, H_{h}^{t}\big(\widehat{\Theta 2_{h}^{s}}\big), \hat{\varepsilon}_{h}^{t}\big), y_{h}^{NL} \mid^{t}\Big). \quad (5.13)$$

This counterfactual distribution can then be transformed to a new distribution of consumption using equation (5.6), as before, and compared with the actual distribution in equation (5.9). The contribution of the change in educational structure to the change in poverty between s and t can be estimated by the difference between poverty indices of the actual (equation [5.9]) and counterfactual (equation [5.13]) distribution: $\Delta P_{\Theta 2}^{s\to t} = P\{y_h^t\}_h - P\{(y_h)_{\Theta 2}^{s\to t}\}_h$.

The difference between the distributions generated by the series of changes in demographics, educational structure, sector choices, and activity choices is comparable to the *endowment effect* in the standard Oaxaca (1973) and Blinder (1973) decomposition. This difference is that, in each case, a new counterfactual distribution is generated, and as a result we can look at the contributions to any distributional summary statistic, including changes in poverty.

Changes in Poverty due to Changes in Returns to Endowments

Poverty rates may have changed not only because of changes in endowments but also because changing market conditions may have changed the *returns* to existing endowments. For instance, higher educational attainment would likely increase incomes and therefore reduce poverty. However, if the *supply* of educated workers outpaces the *demand* for such workers, the premium for having higher educational levels would fall, and thus the returns to higher education likely would also fall. This idea is often associated with Tinbergen's (1975) "race" between technological progress (which he saw as raising the demand for skills) and the expansion of formal education, which raises the supply of skills (Ferreira 2012).

To ascertain the extent to which changes in the *returns* to endowments contributed to poverty reduction, we simulate the counterfactual household income distribution by substituting the estimated returns to individual and household characteristics ($\hat{\Omega}$) computed for period s into the earnings of every household at time t, holding everything else constant:

$$\log\left(y_h\right)_{\Omega}^{s\to t} = f\Big(NF\Big(\widehat{\Omega}_{NF}^{S}, Z_{hi}^{t}, H_{hi}^{t}, \hat{\varepsilon}_{hi}^{t}\Big), O\Big(\widehat{\Psi}^{t}, Z_{hi}^{t}, X2_{hi}^{t}, \hat{\upsilon}_{hi}^{t}\Big),$$
$$F\Big(\widehat{\Omega}_{F}^{S}, W_{h}^{t}, H_{h}^{t}, \hat{\varepsilon}_{h}^{t}\Big), y_h^{NL} \,|^{t}\Big). \quad (5.14)$$

This simulation yields the earnings of each household in the sample if the returns to each observed characteristic had been those observed at time s rather than the actual returns observed at time t, keeping everything else constant.[5] The contribution to the overall change in the distribution assigned to a change in returns ($\Omega^{s\to t}$) between periods s and t can be obtained by comparing equation (5.9) with equation (5.14). Therefore, the effect of a change in endowment *returns* on a change in poverty is $\Delta P_{\Omega}^{s\to t} = P\left\{y_h^t\right\}_h - P\left\{(y_h)_{\Omega}^{s\to t}\right\}_h$.

The difference between this simulated distribution of household incomes, $\left\{y_i\right\}_{\Omega}^{s\to t}$, and the actual distribution is equivalent to the *price effect* in the standard Oaxaca (1973) and Blinder (1973) decomposition.

Changes in Poverty due to Unobservable Factors

Note that, up to this point, we have accounted for changes in the distribution due to observable factors. However, it is likely that factors that are unobservable at the household and individual levels nevertheless affect the distribution of consumption and therefore affect changes in poverty. Although we cannot completely capture these effects, we can simulate the effect of changes in the residuals in the earnings equations.[6] To do so, we rescale the estimated residuals of the earning and net revenue equations for nonfarm and farm workers of time t by the ratio of their standard deviations. This counterfactual is defined as follows:

$$\log(y_h)_{\varepsilon}^{s\to t} = f\left(NF\left(\widehat{\Omega}_{NF}^{t}, Z_{hi}^{t}, H_{hi}^{t}, \hat{\varepsilon}_{hi}^{t}\left(\frac{\hat{\sigma}_{\varepsilon}^{S}}{\hat{\sigma}_{\varepsilon}^{t}}\right)\right), O\left(\widehat{\Psi}^{t}, Z_{hi}^{t}, X2_{hi}^{t}, \hat{\upsilon}_{hi}^{t}\right),\right.$$
$$\left. F\left(\widehat{\Omega}_{F}^{t}, W_{h}^{t}, H_{h}^{t}, \hat{\varepsilon}_{h}^{t}\left(\frac{\hat{\sigma}_{\varepsilon}^{S}}{\hat{\sigma}_{\varepsilon}^{t}}\right)\right), y_h^{NL}\mid^{t}\right). \tag{5.15}$$

The contribution to a change in poverty from a change in unobservable factors ($\varepsilon^{s\to t}$) can be obtained by calculating the poverty rate for the counterfactual distribution generated by equation (5.15) with the original poverty rate at time t as follows: $\Delta P_{\varepsilon}^{s\to t} = P\left\{y_h^t\right\}_h - P\left\{(y_h)_{\varepsilon}^{s\to t}\right\}_h$.

Changes in Poverty as a Result of Changes in Nonlabor Income

To account for changes in nonlabor income, the nonparametric technique first described in chapter 2 can be used. To do so, cells of household heads with the same educational level, gender, and area (urban or rural) must be created. Then, quantiles of nonlabor income must be created for each cell.

The counterfactual distribution of nonlabor income in year t is estimated by assigning the mean value of nonlabor income of quantile q in cell c in year s, to the same quantile and cell in year t. In other words, we rank the two distributions by per capita household nonlabor income, and if q is the rank of a household with income y_h^{NL} at time t, we replace it with the nonlabor income of the household with the same rank at time s. This counterfactual distribution can be expressed formally as follows:

$$\log(y_h)_{y_h^{NL}}^{s\to t} = f\left(NF\left(\widehat{\Omega}_{NF}^{t}, Z_{hi}^{S}, H_{hi}^{t}, \hat{\varepsilon}_{hi}^{t}\right) O\left(\widehat{\Psi}^{t}, Z_{hi}^{S}, X2_{hi}^{S}, \hat{\upsilon}_{hi}^{t}\right),\right.$$
$$\left. F\left(\widehat{\Omega}_{F}^{t}, W_{h}^{S}, H_{h}^{t}, \hat{\varepsilon}_{h}^{t}\right), y_h^{NL}\mid_{q}^{S}\right). \tag{5.16}$$

As before, we can compare with the actual distribution described in equation (5.9), calculate poverty indices, and obtain the contribution of nonlabor income to poverty change between years s and t as follows: $\Delta P_{y_h^{NL}}^{s\to t} = P\left\{y_h^t\right\}_h - P\left\{(y_h)_{y_h^{NL}}^{s\to t}\right\}_h$.

Changes in Poverty as a Result of Changes in Consumption-Income Ratio

Finally, it is important to note that each of the counterfactual distributions simulated so far assumes that the consumption-to-income ratio in period t remains constant. However, in practice, this ratio could change either because of changes in households' savings rates or changes in measurement error.

To account for changes in the consumption-income ratio, the nonparametric technique described above can be used. In particular, cells of household heads with the same level of education, gender, and area (urban or rural) must be created. Then, quantiles of consumption must be created for each cell. The counterfactual distribution of the consumption-to-income ratio in year t is estimated by assigning the mean value of this ratio for quantile q in cell c in year s to the same quantile and cell in year t. In other words, we rank the two distributions by consumption, and if q is the rank of a household with consumption-to-income ratio ϑ_h^t at time t, we replace it with the consumption-to-income ratio of the household with the same rank at time s. Equation (5.6) then becomes

$$C_h^{s\to t} = \frac{\vartheta_h^s}{n}\left[y_h^t\right], \tag{5.17}$$

which creates a counterfactual distribution from which a new poverty rate can be calculated and compared with the poverty rate obtained in period t.

The Cumulative Decomposition Technique

All of the decompositions described above can be done on their own, holding everything else constant. We refer to the results from that analysis as the marginal effects. However, as mentioned before, all of these changes are likely to occur over the course of a decade. Moreover, the effects of interaction between these elements could be important in accounting for the changes in poverty. For instance, changes in the educational composition could reinforce changes in the sectoral composition of employment. Therefore, it is important to take these potential interactions into account.

The cumulative decomposition technique allows us to account for these interactions by calculating each effect successively and cumulating them into a set of counterfactuals that contain the cumulative effects of multiple changes. We attribute all of the additional contribution to poverty change to each specific factor successively being added.

As described in chapters 2 and 3, it is important to note that the magnitude of the contribution will depend on the path chosen for the decomposition. However, the large number of factors involved in calculating Shapley values (from s to t and vice versa) is beyond the scope of this chapter. Instead, we use theory to better inform the path to be adopted. In particular, we follow Bourguignon, Ferreira, and Leite (2008) by first calculating the effects of changes in the characteristics of the population—beginning with the most exogenous variables (such as age, gender, region, and area) and following with changes in the population's sectoral, educational, and activity structure. With these results, we then calculate the changes in farm and nonfarm earnings resulting from changes in the returns to these characteristics, the changes in nonlabor incomes, and the changes in the consumption-to-income ratio.[7]

Final Remarks

This chapter has presented a methodology to account for the finding in chapter 3 that total labor income increased across countries where poverty declined substantially over the past decade. As chapter 4 then described in detail, there are both statistical and structural approaches to account for the contribution of endowment and price effects in explaining distributional changes. In contrast to statistical methods, structural methods aim to account for the factors underpinning observed changes in poverty outcomes by specifying an economic model while also incorporating statistical analysis. In particular, these structural models take into account the behavior of agents in response to changes in their socioeconomic environments.

The approach proposed in this chapter rests on the typical economic assumption that agents seek to maximize their utility subject to constraints. In particular, throughout this chapter, we consider the Roy (1951) model of choice and consequences, which stems from the optimization principle and applies to discrete choice problems. We use it to model individuals' educational levels, sectoral (industry) choices, and activity choices or occupational statuses.

These models are set up sequentially, so that changes in education affect sectoral and activity choice. All of these, in turn, affect earnings, which are modeled separately for nonfarm individuals (in the form of standard Mincer equations) and as net revenue functions for farm households. This setup allows us to distinguish between distributional changes resulting from changes in endowments and those resulting from returns to those endowments (following Bourguignon, Ferreira, and Leite [2008]).

Once all of these models are estimated for individuals and households in each time period, the estimated coefficients from one year can be replaced with the estimates from another year to simulate the impact of changes in each element at a time. The resulting series of counterfactual income distributions can then be used to estimate a counterfactual poverty measure for comparison with the observed outcome while holding everything else constant. By changing one element at a time, these decompositions allow us to account for the observed changes in poverty. In addition, we present a method to estimate these counterfactuals cumulatively, thereby accounting for the impact of concurrent changes.

The method presented here makes some important innovations relative to previous work. First, it models farm income at the household level and models the earnings of individuals in those farm households who have secondary occupations, thus recognizing both that farm households typically make labor decisions as a unit and that these households can be highly diversified. Second, it measures welfare using a consumption aggregate, thus accounting for the contribution of changes in the consumption-to-income ratio. Finally, it ensures that changes in the composition of the work force's activity, sectoral, and educational choices are consistent with the counterfactual choices.

The next chapter concludes the volume by applying the methodology presented in this chapter to three countries that reduced poverty drastically between 2000 and 2010: Bangladesh, Peru, and Thailand.

Annex 5A: Estimating the Residual Term in Multinomial Logit

The allocation of individuals across activities is represented through a multinomial logit model. To calculate the utility of activity s and therefore allow for people to change activities in the simulation exercise when either Z_{hi} or ψ^s changes, we must estimate the residual terms of the choice model (v_i^s), which are unobserved.

The residual terms must be drawn from extreme value distributions in a way that is consistent with the observed choices. Train and Wilson (2008) define the distribution functions of the extreme value errors conditional on the chosen alternative. In particular, assume that the alternative zero is chosen ($j = 0$), and denote $Z_{hi}\widehat{\Psi}^j = V_{hi}^j$ for $j = 0,\ldots,J$. Define $\widehat{V}_{hi}^{0j} = V_{hi}^0 - V_{hi}^j$ and $D_{hi}^0 = \sum_{j=0}^{J} \exp\left(-\widehat{V}_{hi}^{0j}\right)$, where $P_{hi}^0 = 1/D_{hi}^0$ is the logit choice probability. Then the cumulative distribution function (cdf) for the alternative chosen v_{hi}^0 is

$$F\left(v_{hi}^0 \mid \text{alternative 0 is chosen}\right) = \exp(-D_{hi}^0 \exp\left(V_{hi}^0\right). \tag{5A.1}$$

Calculating the inverse of this distribution, we have

$$\hat{v}_{hi}^0 = \ln\left(D_{hi}^0\right) - \ln\left(-\ln(\mu)\right), \tag{5A.2}$$

where μ is drawn from a uniform distribution between zero and one. Error terms for other alternatives v_{hi}^j with $j \neq 0$ must be calculated conditioned on the error terms of the alternative chosen ($\hat{v}_{hi}^{0j}$). The distribution for these errors is

$$F\left(v_{hi}^j \mid \text{alternative 0 is chosen, } j \geq 1\right) = \frac{\exp\left(-\exp\left(v_{hi}^j\right)\right)}{\exp\left(-\exp\left(-\left(\widehat{V}_{hi}^{0j} + \hat{v}_{hi}^0\right)\right)\right)} \tag{5A.3}$$

for $v_{hi}^j < \left(\widehat{V}_{hi}^{0j} + v_{hi}^0\right)$. The inverse of this distribution is

$$\hat{v}_{hi}^j = -\ln\left(-\ln\left(m\left(\hat{v}_{hi}^0\right)\mu\right)\right), \tag{5A.4}$$

where $m\left(\hat{v}_{hi}^0\right) = \exp\left(-\exp\left(-\left(\widehat{V}_{hi}^{0j} + \hat{v}_{hi}^0\right)\right)\right)$, and μ is drawn from a uniform distribution between zero and one. We repeat this same method when an alternative other than zero is chosen. A similar approach is taken for the sectoral and educational choice models.

Annex 5B: The Cumulative Decomposition Technique

The cumulative decomposition technique allows us to account for these interactions by calculating each effect successively and cumulating them into a set of counterfactuals that contain multiple changes. We attribute all of the additional contribution to poverty change to each specific factor being added. However, the magnitude of that contribution will depend on the path chosen for the decomposition. We follow the path suggested by Bourguignon, Ferreira, and Leite (2008)—creating a cumulative counterfactual distribution from which poverty headcount rates can be calculated at every point in the adopted path and compared with the actual poverty rates to estimate the contribution of each additional change on the observed change in poverty.

We begin by calculating the effects of changes in the characteristics of the population, beginning with what we consider to be the most exogenous variables, including age, gender, region, and area (Z^s_{hi}, W^s_h). Specifically, first we reweigh the demographic characteristics of year t in such a way that their structure replicates the demographic characteristics of year s as follows:

$$\begin{aligned}\Delta P^{s\rightarrow t} = {} & P\Big\{f\Big(NF\big(\widehat{\Omega}^t_{NF}, Z^t_{hi}, H^t_{hi}, \hat{\varepsilon}^t_{hi}\big), O\big(\widehat{\Psi}^t, Z^t_{hi}, H^t_{hi}, \hat{\upsilon}^t_{hi}\big), \\ & F\big(\widehat{\Omega}^t_F, W^t_h, H^t_h, \hat{\varepsilon}^t_h\big), y^{NL}_h |^t_q\Big)\Big\}_h \\ & - P\Big\{f\Big(NF\big(\widehat{\Omega}^t_{NF}, Z^s_{hi}, H^t_{hi}, \hat{\varepsilon}^t_{hi}\big), O\big(\widehat{\Psi}^t, Z^s_{hi}, H^t_{hi}, \hat{\upsilon}^t_{hi}\big), \\ & F\big(\widehat{\Omega}^t_F, W^s_h, H^t_h, \hat{\varepsilon}^t_h\big), y^{NL}_h |^t_q\Big\}_h.\end{aligned} \tag{5B.1}$$

Second, keeping the demographic effects, we add the education structure change ($\widehat{\Theta 2}^s_{hi}$):

$$\begin{aligned} = {} & P\Big\{f\Big(NF\big(\widehat{\Omega}^t_{NF}, Z^s_{hi}, H^t_{hi}, \hat{\varepsilon}^t_{hi}\big), O\big(\widehat{\Psi}^t, Z^s_{hi}, H^t_{hi}, \hat{\upsilon}^t_{hi}\big), \\ & F\big(\widehat{\Omega}^t_F, W^s_h, H^t_h, \hat{\varepsilon}^t_h\big), y^{NL}_h |^t_q\Big)\Big\}_h \\ & - P\Big\{f\Big(NF\big(\widehat{\Omega}^t_{NF}, Z^s_{hi}, H^s_{hi}\big(\widehat{\Theta 1}^t_{hi}, \widehat{\Theta 2}^s_{hi}\big), \hat{\varepsilon}^t_{hi}\big), O\big(\widehat{\Psi}^t, Z^s_{hi}, H^s_{hi}, \widehat{\Theta 2}^s_{hi} \hat{\upsilon}^t_{hi}\big), \\ & F\big(\widehat{\Omega}^t_F, W^s_h, H^s_h\big(\widehat{\Theta 1}^t_{hi}, \widehat{\Theta 2}^s_{hi}\big), \hat{\varepsilon}^t_{hi}\big), y^{NL}_h |^t_q\Big)\Big\}_h.\end{aligned} \tag{5B.2}$$

Third, preserving the previous changes, we include the change in occupation structure ($\widehat{\Psi}^s$):

$$\begin{aligned} = {} & P\Big\{f\Big(NF\big(\widehat{\Omega}^t_{NF}, Z^s_{hi}, H^s_{hi}\big(\widehat{\Theta 1}^t_{hi}, \widehat{\Theta 2}^s_{hi}\big), \hat{\varepsilon}^t_{hi}\big), O\big(\widehat{\Psi}^t, Z^s_{hi}, H^s_{hi}\big(\widehat{\Theta 2}^s_{hi}\big), \hat{\upsilon}^t_{hi}\big), \\ & F\big(\widehat{\Omega}^t_F, W^s_h, H^s_h\big(\widehat{\Theta 1}^t_{hi}, \widehat{\Theta 2}^s_{hi}\big), \hat{\varepsilon}^t_h\big), y^{NL}_h |^t_q\Big)\Big\}_h \\ & - P\Big\{f\Big(NF\big(\widehat{\Omega}^t_{NF}, Z^s_{hi}, H^s_{hi}\big(\widehat{\Theta 1}^t_{hi}, \widehat{\Theta 2}^s_{hi}\big), \hat{\varepsilon}^t_{hi}\big), O\big(\widehat{\Psi}^s, Z^s_{hi}, H^s_{hi}, \big(\widehat{\Theta 2}^s_{hi}\big), \hat{\upsilon}^t_{hi}\big), \\ & F\big(\widehat{\Omega}^t_F, W^s_h, H^s_h\big(\widehat{\Theta 1}^t_{hi}, \widehat{\Theta 2}^s_{hi}\big), \hat{\varepsilon}^t_h\big), y^{NL}_h |^t_q\Big)\Big\}_h.\end{aligned} \tag{5B.3}$$

Fourth, we add the change in the structure of economic sectors $(\widehat{\Theta 1}^{s}_{hi})$:

$$
\begin{aligned}
&= P\Big\{ f\Big(NF\big(\hat{\Omega}^{t}_{NF}, Z^{s}_{hi}, H^{s}_{hi}\big(\widehat{\Theta 1}^{t}_{hi}, \widehat{\Theta 2}^{s}_{hi}\big), \hat{\varepsilon}^{t}_{hi}\big), O\big(\hat{\Psi}^{s}, Z^{s}_{hi}, H^{s}_{hi}\big(\widehat{\Theta 2}^{s}_{hi}\big), \hat{\upsilon}^{t}_{hi}\big),\\
&\quad F\big(\hat{\Omega}^{t}_{F}, W^{s}_{h}, H^{s}_{h}\big(\widehat{\Theta 1}^{t}_{hi}, \widehat{\Theta 2}^{s}_{hi}\big)\hat{\varepsilon}^{t}_{h}\big), y^{NL}_{h} \big|^{t}_{q} \Big) \Big\}_{h}\\
&- P\Big\{ f\Big(NF\big(\hat{\Omega}^{t}_{NF}, Z^{s}_{hi}, H^{s}_{hi}\big(\widehat{\Theta 1}^{s}_{hi}, \widehat{\Theta 2}^{s}_{hi}\big), \hat{\varepsilon}^{t}_{hi}\big), O\big(\hat{\Psi}^{s}, Z^{s}_{hi}, H^{s}_{hi}\big(\widehat{\Theta 2}^{s}_{hi}\big), \hat{\upsilon}^{t}_{hi}\big)\Big),\\
&\quad F\big(\hat{\Omega}^{t}_{F}, W^{s}_{h}, H^{s}_{h}\big(\widehat{\Theta 1}^{s}_{hi}, \widehat{\Theta 2}^{s}_{hi}\big)\hat{\varepsilon}^{t}_{h}\big), y^{NL}_{h} \big|^{t}_{q} \Big) \Big\}_{h}.
\end{aligned}
\tag{5B.4}
$$

Fifth, we include the returns to the nonfarm sector $(\hat{\Omega}^{s}_{NF})$:

$$
\begin{aligned}
&= P\Big\{ f\Big(NF\big(\hat{\Omega}^{t}_{NF}, Z^{s}_{hi}, H^{s}_{hi}\big(\hat{\Theta}^{s}_{hi}\big), \hat{\varepsilon}^{t}_{hi}\big), O\big(\hat{\Psi}^{s}, Z^{s}_{hi}, H^{s}_{hi}\big(\widehat{\Theta 2}^{s}_{hi}\big), \hat{\upsilon}^{t}_{hi}\big)\\
&\quad F\big(\hat{\Omega}^{t}_{F}, W^{s}_{h}, H^{s}_{h}\big(\hat{\Theta}^{s}_{hi}\big), \hat{\varepsilon}^{t}_{h}\big), y^{NL}_{h} \big|^{t}_{q} \Big) \Big\}_{h}\\
&- P\Big\{ f\Big(NF\big(\hat{\Omega}^{s}_{NF}, Z^{s}_{hi}, H^{s}_{hi}\big(\hat{\Theta}^{s}_{hi}\big), \hat{\varepsilon}^{t}_{hi}\big), O\big(\hat{\Psi}^{s}, Z^{s}_{hi}, H^{s}_{hi}\big(\widehat{\Theta 2}^{s}_{hi}\big), \hat{\upsilon}^{t}_{hi}\big),\\
&\quad F\big(\hat{\Omega}^{t}_{F}, W^{s}_{h}, H^{s}_{h}\big(\hat{\Theta}^{s}_{hi}\big), \hat{\varepsilon}^{t}_{h}\big), y^{NL}_{h} \big|^{t}_{q} \Big) \Big\}_{h}.
\end{aligned}
\tag{5B.5}
$$

Sixth, we change the returns to the farm sector $(\hat{\Omega}^{s}_{F})$:

$$
\begin{aligned}
&= P\Big\{ f\Big(NF\big(\hat{\Omega}^{s}_{NF}, Z^{s}_{hi}, H^{s}_{hi}\big(\hat{\Theta}^{s}_{hi}\big), \hat{\varepsilon}^{t}_{hi}\big), O\big(\hat{\Psi}^{s}, Z^{s}_{hi}, H^{s}_{hi}\big(\widehat{\Theta 2}^{s}_{hi}\big), \hat{\upsilon}^{t}_{hi}\big),\\
&\quad F\big(\hat{\Omega}^{t}_{F}, W^{s}_{h}, H^{s}_{h}\big(\hat{\Theta}^{s}_{hi}\big), \hat{\varepsilon}^{t}_{h}\big), y^{NL}_{h} \big|^{t}_{q} \Big) \Big\}_{h}\\
&- P\Big\{ f\Big(NF\big(\hat{\Omega}^{s}_{NF}, Z^{s}_{hi}, H^{s}_{hi}\big(\hat{\Theta}^{s}_{hi}\big), \hat{\varepsilon}^{t}_{hi}\big), O\big(\hat{\Psi}^{s}, Z^{s}_{hi}, H^{s}_{hi}\big(\widehat{\Theta 2}^{s}_{hi}\big), \hat{\upsilon}^{t}_{hi}\big),\\
&\quad F\big(\hat{\Omega}^{s}_{F}, W^{s}_{h}, H^{s}_{h}\big(\hat{\Theta}^{s}_{hi}\big), \hat{\varepsilon}^{t}_{h}\big), y^{NL}_{h} \big|^{t}_{q} \Big) \Big\}_{h}.
\end{aligned}
\tag{5B.6}
$$

Seventh, we change residuals of both earnings and net revenues equations:

$$= P\Big\{ f\Big(NF\big(\hat{\Omega}_{NF}^{s}, Z_{hi}^{s}, H_{hi}^{s}\big(\hat{\Theta}_{hi}^{s}\big), \hat{\varepsilon}_{hi}^{t}\big), O\big(\hat{\Psi}^{s}, Z_{hi}^{s}, H_{hi}^{s}\big(\widehat{\Theta 2}_{hi}^{s}\big), \hat{\upsilon}_{hi}^{t}\big),$$

$$F\big(\hat{\Omega}_{F}^{s}, W_{h}^{s}, H_{h}^{s}\big(\hat{\Theta}_{hi}^{s}\big), \hat{\varepsilon}_{h}^{t}\big), y_{h}^{NL}\big|_{q}^{t} \Big)\Big\}_{h}$$

$$- P\left\{ f\left(NF\left(\hat{\Omega}_{NF}^{s}, Z_{hi}^{s}, H_{hi}^{s}\big(\hat{\Theta}_{hi}^{s}\big), \hat{\varepsilon}_{hi}^{t}\left(\frac{\hat{\sigma}_{\varepsilon}^{s}}{\hat{\sigma}_{\varepsilon}^{t}}\right)\right), O\big(\hat{\Psi}^{s}, Z_{hi}^{s}, H_{hi}^{s}\big(\widehat{\Theta 2}_{hi}^{s}\big), \hat{\upsilon}_{hi}^{t}\big), \right. \right. \tag{5B.7}$$

$$\left.\left. F\left(\hat{\Omega}_{F}^{s}, W_{h}^{s}, H_{h}^{s}\big(\hat{\Theta}_{hi}^{s}\big), \hat{\varepsilon}_{h}^{t}\left(\frac{\hat{\sigma}_{\varepsilon}^{s}}{\hat{\sigma}_{\varepsilon}^{t}}\right)\right), y_{h}^{NL}\big|_{q}^{t} \right)\right\}_{h}.$$

Eighth, we add the change in nonlabor income components and the consumption ratio. The latter is not formally displayed in this example:

$$= P\left\{ f\left(NF\left(\hat{\Omega}_{NF}^{s}, Z_{hi}^{s}, H_{hi}^{s}\left(\hat{\Theta}_{hi}^{s}\right), \hat{\varepsilon}_{hi}^{t}\left(\frac{\hat{\sigma}_{\varepsilon}^{s}}{\hat{\sigma}_{\varepsilon}^{t}}\right)\right), O\left(\hat{\psi}^{s}, Z_{hi}^{s}, H_{hi}^{s}\left(\widehat{\Theta 2}_{hi}^{s}\right), \hat{v}_{hi}^{t}\right), \right.\right.$$

$$\left.\left. F\left(\hat{\Omega}_{F}^{s}, W_{h}^{s}, H_{hi}^{s}\left(\hat{\Theta}_{hi}^{s}\right), \hat{\varepsilon}_{h}^{t}\left(\frac{\hat{\sigma}_{\varepsilon}^{s}}{\hat{\sigma}_{\varepsilon}^{t}}\right)\right), y_{h}^{NL}\big|_{q}^{t} \right)\right\}_{h} \tag{5B.8}$$

$$- P\left\{ f\left(NF\left(\hat{\Omega}_{NF}^{s}, Z_{hi}^{s}, H_{hi}^{s}\left(\hat{\Theta}_{hi}^{s}\right), \hat{\varepsilon}_{hi}^{t}\left(\frac{\hat{\sigma}_{\varepsilon}^{s}}{\hat{\sigma}_{\varepsilon}^{t}}\right)\right), O\left(\hat{\psi}^{s}, Z_{hi}^{s}, H_{hi}^{s}\left(\widehat{\Theta 2}_{hi}^{s}\right), \hat{v}_{hi}^{t}\right), \right.\right.$$

$$\left.\left. F\left(\hat{\Omega}_{F}^{s}, W_{h}^{s}, H_{hi}^{s}\left(\hat{\Theta}_{hi}^{s}\right), \hat{\varepsilon}_{h}^{t}\left(\frac{\hat{\sigma}_{\varepsilon}^{s}}{\hat{\sigma}_{\varepsilon}^{t}}\right)\right), y_{h}^{NL}\big|_{q}^{s} \right)\right\}_{h}.$$

Finally, we take into account changes in the consumption-to-income ratio as described in the main text. The cumulative counterfactual change in poverty and the observed change in poverty are compared. Any change that is not accounted for is described as a residual change.

As before, the cumulative decomposition technique is performed both considering s as the initial year and then considering t as the initial year. The average of these decomposition effects is the final result reported in the analysis.

Notes

1. By "activity choice," we refer to the individual's occupational status, which may include paid employment, self-employment, unpaid labor, or unemployment.
2. Note that earnings may be underestimated to the extent that individuals opt out of the labor force because their reservation wage is lower than their market wage (Heckman 1979). Although this is a well-known bias, we do not attempt to correct for it given the complexity of the decompositions that follow.
3. Bear in mind that this approach does not solve all path-dependence problems. Shapley values must be estimated to tackle this difficulty.
4. The notation $s \rightarrow t$ refers to using the parameters estimated in period s in the equation for time t.
5. The returns to the unobserved characteristics behind the residual term $\hat{\varepsilon}^t$ are assumed to be unchanged.
6. The estimated error terms for the multinomial logit models are not rescaled.
7. For a full description of the cumulative approach, please refer to annex 5B.

Bibliography

Blinder, Alan S. 1973. "Wage Discrimination: Reduced Form and Structural Estimates." *Journal of Human Resources* 8 (4): 436–55.

Bourguignon, François, and Francisco H. G. Ferreira. 2005. "Decomposing Changes in the Distribution of Household Incomes: Methodological Aspects." In *The Microeconomics of Income Distribution Dynamics in East Asia and Latin America*, edited by François Bourguignon, Francisco H. G. Ferreira, and Nora Lustig, 17–46. Washington, DC: World Bank.

Bourguignon, François, Francisco H. G. Ferreira, and Nora Lustig, eds. 2005. *The Microeconomics of Income Distribution Dynamics in East Asia and Latin America.* Washington, DC: World Bank.

Bourguignon, François, Francisco H. G. Ferreira, and Phillippe G. Leite. 2008. "Beyond Oaxaca-Blinder: Accounting for Differences in Household Income Distributions." *Journal of Economic Inequality* 6 (2): 117–48.

Davis, Benjamin, Paul. Winters, Calogero Carletto, Katia Covarrubias, Esteban J. Quiñones, Alberto Zezza, Carlo Azzarri, Kostas Stamoulis, and Stefania DiGiuseppe. 2010. "A Cross-Country Comparison of Rural Income Generating Activities." *World Development* 38 (1): 48–63.

Ferreira, Francisco H. G. 2012. "Distributions in Motion: Economic Growth, Inequality, and Poverty Dynamics." In *The Oxford Handbook of the Economics of Poverty*, edited by Philip N. Jefferson, 427–62. New York: Oxford University Press.

Haggblade, Steven, Peter B. R. Hazell, and Thomas Reardon. 2007. *Transforming the Rural Non-Farm Economy: Opportunities and Threats in the Developing World.* Baltimore, MD: Johns Hopkins University Press.

———. 2010. "The Rural Non-Farm Economy: Prospects for Growth and Poverty Reduction." *World Development* 38 (10): 1429–41.

Heckman, James J. 1979. "Sample Selection Bias as a Specification Error." *Econometrica* 47 (1): 153–61.

McFadden, Daniel. 1974a. "Conditional Logit Analysis of Qualitative Choice Behavior." In *Frontiers in Econometrics*, edited by Paul Zarembka, 105–42. New York: Academic Press.

———. 1974b. "The Measurement of Urban Travel Demand." *Journal of Public Economics* 3 (4): 63–82.

Oaxaca, Ronald L. 1973. "Male-Female Wage Differentials in Urban Labor Markets." *International Economic Review* 14 (3): 693–709.

Roy, Arthur D. 1951. "Some Thoughts on the Distribution of Earnings." *Oxford Economic Papers* 3 (2): 135–46.

Tinbergen, Jan. 1975. *Income Differences: Recent Research*. Amsterdam, the Netherlands: North-Holland.

Train, Kenneth E., and Wesley W. Wilson. 2008. "Estimation on Stated-Preference Experiments Constructed from Revealed-Preference Choices." *Transportation Research Part B: Methodological* 42 (3): 191–203.

CHAPTER 6

Understanding Poverty Reduction in Bangladesh, Peru, and Thailand

Introduction

The decomposition method proposed in chapter 2 and implemented in chapter 3 distinguished labor income growth as the main contributor to poverty reduction. However, the method's main limitation is that it cannot explain *why* labor incomes increased: Did they grow because the populations increased their own human capital endowments (such as higher educational levels or other productive assets) or because of changes in *returns* to those endowments? For this answer, we have turned to an alternative decomposition technique that imposes an underlying labor model and greater structure.

This chapter implements chapter 5's proposed approach: to distinguish between distributional changes on account of (a) changes in endowments and the returns to those endowments; (b) changes in occupational and sectoral choice; (c) changes in the population's geographical, age, and gender structure; and (d) the contribution of the nonlabor income dimensions (such as public transfers, remittances, and other private transfers) previously explored in chapter 3. This microdecomposition approach is adapted from Bourguignon, Ferreira, and Leite (2008).

In focusing on Bangladesh, Peru, and Thailand, the chapter highlights their impressive reductions in poverty while taking advantage of the availability, comparability, and transparency of their microdata. The moderate national poverty headcount rate in each of these countries fell by more than 12 percentage points during the past decade, partly because of high gross domestic product (GDP) growth, which was well above 4 percent per year during the 2002–08 period.[1] In the cases of Peru and Thailand, GDP sharply decelerated in the wake of the financial crisis in 2009, only to rebound quickly the following year. In contrast, GDP growth in Bangladesh got through the crisis unscathed.

In all three countries, employment and public social transfers increased, as did remittances. However, the changing patterns of income distribution varied across countries, as did the roles of different factors in reducing poverty. Moreover, the countries progressed from very different starting points: Bangladesh, despite strong growth, remains a low-income country with a GDP per capita of $1,710. Peru and Thailand are firmly in the middle-income ranks, with GDP per capita of $10,439 and $9,630, respectively (all figures in purchasing power parity terms). In addition, Peru is highly urbanized, as opposed to Bangladesh and Thailand, whose shares of urban population remain below 30 percent.

To understand how these diverse economies each reduced poverty so substantially over a similar period of time, we applied the structural decomposition approach progressively developed in the previous chapters of this volume. Chapter 5 had proposed a method to estimate an educational choice model, a sectoral choice model, a work-activity choice model, and individual and household earnings equations. Once all of these models are estimated for individuals and households in each time period, the estimated coefficients from one year can be replaced with the estimates from another year to simulate the impact of changes in each element at a time.

This process enables us to build a series of counterfactual income distributions to estimate a counterfactual poverty measure for comparison with the observed outcome while holding everything else constant. By changing one element at a time, these decompositions allow us to account for the observed changes in poverty. In addition, we can estimate these counterfactuals cumulatively, thereby accounting for the impact of concurrent changes.

The chapter next describes the evolution of poverty and economic growth in Bangladesh, Peru, and Thailand—highlighting the countries' similarities and differences in their initial- and end-period outcomes. "The Decomposition Approach" then presents the results of the decomposition exercise for each country. The chapter ends the volume by summarizing our findings and laying out the possibilities for further application.

Country Context

For all their differences, Bangladesh, Peru, and Thailand have at least one thing in common: they drastically reduced poverty rates over the past decade (figure 6.1). The share of households living at or below the international poverty line corresponding to $2.50 per day (as shown in table 6.1) fell by an average of 1.8 percentage points per year in Bangladesh (2000–10), 2.7 percentage points per year in Peru (2004–10), and 1.6 percentage points per year in Thailand (2000–09).

To calculate the share of population living below the moderate poverty line, the three countries use the "cost of basic needs" approach, although the "basket" for basic needs and specific lines are different.[2] Moreover, this reduction in poverty coincided with strong GDP growth over the decade, which averaged 5.8 percent in Bangladesh, 6 percent in Peru, and 4.4 percent in Thailand (figure 6.2).

There is considerable evidence that economic growth is strongly and negatively correlated with changes in poverty (Ravallion and Chen 2007). Indeed, in these three countries, using the standard Datt and Ravallion (1992) decomposition, growth does indeed explain most of the observed poverty reduction

Figure 6.1 Change in Moderate Poverty Rates in Bangladesh, Peru, and Thailand, 2000s

Population (%)

Bangladesh 2000–10 | Peru 2004–10 | Thailand 2000–09

■ Initial ■ Final

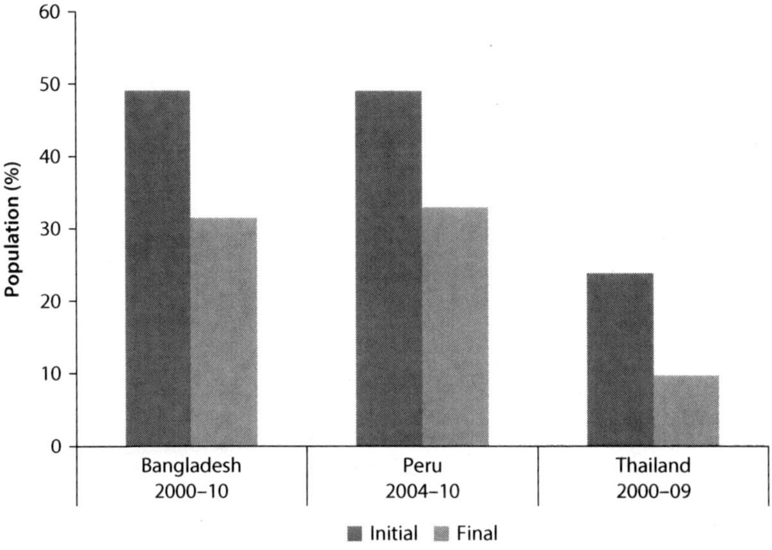

Sources: Household survey results from Bangladesh (HIES 2000–10), Peru (ENAHO 2004–10), and Thailand (SES 2000–09).
Note: "Moderate poverty" headcounts are based on each country's national moderate poverty line. HIES = Household Income and Expenditure Survey (Bangladesh Bureau of Statistics); ENAHO = Encuesta Nacional de Hogares (Peru National Institute of Statistics and Information); SES = Household Socio-Economic Survey (Thailand National Statistical Office).

Table 6.1 Change in Poverty Rates, by Level, in Bangladesh, Peru, and Thailand, 2000s

	Poverty lines				
	$1.25	*$2.50*	*$4.00*	*National extreme*	*National moderate*
Poverty rate in Bangladesh, 2000–10					
Initial period (%)	57.7	89.2	—	34.5	49.1
Final period (%)	40.3	84.0	—	17.6	31.5
Change (ppts)	−17.4	−5.2	—	−16.9	−17.6
Average annual change (ppts)	−1.7	−0.5	—	−1.7	−1.8
Annualized percentage change (%)	−3.5	−0.6	—	−6.5	−4.3
Poverty rate in Peru, 2004–10					
Initial period (%)	3.5	22.9	45.8	17.4	49.1
Final period (%)	0.8	11.7	30.0	10.5	33.0
Change (ppts)	−2.6	−11.2	−15.8	−6.9	−16.2
Average annual change (ppts)	−0.4	−1.9	−2.6	−1.2	−2.7
Annualized percentage change (%)	−21.1	−10.6	−6.8	−8.1	−6.4

table continues next page

Table 6.1 Change in Poverty Rates, by Level, in Bangladesh, Peru, and Thailand, 2000s *(continued)*

	Poverty lines				
	$1.25	*$2.50*	*$4.00*	*National extreme*	*National moderate*
Poverty rate in Thailand, 2000–09					
Initial period (%)	0.2	7.9	31.4	—	23.9
Final period (%)	0.0	2.5	16.6	—	9.8
Change (ppts)	–0.2	–5.3	–14.8	—	–14.1
Average annual change (ppts)	. . .	–0.6	–1.6	—	–1.6
Annualized percentage change (%)	–16.8	–11.8	–6.8	—	–9.4

Sources: Household survey results from Bangladesh (HIES 2000–10), Peru (ENAHO 2004–10), and Thailand (SES 2000–09).
Note: . . . = negligible; — = not available; ppts = percentage points; HIES = Household Income and Expenditure Survey (Bangladesh Bureau of Statistics); ENAHO = Encuesta Nacional de Hogares (Peru National Institute of Statistics and Information). SES = Household Socio-Economic Survey (Thailand National Statistical Office). The $1.25, $2.50, and $4.00 poverty lines are daily household income amounts that correspond to international measurements of varying poverty levels in low- and moderate-income countries. The "National extreme" and "National moderate" poverty levels refer to country-based poverty lines calculated based on the "cost of basic needs," such as specified calorie levels per person per day, and other essentials, such as clothing and shelter.

Figure 6.2 GDP in Bangladesh, Peru, and Thailand, 2000–10

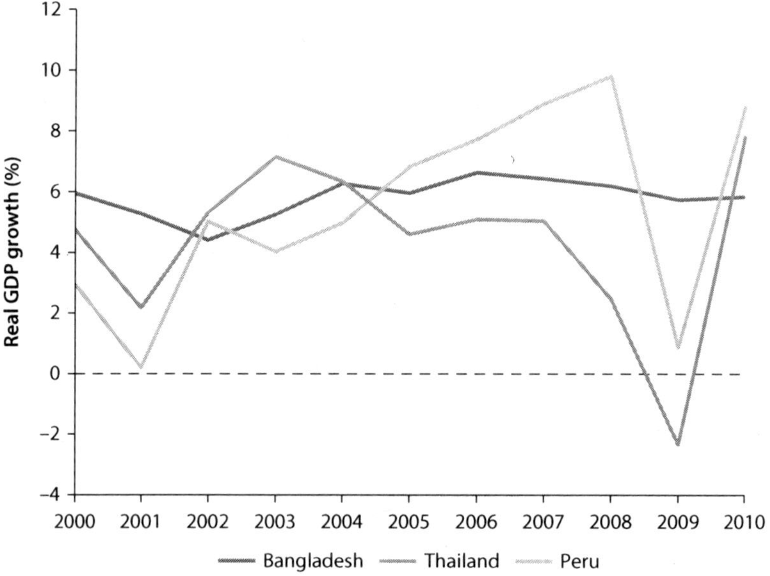

Source: World Bank 2011.
Note: GDP = gross domestic product.

(table 6.2). In each case, more than 80 percent of the reduction in poverty is explained by growth in mean income, whereas better income distribution explains less than 20 percent of the reduction.

Although these estimates of the reduced-form relationships between economic growth, inequality, and poverty have been useful in identifying empirical regularities, they cannot explicitly link *how* growth and poverty reduction are

Table 6.2 Growth and Redistribution Decomposition of Moderate Poverty Rate Changes in Bangladesh, Peru, and Thailand, 2000s
Percent

	Bangladesh 2000 vs. 2010	*Peru 2004 vs. 2010*	*Thailand 2000 vs. 2009*
Poverty headcount rate: FGT(0)[a]			
*t*0	48.9 (1.2)	49.1 (0.2)	23.9 (0.2)
*t*1	31.5 (0.9)	33.0 (0.2)	9.8 (0.1)
Actual percentage change	−17.3 (1.5)	−16.1 (0.3)	−14.1 (0.2)
Change resulting from growth	−15.8 (1.6)	−13.8 (0.4)	−14.2 (0.3)
Change resulting from redistribution	−1.6 (1.5)	−2.4 (0.3)	0.1 (0.3)
Contributions to the decline in FGT(0)			
Growth	91	85	101
Redistribution	9	15	−1
Poverty gap FGT(1)[b]			
*t*0	12.8 (0.5)	16.4 (0.1)	5.5 (0.1)
*t*1	6.5 (0.2)	9.3 (0.1)	1.8 (0.0)
Actual percentage change	−6.2 (0.5)	−7.1 (0.1)	−3.6 (0.1)
Change resulting from growth	−5.6 (0.6)	−5.9 (0.2)	−3.7 (0.1)
Change resulting from redistribution	−0.6 (0.6)	−1.1 (0.2)	0.0 (0.1)
Contributions to the decline in FGT(1)			
Growth	90	84	103
Redistribution	10	16	−3

Sources: Household survey results from Bangladesh (HIES 2000–10), Peru (ENAHO 2004–10), and Thailand (SES 2000–09).
Note: Poverty rates are based on per capita consumption. The Datt and Ravallion (1992) decomposition reported here uses the Shapley (1953) approach described in chapter 2. Standard errors shown in parentheses. *t*0 = the initial year and *t*1 = the last year. HIES = Household Income and Expenditure Survey (Bangladesh Bureau of Statistics); ENAHO = Encuesta Nacional de Hogares (Peru National Institute of Statistics and Information); SES = Household Socio-Economic Survey (Thailand National Statistical Office).
a. FGT(0) = the poverty headcount rate. FGT refers to the Foster, Greer, and Thorbecke (1984) metric, a generalized measure of poverty in an economy.
b. FGT(1) = the poverty gap, which estimates the depth of poverty, defined as the average percentage distance between the incomes of the incomes of the poor and the poverty line (Foster, Greer, and Thorbecke 1984).

related (Ferreira 2010). In particular, we would like to capture the heterogeneity of impacts throughout the distribution and to be able to account for the contributions of demographics, sectoral, occupational, and other labor and nonlabor dimensions toward reducing poverty.

Elements That Could Affect Poverty Reduction

Changes in poverty can be decomposed into those resulting from changes in demographics, changes in labor incomes, changes in nonlabor incomes, and changes in consumption-to-income ratios. Changes in the population's demographics include changes in age, gender, and regional structure. Changes in labor incomes could result from improvements in human capital (such as education) and other endowments (such as greater access to productive assets), all of which would have increased labor productivity. Alternatively, labor incomes could have risen simply because demand for certain characteristics outstripped supply—representing increased *returns* to a population's endowments. In addition, increases in nonlabor incomes could have reduced poverty through higher remittances or public transfers. Finally, households are likely to change the share of income they dedicate to consumption, which affects the very measurements of consumption from which poverty rates are calculated. We look at each of these types of changes in turn.

Demographic Changes

Population growth slowed considerably in each of the countries considered over the past decade (figure 6.3). The change has been significant enough that in Bangladesh and Peru, the youth bulge observed in earlier periods has now reached working age (15–64 years old).[3] As a result, the share of adults per household increased in each case (table 6.3). In other demographic changes, the share of employed women in all three countries increased slightly. Finally, there have been population shifts across regions, with a clear tendency toward greater urbanization in Bangladesh and Thailand.

Changes in Labor Income

Labor income growth is a primary factor to examine regarding the observed poverty reduction. The growth incidence curves in figure 6.4 show that labor income in the 2000s grew across the income distribution in each country.

Figure 6.3 Population Growth in Bangladesh, Peru, and Thailand, 2000–10

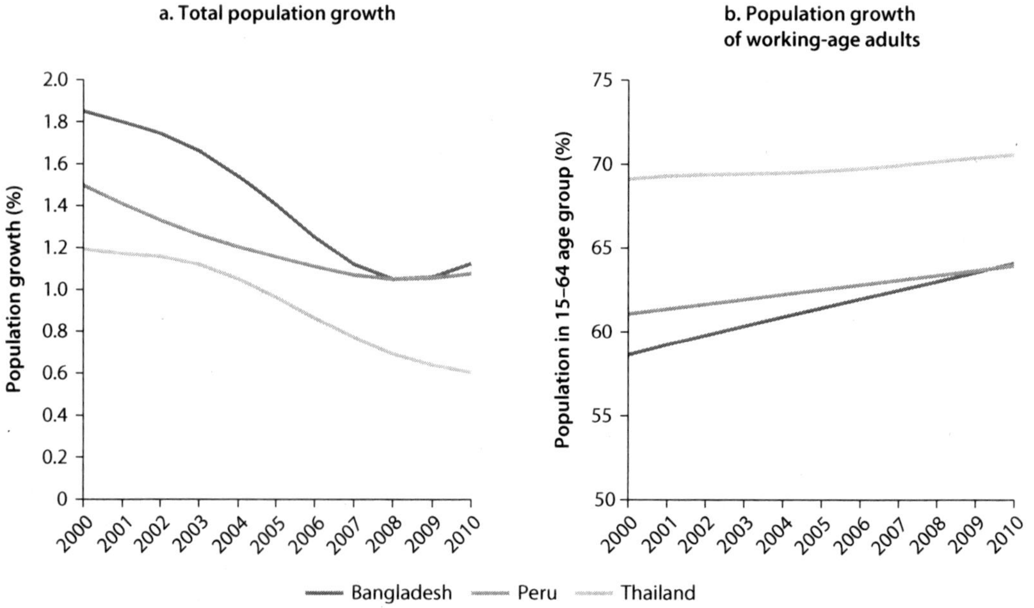

a. Total population growth

b. Population growth of working-age adults

Bangladesh Peru Thailand

Source: World Bank 2011.
Note: "Working-age adults" are defined as those aged 15–64 years.

Table 6.3 Population and Labor Force Characteristics in Bangladesh, Peru, and Thailand, 2000s

	Bangladesh		*Peru*		*Thailand*	
	2000	*2010*	*2004*	*2010*	*2000*	*2009*
Population and demographics						
Total (millions)	71.0	89.8	27.6	31.4	59.8	64.7
Men (%)	50.4	48.4	49.7	49.2	47.8	47.9
Women (%)	49.6	51.6	50.3	50.8	52.2	52.1
Urban (%)	21.8	28.0	64.5	63.5	30.9	31.0
Rural (%)	78.2	72.0	35.5	36.5	69.1	69.0
Average household size (no. of members)	5.2	4.5	4.4	4.2	3.6	3.3
Average adults per household (no.)	3.1	2.9	2.7	2.6	2.5	2.4
Average adults per household (%)	63.4	68.4	68.0	70.7	75.2	78.9
Average occupied adults per household (% of no. of adults)	48.4	50.1	73.2	75.7	77.7	77.4
Labor force participation (% of working-age population)						
All	49.4	49.2	73.5	76.2	80.4	80.5
Men	83.3	84.9	83.1	84.4	87.0	86.7
Women	14.9	15.6	64.1	68.4	74.5	74.9
Employment rate (% of working-age population)						
All	46.6	47.8	71.2	74.9	78.3	79.8
Men	81.6	82.9	80.9	83.4	84.3	85.8
Women	11.1	14.8	61.6	66.8	73.0	74.4
Unemployment rate (% of labor force)						
All	5.6	1.4	5.1	3.8	2.5	0.9
Men	2.0	2.0	4.5	3.3	3.1	1.0
Women	25.9	0.8	5.8	4.4	2.0	0.7
Educational level (% of working-age population)						
Illiterate and incomplete primary	57.2	47.1	19.5	16.4	44.3	34.4
Primary and lower secondary	33.8	43.4	31.6	29.4	32.2	39.0
Higher secondary and tertiary	8.9	9.4	47.4	52.2	23.6	26.7
Labor relationship (% of employed population)						
Daily workers[a]	33.5	32.4	—	—	—	—
Self-employed	46.3	42.3	61.3	57.0	58.8	57.4
Wage workers	20.2	25.4	38.7	43.0	41.2	42.6
Economic sector (% of employed population)						
Agriculture	49.2	41.8	35.9	30.0	49.3	40.6
Manufacturing[a]	18.5	19	—	—	—	—
Industry	4.4	5.5	9.8	10.4	17.3	20.1
Services	27.9	33.7	46.0	50.8	24.6	30.2
Area (% of employed population)						
Rural	78.6	71.6	36.5	34.6	68.9	68.7
Urban	21.4	28.4	63.5	65.4	31.1	31.3

Sources: Household survey results from Bangladesh (HIES 2000–10), Peru (ENAHO 2004–10), and Thailand (SES 2000–09).
Note: "Working-age population" is defined as adults aged 15–64 years. — = not available; HIES = Household Income and Expenditure Survey (Bangladesh Bureau of Statistics); ENAHO = Encuesta Nacional de Hogares (Peru National Institute of Statistics and Information); SES = Household Socio-Economic Survey (Thailand National Statistical Office).
a. The statistics in Peru and Thailand make no distinctions between "daily" and "wage" workers or between the "manufacturing" and "industrial" sectors.

Figure 6.4 Growth Incidence Curves of Labor Income in Bangladesh, Peru, and Thailand, 2000s

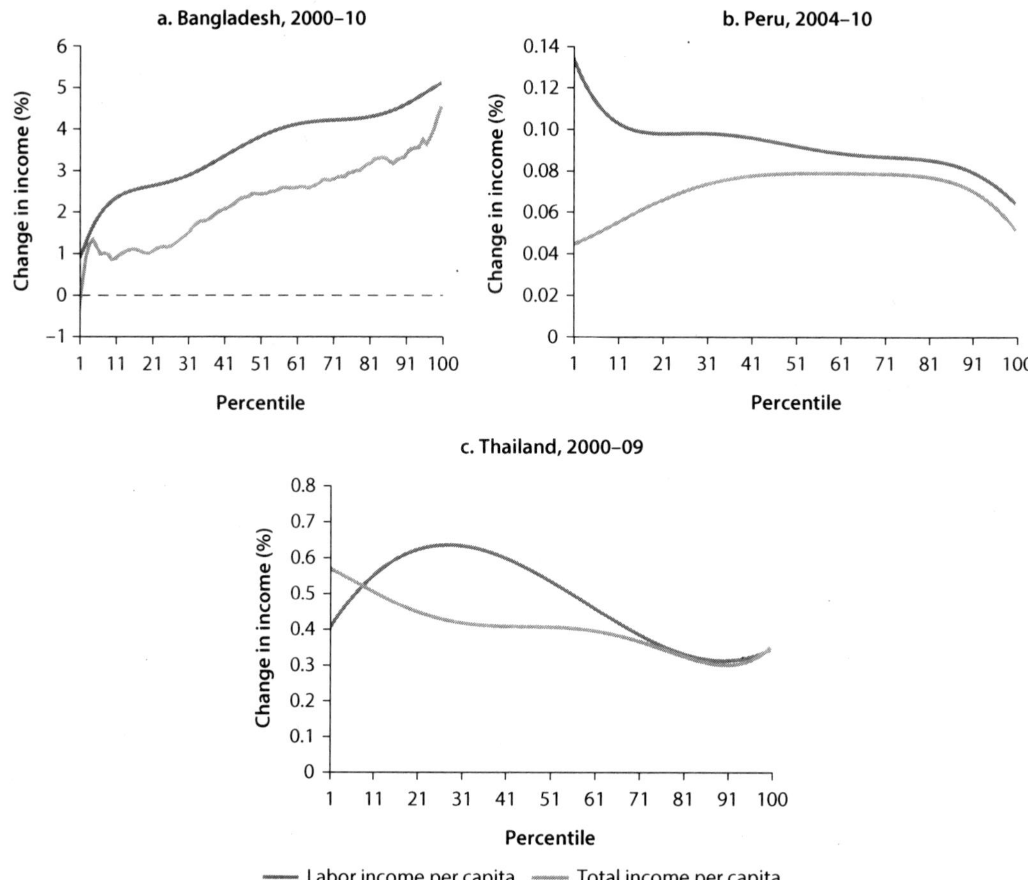

Sources: Household survey results from Bangladesh (HIES 2000–10), Peru (ENAHO 2004–10), and Thailand (SES 2000–09).
Note: The smoothing algorithm is a polynomial regression. The degrees of the polynomial vary by country and were chosen to maximize the fit of the data. "Total income" includes both labor and nonlabor sources of income. HIES = Household Income and Expenditure Survey (Bangladesh Bureau of Statistics); ENAHO = Encuesta Nacional de Hogares (Peru National Institute of Statistics and Information); SES = Household Socio-Economic Survey (Thailand National Statistical Office).

In Bangladesh, labor incomes grew faster for those at the top of the distribution than for those at the bottom, while in Peru the opposite was true. In Thailand, incomes of the poor grew faster than those of the higher deciles (except for those in the poorest decile).

Given the magnitude of the changes, labor income increases likely had an influence in moving people out of poverty. What accounts for these increases? What accounts for the different rates of growth across the distribution?

Labor incomes could have grown for several reasons pertaining to changing labor force characteristics in all three countries:

- *Increased, and better-paying, employment.* In the economically active population, increases in employment, particularly in better-paying jobs, would lead to declines in poverty. Although labor force participation remained relatively stable in Bangladesh and Thailand over the 2000s, employment increased slightly. In Peru, both labor force participation and employment increased, particularly among women.

- *Increases in wage employment.* In addition to higher employment, all three countries saw a clear movement away from self-employed work and toward wage employment. In Bangladesh, there was also a movement away from daily-wage work toward wage work. All of these movements are likely to have led to better-quality employment.
- *Sectoral shifts.* Similarly, employment shifted away from agriculture and toward the manufacturing and services sectors, which tend to be better paying. In Bangladesh, there was also a slight movement toward industry, which is also better paying than agriculture.
- *Educational advancement.* The improved educational composition of the work force over the past 10 years also could have increased labor incomes. In all three countries, a smaller share of the population was illiterate by the end of the decade. In Bangladesh and Thailand, higher shares of the work force had completed primary and lower secondary school; and in Peru and Thailand, higher shares of the population had completed secondary and tertiary school (table 6.3).

Changes in Nonlabor Income

Although labor income has clearly increased, growth in nonlabor income could also be driving the observed reductions in poverty. Indeed, figure 6.5a shows that both public and private transfers steadily increased in Bangladesh, Peru, and Thailand during the 2000s. Although the countries differed widely in terms of the magnitude of public social spending relative to the size of their economies, public spending in each case increased by at least 25 percent during the 2000s.

Whether public transfers are an important means of reducing poverty—and, if so, how important—depends on how effective this spending has been, particularly in terms of targeting the poor. As for private transfers, international remittances have tripled in Bangladesh over the past decade, have grown modestly in Peru, but have declined in Thailand (figure 6.5b). The question is how important have these changes been to poverty reduction?

Changes in Consumption-to-Income Ratio

Finally, in the context of growing overall incomes, households are likely to change the share of income they dedicate to consumption, given different marginal propensities to consume. Figure 6.6 shows that in Bangladesh and Thailand, the consumption-to-income ratio fell over the course of the decade—a large part of which occurred in households below the poverty line, as table 6.4 shows.

Figure 6.5 Nonlabor Income Growth, by Source, in Bangladesh, Peru, and Thailand, 2000s

a. Subsidies and other social transfers

b. International remittances

Peru — Thailand — Bangladesh

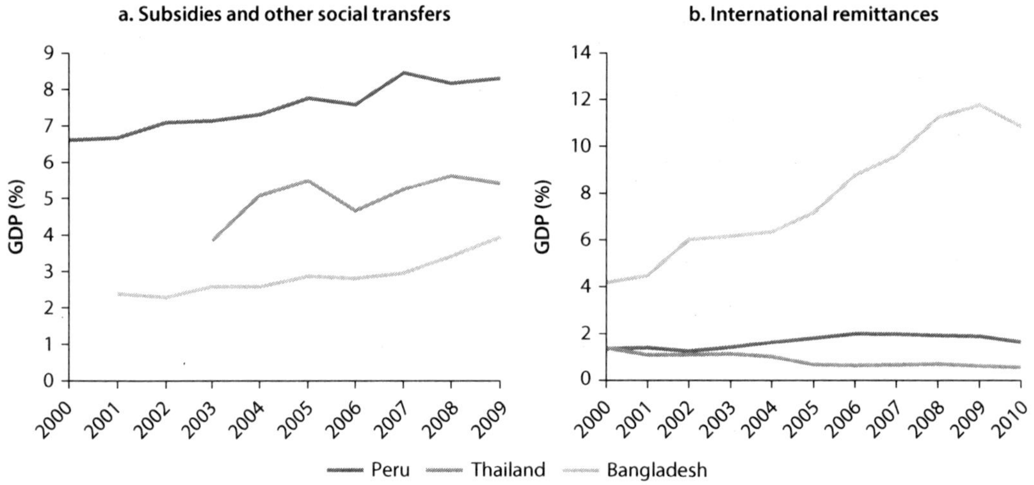

Source: World Bank 2011.
Note: GDP = gross domestic product. Data on subsidies and other social transfers were unavailable for Bangladesh preceding 2001 and for Thailand preceding 2003.

Figure 6.6 Change in Household Consumption-to-Income Ratio in Bangladesh, Peru, and Thailand, 2000s

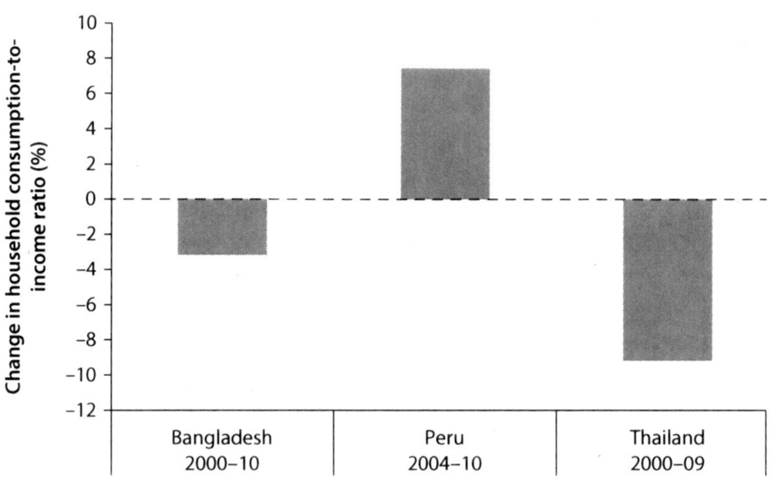

Sources: Household survey results from Bangladesh (HIES 2000–10), Peru (ENAHO 2004–10), and Thailand (SES 2000–09).
Note: HIES = Household Income and Expenditure Survey (Bangladesh Bureau of Statistics); ENAHO = Encuesta Nacional de Hogares (Peru National Institute of Statistics and Information); SES = Household Socio-Economic Survey (Thailand National Statistical Office).

In contrast, the consumption-to-income ratio increased over the course of the decade in Peru, particularly at the bottom of the distribution.

As a result, the observed changes in consumption may be less dramatic than what we would have otherwise expected in Bangladesh and Thailand, but more dramatic in Peru, had the consumption-to-income ratio remained constant.

Table 6.4 Household Consumption-to-Income Ratio, by Income Decile, in Bangladesh, Peru, and Thailand, 2000s

Units of consumption per units of income

	Bangladesh		*Peru*		*Thailand*	
	2000	*2010*	*2004*	*2010*	*2000*	*2009*
Average	1.26	1.22	1.13	1.22	0.98	0.89
Income deciles (per capita)						
1	3.69	3.46	1.96	2.52	2.74	3.01
2	1.39	1.53	1.33	1.50	2.24	1.64
3	1.14	1.29	1.22	1.31	1.77	1.5
4	1.07	1.13	1.18	1.18	1.76	1.46
5	1.05	1.03	1.12	1.13	1.74	1.29
6	1.01	0.92	1.05	1.05	1.56	1.31
7	0.97	0.83	1.00	1.01	1.49	1.21
8	0.95	0.76	0.93	0.92	1.49	1.22
9	0.88	0.67	0.84	0.85	1.59	1.15
10	0.76	0.5	0.71	0.71	1.5	1.1
Spearman rank[a]	0.79	0.56	0.86	0.83	0.81	0.83
Correlation	0.62	0.18	0.76	0.73	0.62	0.51
Coefficient of variation						
Consumption	0.87	0.78	0.97	0.85	0.96	0.99
Income	1.06	2.99	1.35	1.26	1.33	1.49

Sources: Household survey results from Bangladesh (HIES 2000–10), Peru (ENAHO 2004–10), and Thailand (SES 2000–09).
Note: HIES = Household Income and Expenditure Survey (Bangladesh Bureau of Statistics); ENAHO = Encuesta Nacional de Hogares (Peru National Institute of Statistics and Information); SES = Household Socio-Economic Survey.
a. "Spearman rank" refers to Spearman's rank correlation coefficient (named after Charles Spearman), a nonparametric measure of statistical dependence between two variables. The closer the correlation is to one, the more perfect the correlation is.

Since poverty is measured by consumption, actual poverty rates are higher in the final period than they would have been had the consumption-to-income ratio remained constant in Bangladesh and Thailand. In contrast, actual poverty will be lower in the final period in Peru simply because poor households are consuming a higher share of their income.

The Decomposition Approach

As described in chapter 4, we implement the decomposition in four stages:

1. We estimate the determinants of occupational choice, sectoral choice, and educational level for two periods during the past decade.
2. We estimate the earnings regressions for each period for household heads and other household members (distinguishing between wage workers, self-employed, and daily workers) and for net farm revenue for farm households.
3. We use the coefficients from these regressions to simulate counterfactual distributions by replacing one element at a time.
4. We compare these counterfactuals to the observed changes in distribution.

Estimate Educational, Occupational, and Sectoral Choice Structures

As summarized in the first step above, we first estimate the educational, occupational, and sectoral choice models in each period for which data are available. In annex 6A, tables 6A.1, 6A.2, and 6A.3 present simulations for the educational structure, occupation, and economic sectors using these regressions compared with the actual structures during the early and late part of the decade.

Also in the annex, tables 6A.4, 6A.5, and 6A.6 present the multinomial logit regression results for occupational choice in Bangladesh, Peru, and Thailand, respectively. Given the considerable diversification of income sources that is common in rural households (Davis et al. 2010), we estimate the sectoral choice model for the secondary occupation of individuals in farm households, as well as for all nonfarm work.

The simulated structures are close to the true structures, with the errors being relatively small in all three countries. In the case of Bangladesh, the simulated 2010 nonfarm occupational structure has slightly fewer wage workers and more daily workers than the true values, but the regression results show a relatively high coefficient of determination (R2). This gives us confidence that we can use the coefficients from these regressions to simulate shifts in the labor force structure one at a time.

Estimate Earnings Equations

Next, we separate labor income into farm and nonfarm income to estimate the earnings equations.

Nonfarm Household Income

Tables 6A.7, 6A.8, and 6A.9 present the results for individuals engaged in nonfarm activities in Bangladesh, Peru, and Thailand, respectively. The results show that the models fit the data relatively well, with coefficients being statistically significant and of the right sign. In all cases, higher individual earnings are associated with being male, having higher education and experience, living in urban areas, and belonging to the manufacturing sector.

Farm Household Income

Tables 6A.10, 6A.11, and A6A.12 present results of net revenue for farm households in Bangladesh, Peru, and Thailand, respectively.[4] Net revenue for farmers increases with experience, land holdings, access to irrigation, and the number of household members participating in farm work.[5]

Simulate Counterfactual Distributions

In the next step, we use the estimated coefficients from the educational, sectoral, labor, and earnings models to simulate counterfactual distributions. For instance, because we estimated the returns to education in two periods, we can take the estimated parameters in the first period (say, 2000) and evaluate the earnings equations with the 2010 levels of education. This generates counterfactual earnings at the individual level, which we aggregate to get the corresponding household income, then the corresponding level of consumption, and finally a counterfactual poverty rate. In this way—changing one parameter at a time or one characteristic at a time—we can generate multiple counterfactual distributions and recalculate a new poverty rate.

Compare Counterfactuals with Distributional Changes

Finally, we compare these counterfactual poverty rates with the observed poverty rates to quantify the impact of each element being considered. Because replacing the first-period parameters into last-period data will yield results that are different from doing it the other way around, we calculate the counterfactual by doing it both ways and then take the average (in line with Bourguignon, Ferreira, and Lustig 2005; Bourguignon, Ferreira, and Leite 2008).

We first calculate the effects on poverty by changing one element at a time and leaving everything else constant. However, given that changes in multiple factors could have interaction effects, we also calculate the cumulative effect of these decompositions. For this purpose, we adhere to the literature (Bourguignon, Ferreira, and Leite 2008) as follows:

- Begin by calculating the effects on poverty as a result of changes in the population's characteristics, beginning with the most exogenous: age, gender, and region.
- Then calculate the effects on poverty as a result of changes in the population's educational, occupational, and sectoral structure, all of which depend on age, gender, and region.
- Use the preceding results to calculate the effects on poverty as a result of
  - Changes in farm and nonfarm earnings due to changes in the returns to these characteristics;
  - Changes in nonlabor incomes (first private transfers, then public ones); and
  - Changes in the consumption-to-income ratio.

Decomposition Results

Chapter 3 found that, in a set of 21 countries with large declines in poverty, most of these declines could be attributed to increases in labor income. The results of this chapter are in line with that result, while adding a modeling structure that enables us to further conclude that the main contributor to increased labor incomes—and thus to poverty reduction—was the improvement in the returns to individual and household characteristics and endowments.

Endowments and the Returns on Endowments

That these increased *returns* contributed the most to poverty reduction, rather than changes in the populations' endowments or characteristics, points to an increase in the relative price of labor and higher productivity as the main contributors to poverty reduction in each case. In particular, returns to farm and nonfarm endowments amount to 44 percent of poverty reduction in Peru, more than 48 percent in Thailand, and 60 percent in Bangladesh (table 6.5). In both Thailand and Bangladesh, this effect is concentrated in the farm sector, whereas Peru's increased returns were slightly larger in the nonfarm sector.

The overall conclusion—that increased returns to endowments was the largest factor in poverty reduction—holds true whether we (a) calculate one counterfactual at a time, holding all else constant (as shown by the marginal contributions in tables 6.5 and 6.6) or (b) adopt the cumulative decomposition path described (as shown in table 6.7). Although the cumulative results are slightly different in magnitude, the overall messages are the same.

Table 6.5 shows the net effect of changes in returns. However, these net effects reflect the sum of price changes that the labor market assigns to each

Table 6.5 Marginal Contributions to Poverty Reduction in Bangladesh, Peru, and Thailand, 2000s

	Bangladesh, 2000–10		*Peru, 2004–10*		*Thailand, 2000–09*	
	Change (ppts)	*Change (% of total)*	*Change (ppts)*	*Change (% of total)*	*Change (ppts)*	*Change (% of total)*
Nonfarm labor income	−4.56	26	−9.35	58	−3.46	27
Returns to characteristics	−3.52	20	−4.93	31	−1.25	10
Occupational choice	−1.61	9	−3.44	21	0.08	−1
Economic sector	−0.48	3	−0.08	1	−1.01	8
Education	−0.55	3	−0.25	2	−1.34	10
Unobservable factors	1.59	−9	−0.65	4	0.06	0
Farm income	−6.02	35	−2.74	17	−4.91	38
Returns to characteristics	−6.98	40	−2.04	13	−4.83	38
Occupational choice	0.56	−3	−0.25	2	1.31	−10
Economic sector	—	—	−0.14	1	−1.11	9
Education	0.13	−1	−0.08	1	−0.56	4
Unobservable factors	0.26	−2	−0.23	1	0.28	−2
Nonlabor income	1.05	−6	−2.28	14	−5.80	45
Total private transfers	1.05	−6	−0.85	5	−3.30	26
International private transfers	−1.94	11	0.19	−1	−2.19	17
Domestic private transfers	1.10	−6	0.24	−1	—	—
Private donations	—	—	−0.70	4	—	—
Other private transfers	0.58	−3	0.01	0	−1.12	9
Capital	1.31	−8	−0.58	4	0.02	0
Total public transfers	0.00	0	−1.38	9	−2.51	20
Public donations	—	—	−0.45	3	—	—
Public transfers	—	—	−0.90	6	—	—
Pensions	—	—	0.01	0	−2.51	20
Other nonlabor income	—	—	−0.04	0	—	—
Other	−7.50	43	−0.78	5	2.50	−20
Age-gender-regional structure	−3.48	20	−1.17	7	−1.18	9
Consumption-to-income ratio	0.93	−5	−1.73	11	3.43	−27
Unexplained	−4.95	29	2.12	−13	0.26	−2
Total	−17.34	100	−16.13	100	−12.84	100

Sources: Calculations derived from household survey data from Bangladesh (HIES 2000–10), Peru (ENAHO 2004–10), and Thailand (SES 2000–09).
Note: ppts = percentage points; — = not available; HIES = Household Income and Expenditure Survey (Bangladesh Bureau of Statistics); ENAHO = Encuesta Nacional de Hogares (Peru National Institute of Statistics and Information); SES = Household Socio-Economic Survey (Thailand National Statistical Office).

Table 6.6 Contributions to Poverty Reduction by Returns to Endowments in Bangladesh, Peru, and Thailand, 2000s

	Bangladesh				*Peru*				*Thailand*			
	2000–10				*2004–10*				*2000–09*			
	Nonfarm households		*Farm households*		*Nonfarm households*		*Farm households*		*Nonfarm households*		*Farm households*	
	Change (ppts)	*Change (%)*	*Change (ppts)*	*Change (%)*	*Change (ppts)*	*Change (%)*	*Change (ppts)*	*Change (%)*	*Change (ppts)*	*Change (%)*	*Change (ppts)*	*Change (%)*
Total parameter effects	−3.52	20	−6.98	40	−4.93	31	−2.04	13	−1.25	10	−4.83	38
Education	1.77	−10	0.78	−4	0.54	−3	. . .	. . .	−0.28	2	−1.11	9
Age	3.9	−23	4.19	−24	1.0	−6	0.96	−6	−0.90	7	−0.54	4
Female	−0.44	3	−0.20	1	0.77	−5	−0.08	1	−0.01	. . .	−0.33	3
Urban	0.11	−1	0.45	−3	0.20	−1	0.12	−1	−0.40	3	−0.09	1
Region	−0.87	5	−1.82	10	−4.79	30	−0.18	1	−0.27	2	−1.62	13
Sector	5.85	−34	0.21	−1	−1.05	7	−0.19	1	3.50	−27	0.32	−3
Land	n.a.	n.a.	−7.25	42	n.a.	n.a.	−3.18	20	n.a.	n.a.	—	—
Irrigation	n.a.	n.a.	0.30	−2	n.a.	n.a.	−0.11	1	n.a.	n.a.	—	—
Other members	n.a.	n.a.	1.48	−9	n.a.	n.a.	1.07	−7	n.a.	n.a.	—	—
Constant	−14.87	86	−7.74	45	−3.38	21	. . .	. . .	−2.71	21	−1.11	9

Sources: Calculations derived from household survey data from Bangladesh (HIES 2000–10), Peru (ENAHO 2004–10), and Thailand (SES 2000–09).

Note: ppts = percentage points; . . . = negligible; — = not available; n.a. = not applicable. "Region" refers to residence in provinces, states, or other regional subgroups. "Sector" refers to changes in the sectoral choice of workers, including agriculture, manufacturing, industry, and services. "Other members" refers to the number of household members engaged in farm activities. HIES = Household Income and Expenditure Survey (Bangladesh Bureau of Statistics). ENAHO = Encuesta Nacional de Hogares (Peru National Institute of Statistics and Information). SES = Household Socio-Economic Survey (Thailand National Statistical Office).

Table 6.7 Cumulative Contributions to Poverty Reduction in Bangladesh, Peru, and Thailand, 2000s

	Bangladesh, 2000–10		*Peru, 2004–10*		*Thailand, 2000–09*	
	Change (ppts)	*Change (%)*	*Change (ppts)*	*Change (%)*	*Change (ppts)*	*Change (%)*
Demographics	−4.41	25	−0.88	5	−0.41	3
Education	−0.88	5	−0.31	2	−1.74	14
Occupation	−1.38	8	−3.90	24	0.52	−4
Sector	−0.51	3	0.02	0	−1.75	14
Returns nonfarm	−2.93	17	−5.06	31	−1.40	11
Returns farm	−8.18	47	−1.95	12	−3.59	28
Residuals	1.33	−8	0.05	0	0.06	0
Nonlabor income	−1.93	11	−0.13	1	−3.59	28
Others	1.55	−9	−3.96	25	−0.93	7
Total	−17.34	100	−16.13	100	−12.84	100

Sources: Calculations derived from household survey data from Bangladesh (HIES 2000–10), Peru (ENAHO 2004–10), and Thailand (SES 2000–09).
Note: ppts = percentage points. "Demographics" refers to the exogenous structure of the population's age, gender, and regional makeup. For a detailed description of the methodology, refer to chapter 5.
HIES = Household Income and Expenditure Survey (Bangladesh Bureau of Statistics); ENAHO = Encuesta Nacional de Hogares (Peru National Institute of Statistics and Information); SES = Household Socio-Economic Survey (Thailand National Statistical Office).

characteristic or endowment. For example, the price the labor market assigns for each additional level of education or for living in a particular region in the country may be components of this net effect.

Table 6.6 breaks down these changes in returns. The results show that for self-employed farmers, most of the increase in returns has to do with a large increase in the constant, which measures average real farm wages holding everything else constant. This increase could be the result of either higher productivity or higher relative prices in agriculture—potentially resulting from food price increases.

As we have seen, poverty rates changed because of both changes in endowments and changes in the returns to those endowments. However, these two forces could act in opposite directions. For instance, if higher education raises incomes, it also would tend to lower poverty. However, if the supply of educated workers outpaces the demand for such workers, then the *returns* to, or premium for, higher education will likely fall. This idea is often associated with Tinbergen's (1975) "race" between technological progress—which he saw as raising the demand for skills—and the expansion of formal education—which raises the supply of skills (Ferreira 2012). Below, we summarize the results regarding the net impacts of changes in these opposing forces.

Impact of Demographic Changes

Changes in the structure of the populations' age, gender, area (urban or rural), and regional (district) accounted for about 25 percent of the observed poverty reduction in Bangladesh, 5 percent of the reduction in Peru, and 3 percent of the reduction in Thailand when holding all else constant (table 6.7).

These are important contributions that are consistent with the results described in chapter 3, which follow an alternative methodology. Given the increase in the economically active population, the size of the effect is not surprising—particularly in Bangladesh, where fertility rates have declined while a large generation of young people has joined the work force. However, the entrance of young people has coincided with a decline in the premium for experience (as proxied by age), particularly for daily and self-employed workers in Bangladesh. The decline in the returns to experience (shown as a –23 percent decline in the age parameter for Bangladesh in table 6.6) has counteracted the progress in poverty reduction (shown as a combined positive effect of 25 percent for Bangladesh in table 6.7).

In contrast, in Thailand, both the increase in the working-age population and the greater returns to age (interpreted as experience) contributed to poverty reduction. In particular, demographics contributed 3 percent to poverty reduction (table 6.7), while greater returns to experience in the farm and nonfarm households contributed 4 percent and 7 percent, respectively (table 6.6).

A consistent result in all three countries is that the earnings penalty for living outside of the capital city fell over the past decade. This finding points to either an increase in the relative price of labor, higher productivity outside the capitals that helped to reduce poverty, or both. This result is most evident in Peru, where the reduced penalty for living outside of Lima (which table 6.6 reflects through the impact of residency in the "regions") accounted for 30 percent of the reduction in poverty for nonfarm households.[6] In Bangladesh, the penalty for living outside of the capital also declined, accounting for 10 percent and 5 percent of poverty reduction for farm and nonfarm households, respectively. Thailand saw a 13 percent and 2 percent in poverty reduction among farm and nonfarm households, respectively, even though the share of people living outside the capital remained more or less constant.

Impact of Changes in Labor Income

Education

As expected, a more-educated population helped to reduce poverty in all three countries, particularly in the nonfarm sector (table 6.5). However, this effect was modest—being more than offset by a decline in the returns to education in Bangladesh and Peru (table 6.6). In Thailand, in contrast, wage premiums for education increased in farm and nonfarm households, further reducing poverty.

The results of greater education and of returns to education were as follows in the three countries:

- *In Bangladesh*, the large increase in the share of the population who had completed primary school (from 33.8 percent in 2000 to 43.4 percent in 2010, as previously shown in table 6.3) led to only a slight (3 percent) reduction in poverty in the nonfarm sector (table 6.5) because it drove down the premium for completing primary school for all but wage workers.

- *In Peru*, similarly, a more-educated population accounted for 2 percent of the decline in poverty in the nonfarm sector (table 6.5). However, this effect was more than offset by a decline in the returns to education (table 6.6), because the greater supply of more-educated household heads was not met with greater demand for these workers; therefore, the wage premium for education fell. As a result, the increase in education reduced poverty less than expected.

- *In Thailand*, a more-educated population accounted for 10 percent of the reduction in poverty in nonfarm households, and a 4 percent reduction in farm households (table 6.5). In contrast to Peru and Bangladesh, increased returns to education reinforced these gains in poverty reduction, as wage premiums for education and experience increased in both farm and nonfarm households (table 6.6). These results point to greater demand for specialized workers in Thailand than in Bangladesh and Peru.

Collectively, these results point to a relative increase in the price of labor for uneducated workers, an increase that strongly drove poverty reduction in Bangladesh and Peru. Capturing this effect is the large contribution to poverty reduction from the left-out category—the constant—which includes the returns to labor for individuals with no schooling (table 6.6). In Bangladesh, this was true in both the farm and nonfarm sectors for daily and self-employed workers, whose additional years of education did not help to reduce poverty (see the table 6A.7). However, the opposite is true for wage workers, whose returns to education increased. This seeming contrast implies that the population's educational levels grew faster than the rate at which job creation could absorb them. The different job-related returns to education also reflect a sizable increase in the relative price of unskilled labor, which could be driven, at least partly, by higher productivity.

Occupation

Changes in occupational choice were critical to poverty reduction in all three countries among nonfarm workers, who aimed to benefit from better work opportunities. This effect was most important in Peru, where occupational shifts—from being unpaid family workers to being wage workers—accounts for 21 percent of poverty reduction (table 6.5). In the nonfarm sector in Bangladesh, the shift from daily and self-employed work toward wage employment accounted for almost 10 percent of the observed poverty reduction.[7]

In contrast, for workers who remained in agriculture, we find greater specialization on the part of farmers. By the end of the decade, they were less likely to diversify into a secondary occupation, either because they saw increased returns from farm activities or because they lacked the skills to take up a second occupation. For example, the share of Thai farmers with a secondary occupation declined from 32 percent in 2000 to 23 percent in 2009. Meanwhile, in Bangladesh, the drop was even more dramatic: the share of farmers with a secondary occupation fell from 30 percent in 2000 to 10 percent in 2010. This lower diversification increased poverty by 10 percent and 3 percent in Thailand and Bangladesh, respectively (see the "Occupational choice" row under "Farm income" in table 6.5).[8]

Sector of Work

Changes in work sector also affected poverty reduction, particularly shifts away from agriculture and into services. However, in both Bangladesh and Thailand, any related poverty reduction was more than offset by reduced *returns* to working in the service sector, whereas Peru showed the opposite dynamic:

- *In Bangladesh,* the nonfarm sector's shift into the services sector accounted for 3 percent of the observed poverty reduction (table 6.5). However, this was more than offset by a reduction in the service sector wage premium in nonfarm households, leading to a 34 percent higher poverty rate than would have otherwise been expected (table 6.6).
- *In Thailand,* similarly, many workers' movement into manufacturing and services accounted for a 9 percent poverty decrease among farm households and an 8 percent decrease among nonfarm households (table 6.5). However, these effects were countered by a decline in the returns to working in those sectors in farm and nonfarm households (table 6A.9), which led to a 3 percent and 27 percent higher poverty rate, respectively, than would have otherwise been expected (table 6.6).
- *In Peru,* in contrast, despite the increasing share of workers in the service sector, there were increases in the returns to working in the service sector (see table 6A.8) that accounted for 7 percent of the reduction in poverty (table 6.6). This is astonishing, given that Peru has a much larger share of service sector workers than either of the other countries (see table 6.3).

Rural Assets

Among farm households in Bangladesh and Peru, we find some evidence of increased returns to agriculture. In particular, for farm households in Bangladesh, the most important change was the increase in the returns to land, accounting for 42 percent of the reduction in national poverty when holding all other factors constant (table 6.6). These returns increased because average land per capita declined from 0.8 acres to 0.6 acres between 2000 and 2010 given the population increase.

In contrast, in the case of Peru, the average land size for farm households increased while the returns to land increased as well (table 6.6), a boon that accounted for 20 percent of the reduction in poverty. This was complemented by better access to irrigation in Peru, accounting for another 1 percent of the poverty reduction. However, the returns to additional agricultural workers declined. In Bangladesh, although both access to irrigation and the number of agricultural workers increased over the course of the decade, the *returns* to irrigation and having additional household members employed in farming fell, so neither effect helped to reduce poverty.[9]

In considering the increase to rural assets, it is important to note that we cannot disentangle the effects as a result of increased real productivity (real output per worker) from the increase in the real value of output per worker. Given that this period was characterized by an increase in the prices of commodities, this factor might have been an important driver of agricultural returns, through its effect on the real value of agricultural production.

Impact of Changes in Nonlabor Income

Although poverty was reduced primarily because of labor income growth, increases in nonlabor income also played a role that varied by country:

- *In Bangladesh*, the increase in international remittances contributed 11 percent to the decline in poverty. Offsetting this effect, however, was a decline in domestic transfers that led to a slightly higher poverty rate than if both remittance sources had remained constant (table 6.5).
- *In Peru*, public transfers and donations accounted for 9 percent of the reduction in poverty (table 6.5), while capital and private donations accounted for nearly 5 percent of the reduction in poverty (table 6.5).
- *In Thailand*, nonlabor income was important, particularly through private transfers in the form of international remittances and other private transfers (17 percent and 9 percent, respectively) and pensions (20 percent), potentially reflecting the introduction of a new pension scheme in the late 1990s (table 6.5). These results are consistent with those using the simple approach, but they have been further disaggregated to show the relative importance of the different types of sources.

Final Remarks

The past decade affords us a fantastic opportunity to study the most significant factors that worked in favor of the poor. This chapter accounts for the contribution of changes in demographics, labor income, and nonlabor income in the significant poverty reductions observed in Bangladesh, Peru, and Thailand during the 2000s. In contrast to methods that focus on aggregate summary statistics, the methods adopted here generate entire counterfactual distributions, allowing us to identify more precisely the contributions to the observed distributional changes.

Link of Labor Income to Marginal Value of Work

The results show that labor income growth has been the most important contributor to poverty reduction over the past decade. Further—through the microdecomposition methods employed here—we ascertained that the growth in labor income was mainly the result of higher returns to endowments, signaling an increase in the marginal value of work, resulting from increases in either productivity or relative prices of labor.

In Bangladesh and Peru, this increase in the marginal value of work was not driven by higher returns to education, but rather by higher returns to unskilled labor. Thailand, in contrast, demonstrated that greater specialization and higher returns to human capital can boost the marginal value of work, potentially through productivity increases. All three countries showed these results consistently:

- *A falling earnings penalty* for living outside of the capital city served to reduce poverty over the past decade—accounting for as much of 31 percent of the reduction in Peru, 15 percent in Bangladesh, and 15 percent in Thailand.
- *A shift in the sectoral composition of the work force*—away from agriculture and toward services—reduced poverty only slightly in Bangladesh and Peru and a bit more in Thailand. However, this increase in service sector workers led to a declining premium for working in the service sector in Bangladesh and Thailand. In Peru, however, the higher share of service workers was accompanied by increased premiums even though Peru's service sector makes up a far larger share of total employment than it does in the other countries.
- *Occupational choices* among nonfarm workers shifted away from daily-wage and self-employed work and toward wage jobs, all of which contributed to poverty reduction, particularly in Peru.

Roles of Demographic Change and Nonlabor Income Growth

Beyond the effects of labor income growth, the decomposition method adopted in this chapter (as well as the method adopted in chapter 3) showed that a greater share of working-age adults helped to reduce poverty, particularly in Bangladesh.

Finally, although most of the reduction in poverty was the result of labor income growth, it is important to recognize that nonlabor income in the form of transfers did play a role: International remittances accounted for 11 percent and 17 percent of poverty reduction in Bangladesh and Thailand, respectively. Public transfers accounted for about 9 percent of Peru's poverty reduction, particularly for those at the very bottom of the income distribution. And Thailand's generous new pension scheme, combined with various private and other transfers, accounts for more than one-third of its poverty reduction.

An Agenda for Further Research

This volume has proposed two distinct micro-decomposition approaches to understanding changes in poverty over the last decade. The proposed approaches are complementary—the first being quite simple and easy to apply across countries with relatively limited data requirements, and the second providing a more in-depth analysis based on a structural approach.

The approach implemented in this chapter allows for movement across sectors and occupations for nonfarm households. In addition, it allows individuals in farm households to choose a secondary occupation and sector. However, the proposed structure does not model the choice of a household to be either a farm or a nonfarm household. Further research could explore the extent to which this could be incorporated into the decomposition analysis.

In addition, to the extent that demographic changes are important, further work could include a fertility choice model, particularly in settings where there are substantial shifts over time. Finally, as described in chapter 4, other decomposition techniques could be explored and perhaps combined with the two approaches highlighted in this volume.

Annex 6A: Regression and Simulation Results

Table 6A.1 Simulating the Changing Characteristics of Households in Bangladesh, 2000–10

	Household head						*Other members*					
	2000			*2010*			*2000*			*2010*		
	Actual (1)	*Simulated (2)*	*(2) – (1)*	*Actual (1)*	*Simulated (2)*	*(2) – (1)*	*Actual (1)*	*Simulated (2)*	*(2) – (1)*	*Actual (1)*	*Simulated (2)*	*(2) – (1)*
	(%)	*(%)*	*(ppts)*	*(%)*	*(%)*	*(ppts)*	*(%)*	*(%)*	*(ppts)*	*(%)*	*(%)*	*(ppts)*
Education structure												
Illiterate and incomplete primary	63.2	61.9	−1.3	57.0	57.8	0.8	54.4	54.5	0.1	42.1	42.3	0.2
Primary and low secondary	29.0	29.6	0.6	33.1	33.2	0.1	36.2	36.0	−0.3	48.6	48.2	−0.4
Complete tertiary	7.7	8.5	0.8	9.9	9.0	−0.9	9.5	9.6	0.1	9.3	9.4	0.2
Occupation												
Nonemployed	9.6	10.1	0.5	8.0	7.7	−0.4	79.8	83.0	3.2	78.0	80.1	2.2
Daily workers	45.5	40.7	−4.9	43.4	49.9	6.5	8.6	4.7	−3.9	8.2	5.6	−2.7
Self-employed—nonagriculture	24.7	25.1	0.3	24.1	23.9	−0.2	4.4	4.8	0.3	4.1	4.4	0.3
Wage workers	20.2	24.2	4.0	24.5	18.6	−5.9	7.2	7.5	0.3	9.7	9.9	0.2
Economic sectors												
Daily workers												
Agriculture	58.8	56.4	−2.4	51.8	51.8	0.0	54.8	53.4	−1.4	42.7	44.1	1.4
Manufacturing	12.3	12.8	0.5	12.6	13.1	0.6	19.0	18.3	−0.8	21.5	20.4	−1.1
Industry	7.9	8.5	0.6	11.9	12.3	0.4	8.4	8.9	0.6	15.8	16.4	0.5
Services	21.0	22.4	1.4	23.7	22.8	−0.9	17.8	19.4	1.6	20.0	19.2	−0.8
Self-employed												
Manufacturing	34.9	35.3	0.4	17.6	17.0	−0.6	41.1	45.7	4.7	26.8	22.1	−4.8
Industry	6.2	7.8	1.6	1.7	1.9	0.1	7.1	6.9	−0.2	3.1	2.6	−0.5
Services	58.9	57.0	−2.0	80.7	81.1	0.4	51.8	47.4	−4.5	70.1	75.4	5.3
Wage workers												
Agriculture	8.6	7.3	−1.3	5.4	6.9	1.4	4.4	3.4	−1.0	3.0	3.7	0.8
Manufacturing	27.7	26.8	−0.9	33.4	34.3	0.9	42.6	42.4	−0.2	47.3	47.5	0.3
Industry	3.7	3.8	0.1	3.9	4.0	0.1	2.5	2.0	−0.5	2.6	2.7	0.1
Services	60.0	62.2	2.1	57.3	54.9	−2.4	50.5	52.2	1.7	47.2	46.0	−1.2

Source: Household survey results from Bangladesh (HIES 2000–10).
Note: ppts = percentage points. HIES = Household Income and Expenditure Survey (Bangladesh Bureau of Statistics).

Table 6A.2 Simulating the Changing Characteristics of Households in Peru, 2005–09

	Household head						*Other members*					
	2004			*2010*			*2004*			*2010*		
	Actual (1)	*Simulated (2)*	*(2) – (1)*	*Actual (1)*	*Simulated (2)*	*(2) – (1)*	*Actual (1)*	*Simulated (2)*	*(2) – (1)*	*Actual (1)*	*Simulated (2)*	*(2) – (1)*
	(%)	*(%)*	*(ppts)*	*(%)*	*(%)*	*(ppts)*	*(%)*	*(%)*	*(ppts)*	*(%)*	*(%)*	*(ppts)*
Education type												
Less than primary	55.3	55.4	0.1	49.7	49.9	0.3	50.3	50.8	0.6	45.4	44.6	−0.8
Primary	28.2	28.1	−0.1	32.4	32.3	−0.1	36.5	35.6	−0.8	39.7	40.7	1.0
Secondary and above	16.5	16.5	0.0	18.0	17.8	−0.2	13.3	13.6	0.3	15.0	14.7	−0.2
Occupation												
Nonemployed	16.8	17.3	0.5	13.1	12.8	−0.3	57.9	58.7	0.9	49.5	50.4	0.9
Wage workers	48.2	48.1	0.0	50.2	50.0	−0.2	26.2	25.7	−0.5	32.2	31.6	−0.6
Self-employed (nonagriculture)	35.0	34.5	−0.5	36.7	37.2	0.5	15.9	15.6	−0.4	18.3	18.0	−0.3
Economic sectors												
Wage workers												
Agriculture	31.8	29.9	0.0	25.9	27.6	0.1	17.0	17.7	−0.5	14.8	13.9	0.7
Industry	12.1	12.1	1.6	12.0	12.1	−1.0	13.2	12.8	−1.4	13.2	13.9	1.6
Services	35.2	36.8	0.2	40.7	39.7	−1.0	52.8	51.4	1.2	56.7	58.3	−1.4
Public sector	20.9	21.2	0.0	21.5	20.5	0.0	16.9	18.1	0.0	15.3	14.0	0.0

Source: Household survey results from Peru (ENAHO 2004–10).
Note: ppts = percentage points. ENAHO = Encuesta Nacional de Hogares (Peru National Institute of Statistics and Information).

Table 6A.3 Simulating the Changing Characteristics of Households in Thailand, 2000–09

	Household head						*Other members*					
	2000			*2009*			*2000*			*2009*		
	Actual (1)	*Simulated (2)*	*(2) – (1)*	*Actual (1)*	*Simulated (2)*	*(2) – (1)*	*Actual (1)*	*Simulated (2)*	*(2) – (1)*	*Actual (1)*	*Simulated (2)*	*(2) – (1)*
	(%)	*(%)*	*(ppts)*	*(%)*	*(%)*	*(ppts)*	*(%)*	*(%)*	*(ppts)*	*(%)*	*(%)*	*(ppts)*
Education (years)												
<6	59.7	64.8	5.1	46.9	40.8	−6.0	36.6	42.3	5.7	27.3	22.1	−5.2
6–11	23.2	19.3	−3.8	29.3	34.2	4.9	37.1	32.9	−4.2	44.4	49.0	4.6
>11	17.1	15.9	−1.3	23.8	25.0	1.2	26.3	24.8	−1.5	28.3	28.9	0.7
Occupation												
Nonemployed	20.4	21.5	1.1	20.7	19.4	−1.2	49.4	47.0	−2.5	47.3	50.6	3.3
Salaried	57.3	56.4	−0.9	53.9	55.7	1.8	41.0	42.8	1.8	41.9	39.5	−2.4
Self-employed (nonagriculture)	22.3	22.1	−0.2	25.4	24.8	−0.6	9.5	10.3	0.7	10.8	9.9	−0.9
Economic sectors												
Self-employed												
Industry	15.6	14.4	−1.2	17.1	16.7	−0.4	20.0	18.4	−1.6	18.7	16.1	−2.6
Services	84.4	85.6	1.2	82.9	83.3	0.4	80.0	81.7	1.6	81.3	83.9	2.6
Wage workers												
Agriculture	20.6	16.5	−4.0	11.6	15.1	3.5	20.7	18.9	−1.8	9.1	11.0	1.9
Industry	30.7	27.1	−3.6	35.3	37.3	1.9	36.0	32.2	−3.8	38.8	41.2	2.4
Services	23.6	22.8	−0.7	29.3	30.5	1.2	27.2	25.6	−1.5	34.7	35.9	1.2
Public sector	25.1	33.5	8.4	23.8	17.2	−6.6	16.1	23.3	7.2	17.4	11.9	−5.4

Source: Household survey results from Thailand (SES 2000–09).
Note: ppts = percentage points. SES = Household Socio-Economic Survey (Thailand National Statistical Office).

Table 6A.4 Multinomial Logit on Occupational Choice of Working-Age Population, by Household Status, in Bangladesh, 2000 and 2010

	2000			2010		
	Daily workers	*Self-employed*[a]	*Wage worker*	*Daily workers*	*Self-employed*[a]	*Wage worker*
a. Household heads						
Primary & lower secondary education	−1.204***	−0.0182	0.614***	−1.082***	0.122	0.682***
	(0.160)	(0.161)	(0.166)	(0.145)	(0.147)	(0.147)
Higher secondary & tertiary education	−2.408***	0.301	2.002***	−3.461***	−0.599***	1.227***
	(0.368)	(0.294)	(0.287)	(0.267)	(0.203)	(0.194)
Age	0.0408	0.126**	0.114**	0.109**	0.281***	0.238***
	(0.0510)	(0.0544)	(0.0556)	(0.0423)	(0.0449)	(0.0440)
Age squared	−0.00141**	−0.00228***	−0.00208***	−0.00211***	−0.00382***	−0.00360***
	(0.000572)	(0.000611)	(0.000627)	(0.000473)	(0.000504)	(0.000496)
Urban	−0.354**	0.421***	0.795***	−1.150***	−0.411***	−0.00785
	(0.160)	(0.161)	(0.162)	(0.134)	(0.135)	(0.133)
Barisal	0.0892	−0.0402	−0.313	0.101	−0.330	−0.310
	(0.263)	(0.275)	(0.288)	(0.255)	(0.262)	(0.258)
Chittagong	−0.490***	−0.310*	−0.216	0.228	−0.525***	−0.264
	(0.179)	(0.184)	(0.186)	(0.161)	(0.168)	(0.161)
Khulna	0.432*	0.273	0.0118	1.127***	0.352	0.128
	(0.231)	(0.240)	(0.248)	(0.217)	(0.224)	(0.223)
Rajsahi	1.735***	1.400***	0.834***	1.641***	1.141***	0.390**
	(0.227)	(0.234)	(0.242)	(0.190)	(0.194)	(0.197)
Sylhet	0.541*	−0.0682	0.126	0.564**	0.467*	−0.0835
	(0.281)	(0.319)	(0.323)	(0.262)	(0.270)	(0.276)
Attends school	−3.549***	−3.393***	−2.742***	−0.263	−14.93	−1.508
	(0.753)	(0.866)	(0.724)	(1.439)	(565.3)	(1.281)
Remittances	−0.646***	−1.014***	−0.715***	−0.129	−0.00592	−0.178
	(0.172)	(0.178)	(0.181)	(0.214)	(0.215)	(0.218)
Female	−2.213***	−2.993***	−1.178***	−1.903***	−2.802***	−1.019***
	(0.409)	(0.489)	(0.444)	(0.376)	(0.444)	(0.379)
Remittances × Female	−0.328	−0.985*	−1.450***	−1.534***	−1.583***	−2.358***
	(0.321)	(0.595)	(0.431)	(0.338)	(0.506)	(0.380)
Married	0.558	0.683*	0.593	1.295***	1.471***	1.235***
	(0.367)	(0.384)	(0.389)	(0.355)	(0.375)	(0.355)
Married × Female	−2.269***	−1.432**	−1.876***	−2.703***	−1.877***	−1.897***
	(0.496)	(0.651)	(0.569)	(0.467)	(0.590)	(0.464)
Other member employed	−0.521***	−0.385***	−0.513***	−0.395***	−0.492***	−0.363***
	(0.0700)	(0.0717)	(0.0762)	(0.0730)	(0.0760)	(0.0736)
Number of children	0.246***	0.267***	0.213***	0.114	0.0960	−0.115
	(0.0484)	(0.0503)	(0.0521)	(0.0697)	(0.0713)	(0.0722)
Constant	3.198***	0.0640	−0.443	1.710*	−3.336***	−2.206**
	(1.030)	(1.094)	(1.113)	(0.915)	(0.976)	(0.943)
Observations	4,974	4,974	4,974	7,862	7,862	7,862
Pseudo R^2	0.233	0.233	0.233	0.259	0.259	0.259

table continues next page

Table 6A.4 Multinomial Logit on Occupational Choice of Working-Age Population, by Household Status, in Bangladesh, 2000 and 2010 *(continued)*

	2000			*2010*		
	Daily workers	*Self-employed*[a]	*Wage worker*	*Daily workers*	*Self-employed*[a]	*Wage worker*
b. Other household members						
Primary & lower secondary education	−0.964***	−0.0334	0.259***	−0.802***	0.321***	0.240***
	(0.0977)	(0.117)	(0.0965)	(0.0739)	(0.0986)	(0.0704)
Higher secondary & tertiary education	−2.894***	0.0292	1.227***	−2.253***	0.114	1.460***
	(0.358)	(0.197)	(0.155)	(0.264)	(0.171)	(0.111)
Age	0.180***	0.231***	0.190***	0.154***	0.336***	0.183***
	(0.0239)	(0.0311)	(0.0255)	(0.0207)	(0.0281)	(0.0194)
Age squared	−0.00286***	−0.00345***	−0.00308***	−0.00243***	−0.00459***	−0.00303***
	(0.000345)	(0.000454)	(0.000381)	(0.000296)	(0.000407)	(0.000285)
Urban	−0.172	0.623***	0.781***	−0.134	0.358***	0.966***
	(0.108)	(0.112)	(0.0884)	(0.0826)	(0.0907)	(0.0617)
Barisal	0.219	−0.117	−0.284	0.0287	−0.406**	−0.677***
	(0.179)	(0.206)	(0.174)	(0.157)	(0.183)	(0.136)
Chittagong	0.107	−0.0791	0.0725	0.189*	−0.704***	−0.429***
	(0.119)	(0.136)	(0.103)	(0.100)	(0.124)	(0.0766)
Khulna	0.504***	0.155	−0.540***	0.902***	0.219*	−0.506***
	(0.141)	(0.166)	(0.155)	(0.109)	(0.128)	(0.0996)
Rajsahi	1.508***	0.433***	−0.141	0.976***	0.0781	−0.748***
	(0.109)	(0.142)	(0.121)	(0.0901)	(0.108)	(0.0847)
Sylhet	0.414**	0.0886	0.193	0.791***	0.0883	−0.629***
	(0.171)	(0.222)	(0.168)	(0.130)	(0.163)	(0.132)
Attends school	−3.253***	−3.346***	−3.866***	−3.964***	−3.359***	−3.996***
	(0.281)	(0.287)	(0.228)	(0.251)	(0.239)	(0.151)
Remittances	−0.319**	−0.440***	−0.367***	−0.516***	−0.295**	−0.394***
	(0.127)	(0.139)	(0.125)	(0.110)	(0.123)	(0.106)
Female	−3.038***	−3.288***	−1.753***	−3.197***	−3.580***	−1.563***
	(0.161)	(0.269)	(0.136)	(0.146)	(0.256)	(0.0973)
Remittances × Female	0.143	−0.0907	0.0784	0.0908	0.140	−0.352**
	(0.201)	(0.329)	(0.189)	(0.202)	(0.251)	(0.166)
Married	0.822***	1.240***	0.932***	0.817***	0.794***	0.639***
	(0.148)	(0.159)	(0.149)	(0.116)	(0.128)	(0.114)
Married × Female	−2.151***	−2.283***	−2.376***	−1.856***	−1.477***	−2.115***
	(0.202)	(0.309)	(0.189)	(0.176)	(0.276)	(0.138)
Employed Hd head	−0.413***	−0.412***	−0.331***	0.170	−0.0691	0.0817
	(0.121)	(0.135)	(0.112)	(0.123)	(0.135)	(0.0982)
Household head with primary & lower secondary education	−0.952***	−0.244**	−0.379***	1.414***	0.171	0.213**
	(0.104)	(0.115)	(0.0948)	(0.240)	(0.160)	(0.106)
Household head with higher secondary & tertiary education	−1.844***	−0.492**	−0.465***	0.630***	0.0284	−0.0465
	(0.314)	(0.204)	(0.156)	(0.244)	(0.156)	(0.100)
Constant	−1.512***	−3.638***	−2.838***	−3.080***	−5.940***	−2.808***
	(0.364)	(0.475)	(0.387)	(0.414)	(0.482)	(0.329)
Observations	14,058	14,058	14,058	21,715	21,715	21,715
Pseudo R^2	0.362	0.362	0.362	0.359	0.359	0.359

Source: Household survey results from Bangladesh (HIES 2000–10).
Note: "Working-age" = 15–64 years; Hd = household. Dhaka is the base region. "Nonemployed" is the base category.
Remittances × Female = interaction effect between remittances and female. Married × Female = interaction effect between married and female.
Standard errors in parentheses. HIES = Household Income and Expenditure Survey (Bangladesh Bureau of Statistics).
a. Nonagricultural self-employment.
$^{*}p < 0.1$, $^{**}p < 0.05$, $^{***}p < 0.01$

Table 6A.5 Multinomial Logit on Occupational Choice of Working-Age Population, by Household Status, in Peru, 2004 and 2010

	2004						2010					
	Head		*Spouse*		*Other*		*Head*		*Spouse*		*Other*	
	Salaried job	*Self-employed*	*Salaried job*	*Self-employed*	*Salaried job*	*Self-employed*	*Salaried job*	*Self-employed*	*Salaried job*	*Self-employed*	*Salaried job*	*Self-employed*
At least high school education					0.609***	0.416***					0.809***	0.527***
					(0.0476)	(0.0690)					(0.0510)	(0.0748)
Head or spouse with at least high school education	0.395***	−0.0337	0.547***	0.0410	−0.323***	−0.572***	0.185*	−0.128	0.675***	0.119	−0.324***	−0.384***
	(0.0882)	(0.0881)	(0.0940)	(0.0685)	(0.0517)	(0.0730)	(0.102)	(0.103)	(0.0917)	(0.0763)	(0.0562)	(0.0787)
Age (years)												
26–35	0.737***	1.052***	0.709***	0.693***	0.777***	1.305***	0.401*	0.844***	0.439***	0.856***	0.863***	1.181***
	(0.187)	(0.205)	(0.165)	(0.125)	(0.0567)	(0.0774)	(0.233)	(0.257)	(0.161)	(0.154)	(0.0648)	(0.0866)
36–45	0.673***	1.208***	0.859***	0.746***	0.564***	1.312***	0.286	0.894***	0.570***	0.946***	0.796***	1.425***
	(0.176)	(0.194)	(0.172)	(0.128)	(0.0941)	(0.113)	(0.224)	(0.246)	(0.165)	(0.154)	(0.0997)	(0.122)
46–55	0.127	0.778***	0.192	0.179	0.372***	1.211***	−0.189	0.603**	0.296*	0.757***	0.316**	1.458***
	(0.179)	(0.196)	(0.190)	(0.139)	(0.144)	(0.167)	(0.229)	(0.250)	(0.177)	(0.162)	(0.154)	(0.163)
56–65	−1.287***	−0.128	−0.479*	−0.200	−0.790***	0.455**	−1.307***	−0.204	−0.727***	0.260	−1.248***	0.911***
	(0.182)	(0.198)	(0.272)	(0.153)	(0.215)	(0.227)	(0.232)	(0.250)	(0.210)	(0.173)	(0.274)	(0.222)
At least one family worker	0.0356	1.314***	−1.118***	0.689***	−0.261***	0.218**	−0.0482	1.003***	−0.844***	0.811***	−0.202***	0.221**
	(0.239)	(0.208)	(0.234)	(0.0909)	(0.0633)	(0.0938)	(0.330)	(0.314)	(0.188)	(0.0940)	(0.0668)	(0.0984)
Farm household	−0.315**	−0.900***	−0.829***	−0.480***	−0.317***	−0.568***	−0.162	−0.573***	−0.927***	−0.591***	−0.244***	−0.402***
	(0.150)	(0.170)	(0.134)	(0.103)	(0.0711)	(0.104)	(0.171)	(0.185)	(0.143)	(0.107)	(0.0771)	(0.116)
Female	−1.640***	−0.949***	−2.191***	−0.974***	−0.712***	−0.643***	−1.412***	−1.193***	−1.975***	−0.736***	−0.685***	−0.623***
	(0.129)	(0.127)	(0.231)	(0.245)	(0.0448)	(0.0630)	(0.152)	(0.155)	(0.224)	(0.234)	(0.0477)	(0.0661)
Attends school	−0.773***	−1.019***	0.995***	−0.00837	−1.110***	−0.803***	0.0414	−0.673**	0.714**	−0.461	−1.163***	−0.917***
	(0.206)	(0.252)	(0.298)	(0.340)	(0.0600)	(0.0840)	(0.275)	(0.301)	(0.279)	(0.350)	(0.0578)	(0.0842)
Married	−0.141	−0.0760			0.00307	0.267***	−0.185	−0.236			−0.109	0.138
	(0.128)	(0.128)			(0.0608)	(0.0833)	(0.155)	(0.158)			(0.0689)	(0.0866)

table continues next page

Table 6A.5 Multinomial Logit on Occupational Choice of Working-Age Population, by Household Status, in Peru, 2004 and 2010 *(continued)*

	2004						*2010*					
	Head		*Spouse*		*Other*		*Head*		*Spouse*		*Other*	
	Salaried job	*Self-employed*	*Salaried job*	*Self-employed*	*Salaried job*	*Self-employed*	*Salaried job*	*Self-employed*	*Salaried job*	*Self-employed*	*Salaried job*	*Self-employed*
Head employed			−0.00833	−0.431***	−0.0719	0.0156			0.203	−0.212*	−0.0477	0.117
			(0.155)	(0.106)	(0.0586)	(0.0775)			(0.163)	(0.125)	(0.0706)	(0.0889)
Spouse employed					0.0886*	0.0435					0.0948*	0.0138
					(0.0496)	(0.0688)					(0.0513)	(0.0733)
Costa	−0.00486	0.0614	−0.153	0.307***	−0.0886	0.201**	−0.0765	0.121	0.0767	0.367***	−0.366***	−0.0823
	(0.103)	(0.103)	(0.107)	(0.0891)	(0.0586)	(0.0808)	(0.118)	(0.119)	(0.108)	(0.0990)	(0.0671)	(0.0904)
Sierra	−0.0484	0.0569	−0.150	0.340***	−0.418***	−0.0714	−0.0881	0.256**	−0.0680	0.289***	−0.477***	−0.275***
	(0.109)	(0.110)	(0.113)	(0.0921)	(0.0625)	(0.0861)	(0.125)	(0.127)	(0.112)	(0.100)	(0.0715)	(0.0944)
Selva	−0.190	0.105	−0.0935	0.200**	−0.388***	−0.0687	−0.0160	0.304**	0.0924	0.383***	−0.457***	−0.0230
	(0.128)	(0.125)	(0.120)	(0.101)	(0.0715)	(0.0987)	(0.141)	(0.143)	(0.117)	(0.105)	(0.0763)	(0.0987)
Rural	0.314***	−0.414***	−0.457***	−0.674***	−0.0716	−0.570***	−0.00734	−0.609***	−0.308**	−0.737***	−0.0120	−0.543***
	(0.113)	(0.121)	(0.129)	(0.0973)	(0.0716)	(0.103)	(0.148)	(0.152)	(0.139)	(0.106)	(0.0774)	(0.118)
Child ≤5	0.0589	0.176*	−0.300***	−0.349***			−0.0138	−0.0140	−0.313***	−0.179***		
	(0.0971)	(0.102)	(0.0670)	(0.0496)			(0.0861)	(0.0898)	(0.0621)	(0.0418)		
Constant	1.349***	0.477**	0.594*	0.289	−0.0442	−1.454***	2.166***	1.253***	0.687**	−0.165	0.315***	−1.089***
	(0.204)	(0.220)	(0.329)	(0.291)	(0.0809)	(0.114)	(0.273)	(0.288)	(0.306)	(0.299)	(0.100)	(0.131)
Observations	10,087	10,087	12,004	12,004	21,720	21,720	8,312	8,312	9,327	9,327	16,824	16,824
Pseudo R^2	0.0879	0.0879	0.0914	0.0914	0.118	0.118	0.0599	0.0599	0.0950	0.0950	0.136	0.136

Source: Household survey results from Peru (ENAHO 2004–10).
Note: "Working age" = 15–64 years. Standard errors in parentheses. "Other" = household members who are neither household heads nor spouses. ENAHO = Encuesta Nacional de Hogares (Peru National Institute of Statistics and Information).
$^{*}p < 0.1$, $^{**}p < 0.05$, $^{***}p < 0.01$

Table 6A.6 Multinomial Logit on Occupational Choice of Working-Age Population, by Household Status, in Thailand, 2000 and 2009

	2000						2009					
	Head		Spouse		Other		Head		Spouse		Other	
	Wage worker	*Self-employed*	*Wage worker*	*Self-employed*	*Wage worker*	*Self-employed*	*Wage worker*	*Self-employed*	*Wage worker*	*Self-employed*	*Wage worker*	*Self-employed*
6–11 yrs educ.					0.452***	0.541***					0.655***	0.581***
					(0.0846)	(0.133)					(0.0775)	(0.107)
>11 yrs educ.					0.610***	0.443***					1.336***	0.887***
					(0.0881)	(0.142)					(0.0796)	(0.114)
Head of household education (years)												
6–11	0.128	0.0573	−0.157*	0.321***	−0.121	−0.141	0.194**	0.0547	0.0444	0.313***	−0.0690	−0.145
	(0.123)	(0.133)	(0.0898)	(0.123)	(0.0876)	(0.152)	(0.0819)	(0.0855)	(0.0716)	(0.0867)	(0.0624)	(0.120)
>11	0.797***	−0.256*	−0.422***	0.309**	0.173*	−0.224	0.616***	−0.221**	0.0599	0.434***	−0.0296	−0.190
	(0.121)	(0.140)	(0.116)	(0.153)	(0.103)	(0.210)	(0.0842)	(0.0886)	(0.0839)	(0.103)	(0.0681)	(0.125)
Spouse education												
<6	0.316**	0.581***			−0.252***	−0.285***	0.540***	0.581***			−0.258***	−0.169*
	(0.157)	(0.172)			(0.0659)	(0.109)	(0.120)	(0.123)			(0.0563)	(0.0914)
6–11	0.829***	1.204***	0.240**	−0.124	−0.363***	−0.636***	0.478***	0.807***	0.237***	0.0360	−0.390***	−0.307**
	(0.188)	(0.206)	(0.0977)	(0.126)	(0.119)	(0.234)	(0.126)	(0.132)	(0.0757)	(0.0867)	(0.0787)	(0.138)
>11	0.660***	1.021***	1.164***	−0.552***	−0.188	−0.274	0.598***	0.881***	0.842***	−0.200*	−0.422***	−0.358**
	(0.200)	(0.217)	(0.127)	(0.175)	(0.163)	(0.278)	(0.125)	(0.134)	(0.0879)	(0.113)	(0.0905)	(0.165)
Age (years)												
26–35	0.936***	1.936***	0.00906	1.252***	0.597***	1.524***	1.159***	2.171***	0.157	0.743***	0.758***	1.352***
	(0.178)	(0.244)	(0.146)	(0.256)	(0.0681)	(0.131)	(0.156)	(0.227)	(0.114)	(0.245)	(0.0556)	(0.117)
36–45	0.591***	1.977***	−0.328**	1.421***	0.482***	1.888***	0.619***	2.028***	−0.0610	1.234***	0.549***	1.760***
	(0.171)	(0.238)	(0.149)	(0.258)	(0.0988)	(0.166)	(0.150)	(0.219)	(0.111)	(0.237)	(0.0663)	(0.123)
46–55	−0.270	1.263***	−0.881***	1.221***	−0.0748	1.667***	−0.222	1.427***	−0.611***	1.070***	0.225**	1.778***
	(0.182)	(0.243)	(0.160)	(0.269)	(0.140)	(0.206)	(0.140)	(0.212)	(0.118)	(0.240)	(0.0972)	(0.147)
56–65	−1.997***	−0.121	−2.002***	0.282	−2.409***	0.237	−1.934***	0.102	−1.705***	0.240	−1.330***	0.740***
	(0.178)	(0.240)	(0.188)	(0.285)	(0.218)	(0.300)	(0.147)	(0.214)	(0.138)	(0.249)	(0.143)	(0.184)
Female	−1.169***	−0.649***	−0.972***	−0.108	−0.459***	−0.199**	−1.020***	−0.563***	−1.214***	−0.394***	−0.531***	−0.326***
	(0.111)	(0.120)	(0.141)	(0.177)	(0.0532)	(0.0923)	(0.0719)	(0.0734)	(0.0762)	(0.0953)	(0.0426)	(0.0709)

table continues next page

Table 6A.6 Multinomial Logit on Occupational Choice of Working-Age Population, by Household Status, in Thailand, 2000 and 2009 *(continued)*

	2000						*2009*					
	Head		*Spouse*		*Other*		*Head*		*Spouse*		*Other*	
	Wage worker	*Self-employed*	*Wage worker*	*Self-employed*	*Wage worker*	*Self-employed*	*Wage worker*	*Self-employed*	*Wage worker*	*Self-employed*	*Wage worker*	*Self-employed*
Central	−0.0226	0.0373	0.0240	0.0409	−0.404***	−0.153	0.278***	0.302***	0.109	0.248**	0.0418	0.0641
	(0.125)	(0.133)	(0.107)	(0.141)	(0.0940)	(0.167)	(0.0865)	(0.0923)	(0.0788)	(0.107)	(0.0639)	(0.112)
North	0.0286	0.0767	0.382***	0.579***	−0.343***	0.269	−0.188**	0.295***	−0.403***	0.417***	−0.407***	0.110
	(0.129)	(0.139)	(0.114)	(0.146)	(0.102)	(0.170)	(0.0944)	(0.0983)	(0.0886)	(0.109)	(0.0735)	(0.121)
Northeast	−0.502***	−0.502***	−0.0292	0.249*	−0.755***	−0.347**	−0.690***	−0.0869	−0.469***	0.255**	−0.649***	−0.0379
	(0.125)	(0.133)	(0.110)	(0.144)	(0.0956)	(0.173)	(0.0908)	(0.0954)	(0.0864)	(0.109)	(0.0693)	(0.119)
South	0.0191	0.255*	−0.358***	0.372**	−0.874***	−0.161	0.172	0.420***	−0.230**	0.518***	−0.105	0.339**
	(0.140)	(0.149)	(0.116)	(0.145)	(0.102)	(0.178)	(0.108)	(0.114)	(0.0931)	(0.116)	(0.0801)	(0.136)
Urban	0.107	0.842***	−0.345***	−0.0744	−0.162***	0.109	0.0459	0.728***	−0.277***	0.0603	−0.151***	0.144**
	(0.0766)	(0.0855)	(0.0686)	(0.0821)	(0.0534)	(0.0936)	(0.0569)	(0.0597)	(0.0498)	(0.0587)	(0.0420)	(0.0686)
Head employed			0.575***	−0.277**	0.00257	−0.130			0.599***	−0.217***	−0.220***	−0.406***
			(0.111)	(0.119)	(0.0620)	(0.100)			(0.0814)	(0.0837)	(0.0498)	(0.0784)
Spouse employed					0.185***	0.240*					0.276***	0.146
					(0.0710)	(0.130)					(0.0566)	(0.105)
Married	−0.660***	−0.630***			0.111*	0.449***	−0.640***	−0.569***			0.190***	0.711***
	(0.138)	(0.155)			(0.0574)	(0.0986)	(0.112)	(0.116)			(0.0470)	(0.0734)
Attends school	−2.980***	−2.716***	−0.649	0.399	−3.489***	−3.428***	−2.325***	−2.473***	−0.127	−2.850***	−3.016***	−3.195***
	(0.235)	(0.399)	(0.546)	(0.502)	(0.110)	(0.353)	(0.283)	(0.286)	(0.271)	(0.656)	(0.0823)	(0.254)
Number of children < 5 years old	−0.371***	−0.167**	−0.525***	−0.398***			−0.350***	−0.286***	−0.575***	−0.386***		
	(0.0668)	(0.0689)	(0.0582)	(0.0689)			(0.0550)	(0.0562)	(0.0488)	(0.0574)		
Constant	2.002***	−0.884***	0.969***	−1.936***	0.810***	−2.567***	1.825***	−1.034***	1.009***	−1.653***	0.145	−2.818***
	(0.226)	(0.281)	(0.249)	(0.357)	(0.141)	(0.245)	(0.178)	(0.238)	(0.176)	(0.289)	(0.113)	(0.189)
Observations	15,221	15,221	11,386	11,386	19,603	19,603	25,341	25,341	19,176	19,176	31,564	31,564
Pseudo R^2	0.163	0.163	0.0883	0.0883	0.266	0.266	0.145	0.145	0.106	0.106	0.262	0.262

Source: Household survey results from Thailand (SES 2000–09).

Note: "Working age" = 15–64 years; "Other" = household members who are neither heads of households nor spouses. Sample includes individuals who are nonfarmers in main occupation. The omitted occupational category includes family workers, unemployed, and inactive individuals (that is, individuals with zero earnings). Standard errors in parentheses. SES = Household Socio-Economic Survey (Thailand National Statistical Office).

$*p < 0.1$, $**p < 0.05$, $***p < 0.01$

Table 6A.7 Earnings Regressions for Nonfarm Working-Age Population in Bangladesh, 2000 and 2010

	2000			*2010*		
	Daily workers	*Self-employed*[a]	*Wage worker*	*Daily workers*	*Self-employed*[a]	*Wage worker*
a. Household heads						
Primary & lower secondary education	0.132***	0.370***	0.330***	0.0530***	0.312***	0.357***
	(0.0392)	(0.0484)	(0.0499)	(0.0150)	(0.0387)	(0.0387)
Higher secondary & tertiary education	0.420**	0.994***	0.796***	0.248***	0.632***	0.826***
	(0.164)	(0.0810)	(0.0551)	(0.0654)	(0.0625)	(0.0420)
Age	0.0510***	0.0591***	0.0529***	0.0224***	0.0411***	0.0916***
	(0.00989)	(0.0186)	(0.0161)	(0.00426)	(0.0149)	(0.0117)
Age squared	−0.000666***	−0.000664***	−0.000570***	−0.000267***	−0.000541***	−0.00107***
	(0.000119)	(0.000219)	(0.000191)	(5.09e-05)	(0.000172)	(0.000138)
Female	−0.894***	−1.477***	−0.956***	−0.688***	−1.080***	−0.709***
	(0.0621)	(0.166)	(0.0849)	(0.0266)	(0.138)	(0.0609)
Urban	0.0863*	0.234***	0.108**	−0.0217	0.264***	0.117***
	(0.0447)	(0.0495)	(0.0421)	(0.0164)	(0.0396)	(0.0315)
Barisal	0.0601	−0.193**	−0.0421	0.0120	−0.0592	−0.0989
	(0.0641)	(0.0966)	(0.0880)	(0.0293)	(0.0857)	(0.0671)
Chittagong	−0.0891*	−0.0956	−0.0181	0.0488**	−0.152**	−0.0456
	(0.0461)	(0.0622)	(0.0521)	(0.0194)	(0.0597)	(0.0405)
Khulna	0.103**	−0.108	−0.0193	−0.216***	−0.212***	−0.184***
	(0.0478)	(0.0747)	(0.0677)	(0.0194)	(0.0621)	(0.0506)
Rajsahi	−0.182***	−0.242***	−0.195***	−0.179***	−0.314***	−0.112**
	(0.0364)	(0.0589)	(0.0610)	(0.0160)	(0.0466)	(0.0454)
Sylhet	−0.0841	−0.183	−0.370***	−0.0994***	0.302***	−0.0124
	(0.0604)	(0.131)	(0.111)	(0.0298)	(0.0846)	(0.0812)
Manufacturing	0.432***		0.446***	0.0674***		0.107
	(0.0456)		(0.0780)	(0.0196)		(0.0699)
Industry	0.178***	0.00876	0.433***	0.272***	−0.0833	0.250**
	(0.0547)	(0.0962)	(0.121)	(0.0201)	(0.146)	(0.0969)
Services	0.429***	−0.0220	0.403***	0.111***	−0.0844*	0.0882
	(0.0379)	(0.0472)	(0.0740)	(0.0156)	(0.0475)	(0.0670)
Public job			0.178***			0.320***
			(0.0452)			(0.0393)
Constant	6.395***	6.636***	6.256***	7.190***	7.164***	5.698***
	(0.198)	(0.386)	(0.334)	(0.0872)	(0.317)	(0.248)
Observations	2,092	1,269	1,134	3,390	2,007	1,820
R^2	0.216	0.240	0.401	0.289	0.183	0.373
Adjusted R^2	0.211	0.232	0.393	0.286	0.177	0.368
b. Other members						
Primary & lower secondary education	0.133**	0.449***	0.459***	0.0492**	0.0246	0.292***
	(0.0554)	(0.0831)	(0.0674)	(0.0211)	(0.0676)	(0.0372)
Higher secondary & tertiary education	0.114	0.975***	0.837***	0.466***	0.331***	0.954***
	(0.270)	(0.124)	(0.0854)	(0.0992)	(0.107)	(0.0478)
Age	0.0514***	0.0693***	0.0478***	0.0384***	0.124***	0.0693***
	(0.0131)	(0.0222)	(0.0178)	(0.00593)	(0.0167)	(0.00975)
Age squared	−0.000633***	−0.000774**	−0.000444	−0.000470***	−0.00170***	−0.000846***
	(0.000203)	(0.000350)	(0.000282)	(9.17e-05)	(0.000246)	(0.000153)

table continues next page

Table 6A.7 Earnings Regressions for Nonfarm Working-Age Population in Bangladesh, 2000 and 2010 *(continued)*

	2000			*2010*		
	Daily workers	*Self-employed*[a]	*Wage worker*	*Daily workers*	*Self-employed*[a]	*Wage worker*
Female	−1.078***	−1.244***	−0.682***	−0.691***	−1.132***	−0.462***
	(0.0698)	(0.121)	(0.0656)	(0.0301)	(0.0841)	(0.0331)
Urban	−0.0135	0.0209	−0.147**	−0.104***	0.287***	−0.0407
	(0.0737)	(0.0803)	(0.0619)	(0.0276)	(0.0615)	(0.0316)
Barisal	0.216*	−0.0186	−0.228*	0.0885*	0.156	−0.0396
	(0.111)	(0.151)	(0.124)	(0.0502)	(0.127)	(0.0752)
Chittagong	−0.200***	−0.123	−0.178**	0.101***	−0.149*	−0.0281
	(0.0756)	(0.101)	(0.0704)	(0.0321)	(0.0883)	(0.0388)
Khulna	−0.107	−0.0433	−0.215*	−0.204***	−0.297***	−0.237***
	(0.0855)	(0.121)	(0.117)	(0.0338)	(0.0907)	(0.0562)
Rajsahi	−0.227***	−0.396***	−0.295***	−0.103***	−0.00253	−0.0741
	(0.0665)	(0.103)	(0.0910)	(0.0281)	(0.0756)	(0.0481)
Sylhet	−0.231**	−0.481***	−0.636***	0.0448	0.125	−0.0857
	(0.103)	(0.166)	(0.125)	(0.0389)	(0.112)	(0.0741)
Manufacturing	0.300***		0.463***	−0.169***		0.149*
	(0.0674)		(0.145)	(0.0274)		(0.0904)
Industry	0.448***	−0.0366	0.440**	0.174***	0.700***	0.0853
	(0.0897)	(0.148)	(0.221)	(0.0296)	(0.171)	(0.126)
Services	0.469***	0.0881	0.297**	0.0930***	0.195***	−0.0847
	(0.0692)	(0.0777)	(0.144)	(0.0276)	(0.0707)	(0.0905)
Public job			0.555***			0.437***
			(0.0921)			(0.0522)
Constant	6.270***	6.379***	6.198***	6.974***	5.456***	6.227***
	(0.192)	(0.334)	(0.285)	(0.0892)	(0.273)	(0.163)
Observations	1,153	673	1,104	1,857	973	1,984
R^2	0.307	0.317	0.285	0.383	0.343	0.348
Adjusted R^2	0.299	0.304	0.275	0.379	0.334	0.343

Source: Household survey results from Bangladesh (HIES 2000–10).
Note: "Working-age" = 15–64 years. Dhaka is the base region. "Illiterate and incomplete primary" education is the base for educational levels. "Agriculture" is the base sector for "Daily" and "wage" workers, while "Manufacturing" is the base sector for "self-employed." Standard errors in parentheses. HIES = Household Income and Expenditure Survey (Bangladesh Bureau of Statistics).
a. Nonagricultural self-employment.
$^*p < 0.1$, $^{**}p < 0.05$, $^{***}p < 0.01$

Table 6A.8 Earnings Regressions for Nonfarm Working-Age Population in Peru, 2004 and 2010

	2004						2010					
	Head		Spouse		Other		Head		Spouse		Other	
	Salaried job	Self-employed	Salaried job	Self-employed	Salaried job	Self-employed	Salaried job	Self-employed	Salaried job	Self-employed	Salaried job	Self-employed
Education type												
Primary	0.132***		0.296***		0.0984**		0.148***		0.220***		0.142***	
	(0.0383)		(0.0637)		(0.0417)		(0.0367)		(0.0623)		(0.0457)	
Secondary	0.350***		0.558***		0.238***		0.271***		0.519***		0.278***	
	(0.0382)		(0.0663)		(0.0415)		(0.0359)		(0.0633)		(0.0451)	
College	0.837***		0.937***		0.570***		0.627***		0.825***		0.578***	
	(0.0404)		(0.0727)		(0.0452)		(0.0381)		(0.0662)		(0.0477)	
Age (years)												
26–35	0.243***	0.314***	0.280***	0.291***	0.321***	0.389***	0.169***	0.305***	0.249***	0.457***	0.283***	0.556***
	(0.0441)	(0.0842)	(0.0875)	(0.0955)	(0.0206)	(0.0486)	(0.0422)	(0.0946)	(0.0754)	(0.110)	(0.0198)	(0.0539)
36–45	0.358***	0.428***	0.318***	0.372***	0.313***	0.482***	0.192***	0.390***	0.254***	0.591***	0.285***	0.705***
	(0.0436)	(0.0818)	(0.0876)	(0.0946)	(0.0307)	(0.0634)	(0.0413)	(0.0922)	(0.0731)	(0.108)	(0.0289)	(0.0691)
46–55	0.405***	0.277***	0.357***	0.329***	0.396***	0.339***	0.167***	0.253***	0.241***	0.554***	0.251***	0.545***
	(0.0446)	(0.0824)	(0.0922)	(0.0983)	(0.0484)	(0.0935)	(0.0419)	(0.0919)	(0.0759)	(0.110)	(0.0462)	(0.0899)
56–65	0.305***	0.0801	0.541***	0.128	0.548***	0.220	0.0896**	−0.00376	0.405***	0.418***	0.223**	0.711***
	(0.0504)	(0.0845)	(0.107)	(0.106)	(0.0968)	(0.156)	(0.0456)	(0.0940)	(0.0907)	(0.116)	(0.0994)	(0.133)
Female	−0.427***	−0.582***			−0.166***	−0.601***	−0.435***	−0.781***			−0.236***	−0.859***
	(0.0287)	(0.0338)			(0.0182)	(0.0416)	(0.0235)	(0.0337)			(0.0172)	(0.0461)
Informal	−0.373***	−0.554***	−0.539***	−0.568***	−0.336***	−0.538***	−0.383***	−0.596***	−0.731***	−0.829***	−0.373***	−0.580***
	(0.0248)	(0.0323)	(0.0504)	(0.0592)	(0.0194)	(0.0505)	(0.0229)	(0.0317)	(0.0425)	(0.0554)	(0.0187)	(0.0545)
Manufacturing	0.0471		0.327***		0.299***		−0.00185		0.497***		0.153***	
	(0.0383)		(0.0924)		(0.0347)		(0.0371)		(0.0856)		(0.0339)	
Services	−0.0832***	−0.00266	0.402***	0.855***	0.266***	0.478***	0.0911***	0.113***	0.599***	0.723***	0.209***	0.534***
	(0.0322)	(0.0396)	(0.0770)	(0.0569)	(0.0297)	(0.0648)	(0.0312)	(0.0414)	(0.0708)	(0.0575)	(0.0287)	(0.0713)
Public sector	−0.188***		0.352***		0.337***		−0.0215		0.460***		0.287***	
	(0.0357)		(0.0804)		(0.0387)		(0.0351)		(0.0736)		(0.0368)	

table continues next page

Table 6A.8 Earnings Regressions for Nonfarm Working-Age Population in Peru, 2004 and 2010 *(continued)*

	2004						*2010*					
	Head		*Spouse*		*Other*		*Head*		*Spouse*		*Other*	
	Salaried job	*Self-employed*	*Salaried job*	*Self-employed*	*Salaried job*	*Self-employed*	*Salaried job*	*Self-employed*	*Salaried job*	*Self-employed*	*Salaried job*	*Self-employed*
Costa	−0.360***	−0.491***	−0.392***	−0.575***	−0.459***	−0.682***	−0.233***	−0.234***	−0.347***	−0.176***	−0.255***	−0.298***
	(0.0257)	(0.0345)	(0.0502)	(0.0526)	(0.0222)	(0.0501)	(0.0231)	(0.0353)	(0.0457)	(0.0543)	(0.0219)	(0.0563)
Sierra	−0.342***	−0.632***	−0.570***	−0.563***	−0.599***	−0.730***	−0.233***	−0.212***	−0.486***	−0.305***	−0.370***	−0.386***
	(0.0283)	(0.0393)	(0.0537)	(0.0553)	(0.0257)	(0.0612)	(0.0254)	(0.0391)	(0.0494)	(0.0581)	(0.0241)	(0.0676)
Selva	−0.452***	−0.521***	−0.409***	−0.490***	−0.442***	−0.645***	−0.209***	−0.201***	−0.444***	−0.0545	−0.230***	−0.232***
	(0.0381)	(0.0501)	(0.0667)	(0.0686)	(0.0339)	(0.0784)	(0.0347)	(0.0512)	(0.0638)	(0.0703)	(0.0315)	(0.0787)
Rural	−0.186***	−0.200***	−0.104	−0.496***	−0.0519*	−0.524***	−0.208***	−0.196***	−0.196***	−0.513***	−0.112***	−0.348***
	(0.0339)	(0.0595)	(0.0675)	(0.0540)	(0.0289)	(0.0722)	(0.0318)	(0.0575)	(0.0629)	(0.0573)	(0.0259)	(0.0739)
Has two jobs	0.243***	0.229***	0.324***	0.539***	0.316***	0.448***	0.0652***	0.190***	0.163***	0.403***	0.111***	0.361***
	(0.0284)	(0.0435)	(0.0575)	(0.0601)	(0.0317)	(0.0700)	(0.0228)	(0.0387)	(0.0454)	(0.0543)	(0.0262)	(0.0637)
Head/spouse with at least secondary		0.201***		0.156***		−0.241***		0.0844***		0.103**		−0.266***
		(0.0312)		(0.0432)		(0.0457)		(0.0327)		(0.0466)		(0.0477)
At least one family worker		0.307***		0.160***		−0.00777		0.246***		0.283***		−0.00123
		(0.0525)		(0.0535)		(0.0601)		(0.0554)		(0.0552)		(0.0652)
At least secondary						0.178***						0.410***
						(0.0482)						(0.0540)
Constant	6.248***	6.709***	5.268***	5.133***	5.813***	5.949***	6.495***	6.764***	5.462***	5.114***	5.992***	5.530***
	(0.0605)	(0.0954)	(0.115)	(0.127)	(0.0484)	(0.0978)	(0.0592)	(0.107)	(0.105)	(0.137)	(0.0506)	(0.109)
Observations	4,758	3,651	1,665	3,022	6,374	2,375	5,483	4,250	2,326	3,586	7,963	2,817
R^2	0.370	0.300	0.444	0.264	0.414	0.380	0.271	0.265	0.437	0.198	0.300	0.327
Sigma	0.650	0.846	0.761	1.049	0.722	1.025	0.649	0.921	0.801	1.206	0.764	1.162

Source: Household survey results from Peru (ENAHO 2005–09).

Note: "Working age" = 15–64 years. Standard errors in parentheses. "Other" = those who are neither household heads nor spouses. ENAHO = Encuesta Nacional de Hogares (Peru National Institute of Statistics and Information).

$^{*}p < 0.1$, $^{**}p < 0.05$, $^{***}p < 0.01$.

Table 6A.9 Earnings Regressions for Nonfarm Working-Age Population in Thailand, 2000 and 2009

	2000						2009					
	Head		*Spouse*		*Others*		*Head*		*Spouse*		*Others*	
	Wage worker	*Self-employed*	*Wage worker*	*Self-employed*	*Wage worker*	*Self-employed*	*Wage worker*	*Self-employed*	*Wage worker*	*Self-employed*	*Wage worker*	*Self-employed*
Education (years)												
6–11 yrs	0.375***		0.289***		0.330***	0.240***	0.428***		0.378***		0.369***	0.129*
	(0.0240)		(0.0365)		(0.0321)	(0.0788)	(0.0176)		(0.0243)		(0.0264)	(0.0716)
>11 yrs	0.944***		1.104***		0.783***	0.454***	1.089***		1.058***		0.888***	0.376***
	(0.0256)		(0.0413)		(0.0348)	(0.0863)	(0.0180)		(0.0261)		(0.0269)	(0.0733)
Head of household education (years)												
6–11		0.185***		0.171***		0.0273		0.211***		0.194***		0.0753
		(0.0387)		(0.0558)		(0.0969)		(0.0306)		(0.0459)		(0.0654)
>11		0.534***		0.316***		0.291**		0.508***		0.321***		0.0711
		(0.0493)		(0.0733)		(0.117)		(0.0355)		(0.0530)		(0.0767)
Spouse education (years)												
<6		0.108**				0.105*		0.177***				−0.00364
		(0.0480)				(0.0592)		(0.0357)				(0.0459)
6–11		0.285***		0.0293		0.287*		0.270***		0.154***		−0.114
		(0.0523)		(0.0637)		(0.150)		(0.0351)		(0.0488)		(0.0899)
>11		0.460***		0.434***		0.0742		0.344***		0.267***		−0.0660
		(0.0631)		(0.0942)		(0.168)		(0.0384)		(0.0612)		(0.107)
Age (years)												
26–35	0.304***	0.140	0.211***	−0.0875	0.341***	0.485***	0.259***	0.205**	0.209***	1.186***	0.391***	0.367***
	(0.0326)	(0.108)	(0.0451)	(0.168)	(0.0210)	(0.0771)	(0.0258)	(0.102)	(0.0361)	(0.146)	(0.0144)	(0.0671)
36–45	0.534***	0.277***	0.341***	0.203	0.497***	0.745***	0.457***	0.309***	0.361***	1.331***	0.573***	0.592***
	(0.0337)	(0.107)	(0.0500)	(0.169)	(0.0322)	(0.0901)	(0.0252)	(0.0991)	(0.0358)	(0.140)	(0.0181)	(0.0691)
46–55	0.597***	0.414***	0.440***	0.199	0.612***	0.696***	0.656***	0.244**	0.577***	1.364***	0.699***	0.508***
	(0.0367)	(0.109)	(0.0576)	(0.174)	(0.0578)	(0.126)	(0.0266)	(0.0999)	(0.0391)	(0.144)	(0.0292)	(0.0885)
56–65	0.395***	0.0838	0.141*	0.0322	0.348***	−0.0913	0.541***	−0.00722	0.487***	1.169***	0.643***	0.185
	(0.0436)	(0.113)	(0.0746)	(0.182)	(0.130)	(0.183)	(0.0311)	(0.102)	(0.0489)	(0.150)	(0.0597)	(0.126)

table continues next page

Table 6A.9 Earnings Regressions for Nonfarm Working-Age Population in Thailand, 2000 and 2009 *(continued)*

	2000						*2009*					
	Head		*Spouse*		*Others*		*Head*		*Spouse*		*Others*	
	Wage worker	*Self-employed*	*Wage worker*	*Self-employed*	*Wage worker*	*Self-employed*	*Wage worker*	*Self-employed*	*Wage worker*	*Self-employed*	*Wage worker*	*Self-employed*
Female	−0.283***	−0.271***	−0.246***	−0.291***	−0.0594***	−0.0789	−0.242***	−0.254***	−0.243***	−0.278***	−0.0650***	−0.166***
	(0.0193)	(0.0448)	(0.0443)	(0.109)	(0.0191)	(0.0568)	(0.0130)	(0.0286)	(0.0207)	(0.0541)	(0.0124)	(0.0417)
Services	1.159***	0.0232	1.136***	0.665***	1.026***	0.357***	0.635***	−0.0124	0.649***	0.613***	0.518***	0.314***
	(0.0284)	(0.0407)	(0.0402)	(0.0573)	(0.0315)	(0.0703)	(0.0223)	(0.0299)	(0.0307)	(0.0456)	(0.0257)	(0.0533)
Central	−0.0730***	−0.102**	−0.0775*	−0.254***	−0.115***	−0.268***	−0.196***	−0.206***	−0.149***	−0.131**	−0.278***	−0.393***
	(0.0253)	(0.0438)	(0.0412)	(0.0842)	(0.0313)	(0.0978)	(0.0183)	(0.0353)	(0.0280)	(0.0660)	(0.0210)	(0.0765)
North	−0.578***	−0.558***	−0.646***	−0.674***	−0.696***	−0.420***	−0.499***	−0.403***	−0.598***	−0.507***	−0.629***	−0.750***
	(0.0306)	(0.0525)	(0.0481)	(0.0845)	(0.0360)	(0.105)	(0.0232)	(0.0405)	(0.0338)	(0.0692)	(0.0247)	(0.0814)
Northeast	−0.694***	−0.630***	−0.692***	−0.690***	−0.786***	−0.726***	−0.611***	−0.411***	−0.627***	−0.436***	−0.694***	−0.662***
	(0.0292)	(0.0490)	(0.0468)	(0.0838)	(0.0346)	(0.102)	(0.0217)	(0.0373)	(0.0319)	(0.0673)	(0.0227)	(0.0773)
South	−0.247***	−0.248***	−0.305***	−0.326***	−0.379***	−0.172	−0.279***	−0.237***	−0.237***	−0.236***	−0.500***	−0.342***
	(0.0322)	(0.0536)	(0.0515)	(0.0893)	(0.0401)	(0.116)	(0.0228)	(0.0414)	(0.0340)	(0.0710)	(0.0251)	(0.0853)
Urban	0.148***	0.346***	0.141***	0.117**	0.0608**	0.157**	0.268***	0.410***	0.247***	0.360***	0.254***	0.325***
	(0.0202)	(0.0337)	(0.0311)	(0.0516)	(0.0237)	(0.0635)	(0.0140)	(0.0254)	(0.0205)	(0.0399)	(0.0151)	(0.0488)
Manufacturing	1.067***		1.041***		1.071***		0.636***		0.612***		0.482***	
	(0.0261)		(0.0365)		(0.0289)		(0.0214)		(0.0295)		(0.0249)	
Public sector	1.489***		1.458***		1.269***		0.976***		1.116***		0.775***	
	(0.0302)		(0.0478)		(0.0380)		(0.0242)		(0.0356)		(0.0292)	
Constant	7.168***	8.545***	7.183***	8.228***	7.107***	7.745***	7.486***	8.633***	7.498***	6.876***	7.480***	8.219***
	(0.0454)	(0.127)	(0.0810)	(0.218)	(0.0491)	(0.156)	(0.0368)	(0.111)	(0.0561)	(0.169)	(0.0393)	(0.129)
Observations	8,251	4,216	4,138	1,929	7,755	1,350	13,016	7,564	7,216	3,421	13,185	2,587
R^2	0.624	0.236	0.627	0.203	0.473	0.176	0.537	0.213	0.522	0.210	0.438	0.175
Sigma	0.725	0.959	0.762	0.975	0.816	1.005	0.667	0.933	0.700	0.978	0.687	1.001

Source: Household survey results from Thailand (SES 2000–09).
Note: "Working age" = 15–64 years; "Others" = those who are neither heads of households nor spouses. Standard errors in parentheses. SES = Household Socio-Economic Survey (Thailand National Statistical Office).
*$p < 0.1$, **$p < 0.05$, ***$p < 0.01$.

Table 6A.10 Net Revenue Regressions for Farm Households in Bangladesh, 2000 and 2010

	2000	*2010*
Primary & lower secondary education	0.132** (0.0633)	0.0331 (0.0489)
Higher secondary & tertiary education	0.295** (0.147)	−0.00290 (0.119)
Age	0.142*** (0.0214)	0.0795*** (0.0172)
Age squared	−0.00175*** (0.000245)	−0.000843*** (0.000190)
Female	−2.243*** (0.123)	−0.926*** (0.0605)
Urban	0.197 (0.123)	−0.161** (0.0816)
Barisal	−0.285** (0.123)	0.270*** (0.0920)
Chittagong	−0.240** (0.0977)	0.164** (0.0680)
Khulna	0.405*** (0.0955)	0.204*** (0.0751)
Rajshahi	0.0125 (0.0763)	0.303*** (0.0629)
Sylhet	0.0104 (0.126)	0.253** (0.108)
Land (low)	−0.107 (0.0986)	0.743*** (0.0666)
Land (high)	0.457*** (0.111)	1.333*** (0.0786)
Irrigation	0.458*** (0.0941)	0.408*** (0.0707)
Household members (no.)	0.525*** (0.0507)	0.429*** (0.0525)
Constant	4.007*** (0.462)	4.780*** (0.381)
Observations	1,678	2,956
R^2	0.340	0.323
Adjusted R^2	0.334	0.320

Source: Household survey results from Bangladesh (HIES 2000–10).
Note: Results represent net revenue for farm households in Bangladesh. Net revenue was calculated using the available information on total revenue stemming from agricultural production and the cost of inputs. The sample comprises those farm household members of working age (15–64 years) who are self-employed in agriculture. Dhaka is the base region. "Illiterate and incomplete primary" is the base for education. "No-land" is the base category for land tenure. Standard errors appear in parentheses. HIES = Household Income and Expenditure Survey (Bangladesh Bureau of Statistics).
$^{*}p < 0.1$, $^{**}p < 0.05$, $^{***}p < 0.01$.

Table 6A.11 Net Revenue Regressions for Farm Households in Peru, 2004 and 2010

	2004	*2010*
Head/spouse with at least secondary	0.133*** (0.0296)	0.128*** (0.0273)
Age (years)		
26–35	0.267*** (0.0610)	0.231*** (0.0736)
36–45	0.412*** (0.0598)	0.333*** (0.0722)
46–55	0.473*** (0.0600)	0.272*** (0.0724)
56–65	0.373*** (0.0607)	0.214*** (0.0736)
Female	−0.420*** (0.0349)	−0.385*** (0.0318)
Head farmer	0.421*** (0.0409)	0.304*** (0.0351)
More than 1 farmer in household	0.688*** (0.0571)	0.513*** (0.0453)
Land size (ha)		
0.5–2	−0.0127 (0.0377)	0.437*** (0.0281)
2–5	0.288*** (0.0443)	0.799*** (0.0348)
>5	0.604*** (0.0468)	1.055*** (0.0371)
Share of adults >50 percent	0.0476* (0.0254)	0.0206 (0.0251)
Improved irrigation system	0.130*** (0.0340)	0.177*** (0.0249)
Owns land	−0.218*** (0.0336)	0.0647** (0.0252)
Sierra	−0.151*** (0.0336)	0.00957 (0.0326)
Selva	0.0414 (0.0404)	−0.0303 (0.0422)
Rural	0.0757** (0.0302)	0.0935*** (0.0303)
Constant	4.249*** (0.0784)	4.182*** (0.0845)
Observations	6,870	7,117
R^2	0.123	0.238
Sigma	0.922	0.894

Source: Household survey results from Peru (ENAHO 2005–09).
Note: ha = hectares (1 hectare = about 100 acres or 10,000 square meters). Results represent net revenue for farm households in Bangladesh. Net revenue was calculated using the available information on total revenue stemming from agricultural production and the cost of inputs. Standard errors in parentheses. "Other" = those who are neither household heads nor spouses. ENAHO = Encuesta Nacional de Hogares (Peru National Institute of Statistics and Information).
$^*p < 0.1$, $^{**}p < 0.05$, $^{***}p < 0.01$.

Table 6A.12 Net Revenue Regressions for Farm Households in Thailand, 2000 and 2009

	2000	*2009*
Head of household education (years)		
6–11	0.0575 (0.0556)	0.0474 (0.0387)
>11	0.273*** (0.105)	0.0814 (0.0565)
Spouse education (years)		
<6	0.189** (0.0742)	0.343*** (0.0429)
6–11	0.271*** (0.0890)	0.421*** (0.0497)
>11	0.743*** (0.154)	0.629*** (0.0724)
Age (years)		
26–35	0.177 (0.167)	0.369** (0.170)
36–45	0.426** (0.166)	0.573*** (0.165)
46–55	0.455*** (0.169)	0.612*** (0.167)
56–65	0.545*** (0.170)	0.512*** (0.168)
Female	−0.334*** (0.0761)	−0.158*** (0.0388)
North	−0.816*** (0.0607)	−0.512*** (0.0443)
Northeast	−1.078*** (0.0556)	−1.104*** (0.0413)
South	−0.0996 (0.0675)	0.220*** (0.0508)
Urban	−0.171*** (0.0651)	−0.0914* (0.0485)
Household owns land	0.132 (0.101)	0.167*** (0.0585)
Household members older than 18 years of age (%)	−0.161* (0.0947)	−0.0815 (0.0686)
Constant	7.392*** (0.205)	7.394*** (0.177)
Observations	5,801	10,118
R^2	0.119	0.151
Sigma	1.393	1.348

Source: Household survey results from Thailand (SES 2000–09).
Note: HH = household. Standard errors in parentheses. Figure results represent net revenue for farm households in Thailand. Net revenue was calculated using the available information on total revenue stemming from agricultural production and the cost of inputs. Unfortunately, unlike the surveys for Bangladesh and Peru, the household survey for Thailand does not contain information on landholding and access to irrigation. SES = Household Socio-Economic Survey (Thailand National Statistical Office).
$^*p < 0.1$, $^{**}p < 0.05$, $^{***}p < 0.01$.

Notes

1. As first noted in chapter 1, "moderate poverty" is a country-specific poverty line referring to the international poverty line that is closest to the country's moderate poverty rate (in some cases \$1.25 a day, in others \$2.50; and in still others \$4–\$5 per day).
2. The widely used "cost of basic needs" approach to drawing consumption-based poverty lines "first estimates the cost of acquiring enough food for adequate nutrition—usually 2,100 calories per person per day—and then adds the cost of other essentials such as clothing and shelter" (Haughton and Khandker, 2009, 39).
3. Despite this deceleration of population growth, Bangladesh has added 19 billion people to its total, a 15 percent increase between 2000 and 2010. Over the same period, Peru has added 3.2 million (a 12 percent increase) and Thailand 6 million (a 9 percent increase).
4. Net revenue was calculated using the available information on total revenue stemming from agricultural production and the cost of inputs.
5. Unfortunately, the household survey for Thailand does not contain information on landholding and access to irrigation.
6. As mentioned earlier, this decomposition method cannot identify the reason behind this change. However, one possible theory is that improved road networks reduced transportation costs and thus allowed for greater returns in investing outside the capital. An alternative explanation is that internal migration toward the capital led to a greater scarcity of workers in other regions, and therefore relatively better earnings. Given the size of this effect, further research on this would be useful to identify the source of change.
7. The cumulative effects are larger because they include all occupational changes, including the choice between daily, wage, and self-employed work for nonfarm workers, and the choice to have a secondary occupation for farm workers.
8. Note that this is consistent with the findings using the simple approach (see table 6.5).
9. Similar analysis about the returns to agriculture in Thailand was not possible because of lack of similar variables in the database used.

Bibliography

Bourguignon, François, Francisco H. G. Ferreira, and Nora Lustig, eds. 2005. *The Microeconomics of Income Distribution Dynamics in East Asia and Latin America.* Washington, DC: World Bank.

Bourguignon, François, Francisco H. G. Ferreira, and Phillippe G. Leite. 2008. "Beyond Oaxaca-Blinder: Accounting for Differences in Household Income Distributions." *Journal of Economic Inequality* 6 (2): 117–48.

Datt, Gaurav, and Martin Ravallion. 1992. "Growth and Redistribution Components of Changes in Poverty Measures: A Decomposition with Applications to Brazil and India in the 1980s." *Journal of Development Economics* 38 (2): 275–96.

Davis, Benjamin, Paul Winters, Calogero Carletto, Katia Covarrubias, Esteban J. Quiñones, Alberto Zezza, Carlo Azzarri, Kostas Stamoulis, and Stefania DiGiuseppe. 2010. "A Cross-Country Comparison of Rural Income Generating Activities." *World Development* 38 (1): 48–63.

Ferreira, Francisco H. G. 2010. "Distributions in Motion: Economic Growth, Inequality and Poverty Dynamics." Policy Research Working Paper 5424, World Bank.

———. 2012. "Distributions in Motion: Economic Growth, Inequality, and Poverty Dynamics." In *The Oxford Handbook of the Economics of Poverty*, edited by Philip N. Jefferson, 427–62. New York: Oxford University Press.

Foster, James, Joel Greer, and Erik Thorbecke. 1984. "A Class of Decomposable Poverty Measures." *Econometrica* 52 (3): 761–66.

Government of Thailand. 2003. "Thailand's Official Poverty Lines." National Economic and Social Development Board, Government of Thailand, Bangkok.

Haughton, Jonathan, and Shahidur R. Khandker. 2009. *Handbook on Poverty + Inequality*. World Bank Training Series. Washington, DC: World Bank.

Kakwani, Nanak, and Medhi Krongkaew. 1998. "Poverty in Thailand: Defining, Measuring and Analyzing." Working Paper N4, Office of the National Economic and Social Development Board, Development Evaluation Division, Bangkok.

Ravallion, Martin, and Shaohua Chen. 2007. "China's (Uneven) Progress against Poverty." *Journal of Development Economics* 82 (1): 1–42.

Shapley, Lloyd. S. 1953. "A Value for *n*-Person Games." In *Contributions to the Theory of Games*, Vol. 2, edited by H. W. Kuhn and A. W. Tucker, 307–17. Princeton, NJ: Princeton University Press.

Shorrocks, Anthony F. 1999. "Decomposition Procedures for Distributional Analysis: A Unified Framework Based on Shapley Value." University of Essex and Institute for Fiscal Studies, London.

Tinbergen, Jan. 1975. *Income Differences: Recent Research*. Amsterdam, the Netherlands: North-Holland.

World Bank. 2011. *World Development Indicators 2011*. Washington, DC: World Bank. Online database.

Environmental Benefits Statement

The World Bank Group is committed to reducing its environmental footprint. In support of this commitment, the Publishing and Knowledge Division leverages electronic publishing options and print-on-demand technology, which is located in regional hubs worldwide. Together, these initiatives enable print runs to be lowered and shipping distances decreased, resulting in reduced paper consumption, chemical use, greenhouse gas emissions, and waste.

The Publishing and Knowledge Division follows the recommended standards for paper use set by the Green Press Initiative. Whenever possible, books are printed on 50 percent to 100 percent postconsumer recycled paper, and at least 50 percent of the fiber in our book paper is either unbleached or bleached using Totally Chlorine Free (TCF), Processed Chlorine Free (PCF), or Enhanced Elemental Chlorine Free (EECF) processes.

More information about the Bank's environmental philosophy can be found at http://crinfo.worldbank.org/wbcrinfo/node/4.